'[A] fascinating study of the phenomenon known as the flapper.'
– History Books of the Year, *Daily Mail*

'Social anxieties have a way of coalescing around young women's bodies, Linda Simon demonstrates in *Lost Girls*, her riveting, deeply researched counter-history of the flapper. Behind the beads, the bob, the fringe and the Charleston, there is a much darker story to be told.'
– Lauren Elkin, author of *Flâneuse: Women Walk the City in Paris, New York, Tokyo, Venice, and London*

'"The iconic, mythic, post-war flapper," writes Simon in her involving social history of the phenomenon, "emerged from a culture obsessed with the adolescent girl: as a problem, a temptation and finally, in the 1920s and beyond, an aspiration." . . . She has come up with a great deal of fascinating information and her research is impressive.'
– *Wall Street Journal*

'Rich in surprise connections and creepy quotes, *Lost Girls* illuminates a modernist aspiration to blur gender and age that was simultaneously abetted and repressed by a deeply confused society.'

– *TLS*

'We think of flappers as flirty, rebellious young women given to snappy one-liners, short dresses, and flat chests. We rarely give credit to these bright young things as the women who shed their mothers' Victorian corsetry and prudish notions about sex and scotch. Simon's engaging history explores this seminal postwar moment, exploring the evolution of these radical young girls (Simon calls them "girls" in a good way) from "a problem to a temptation, and finally, in the 1920s and beyond, to an aspiration."'
– *Toronto Star*

'[A] deftly written and meticulously researched cultural and experiential history.'
– *History Today*

'Using sources from popular culture and from people of the time, Simon asserts that the image of the flapper did not appear out of a single historical moment but rather was invented over the decades. The flapper did not limit its impact to fashion and women's attitudes, but also intersected with debates about race, immigration, politics, and the like. Simon's book is an excellent and very accessible narrative on the flapper and will be of interest to anyone fascinated with gender and the history of the late-nineteenth to early-twentieth century.'
– *New Books Network*

— LOST GIRLS —

The Invention of the Flapper

Linda Simon

REAKTION BOOKS

To Eva Seligmann and in memory of Brita Seligmann de Juanes

Published by Reaktion Books Ltd
Unit 32, Waterside
44–48 Wharf Road
London N1 7UX, UK
www.reaktionbooks.co.uk

First published 2017, reprinted 2017
First paperback edition published 2019

Printed and bound in Great Britain
by Bell & Bain, Glasgow

A catalogue record for this book is available from the British Library

ISBN 978 1 78914 071 2

—— CONTENTS ——

Russell Patterson, *Where There's Smoke There's Fire,* 1930s, illustration.
The allure of the flapper persisted beyond the 1920s.

Introduction

ॐ

'When we take up the "new" it is only
because we have had a secret need of it and have
unconsciously prepared for its coming.'
Cecil Beaton, *Glass of Fashion* (1954)

In the glorious, boozy party after the First World War, a new being burst defiantly on to the cultural stage: skinny, young, impetuous and flirtatious. She wore skirts above the knee, with stockings rolled provocatively; skimpy little dresses, maybe spangled for evening, and nothing much underneath. Her hair was cut short. She was flat-chested, hipless, wiry. She slouched and strutted, cursed mildly and refused to marry. She was young, eternally so, it seemed, and revelled in her youthfulness. She had the unmistakable physique of an adolescent boy. People called her a flapper. And the question that animates this book is this: how did she happen?

It is easy to blame the war. After all, there was, by many accounts, a spirit of euphoria when the long, brutal conflict finally ended. Euphoria and disillusionment. These combined with cynicism to foster a spirit of rebellion and *carpe diem*: a perfect setting for women to throw off Victorian strictures, along with corsets and long skirts, and kick up their heels.

It is common to blame F. Scott Fitzgerald, whose early stories, collected in 1920 as *Flappers and Philosophers*, followed the adventures of just such young women. Although the collection was not unanimously praised – the writing, many critics said, was inferior to his best-selling *This Side of Paradise* (1920) – a reviewer for the *Chicago Daily Tribune* was enthusiastic. Fitzgerald, she said, 'has crystallized his generation' and created a few stories sure to become classics. 'The Offshore Pirate', especially, featured a 'pure, jaunty flapper, with the snappiest line of conversation yet displayed this season'. Fitzgerald's work 'is youth, uncompromising, unclothed, but not, as youth too often is, dour and morbid. It is youth conscious of its powers and joyous in them.'[1]

Fitzgerald modelled these insouciant characters, he said, on his wife, Zelda, but refused to take credit for inventing the flapper. The birth of the flapper, he said, occurred in 1912, when dancers Vernon and Irene Castle – she with bobbed hair and slinky dresses – 'brought the nice girl into the cabaret and sat her down next to the distinctly not-nice girl'.[2] Not-nice girls seemed to be everywhere, tempting young females to precocious sexuality. They ran to barbers for a 'Castle Bob'.

Fitzgerald, then, dates the advent of the flapper to several years before the war began. In fact, there is evidence of flapperdom even earlier. In 1890s Britain, 'flapper', a term applied to very young prostitutes, soon became generalized and sanitized to describe adolescents: thin and long-legged, but not the cigarette-smoking, bourbon-drinking jazz babies of the 1920s. 'The funny English "flapper" with her gawky legs and soulful eyes is still kept very much in the social background,' noted *Vogue* magazine.[3]

Throughout the early 1900s, in newspapers and magazines, flappers were everywhere. A flapper, wrote the London *Times* in 1908, was 'a young lady who has not yet been promoted to long frocks and the wearing of her hair "up"' – a type, the newspaper added, very much prevalent at the time.[4] A *New York Times* article reiterated that view: the flapper 'is a girl who has just "come out." She is at an awkward age, neither a child nor a woman.'[5] In 1911 the magazine *Home Notes* published '"A Page for Flappers": Who and what is a flapper? How does she "flap" and why? Who christened her, and why has the name stuck to every girl between the ages of fourteen and seventeen?'[6] Clothing stores designed styles just for her: 'very girlish in character', touted an advertisement for the chic New York department store Bonwit Teller, 'yet distinctively different from really little girls' styles'.[7] The flapper girl loved to wear big bows in her hair, the better to advertise that she was adorable.

Although her body was still child-like – flat-chested and boyish – her approach to puberty hinted at her coming sexual maturity. There was something covertly erotic about her – hidden, many people thought, even to the girl herself. 'All the secret thoughts of the average girl emerging from the "flapper" stage turn on love,' one observer noted, 'and she is consumed with curiosity on a hundred matters about which she dare not inquire.' She tried to sate her curiosity by reading novels, with the result that she developed 'a totally erroneous and generally silly conception of life'.[8] But who would set her straight? Mothers, observed an article in the *Washington Post*, wanted to 'keep a girl a child as long as possible', which, the writer thought, 'is decidedly dangerous under present conditions'. The modern girl was eager to learn 'everything about human life', including everything about sex.[9] She resented being swaddled.

In the theatre, the *New York Times* noticed, flappers were in vogue as early as 1907, when 'the little, hair-down-her-back sort of girl' evolved into someone 'more grown-up and womanly' but not 'too big or dignified'. She looked every bit like an adolescent, and often, in fact, was performed by an actress in her teens, but her role was hardly that of a demure, awkward girl. Vaudeville impresarios called for chorus girls around five feet tall, young and with a 'lilylike, slender, graceful figure', rather than the buxom, statuesque performers of the previous decade.[10] The flapper was an ingénue of a particular type: pretending to be innocent and girlish, she was sexy and she knew it. And she could be devious and manipulative.

Men thought she was charming: fresh, nubile, amusing. 'It was really too painful', one woman cabled to the *New York Times* from a visit in London:

> sweet sixteen continues to be the greatest attraction where
> the menfolk are concerned. The woman of the world is
> quite out of it . . . We travel, we study, we are able to talk
> to men as men talk to one another on golf, politics or
> the turf, and along comes a girl who is young, pretty,
> 'innocent', and thoroughly feather-brained, and no one
> has any more use for us.[11]

The shy, long-legged young girl had evolved into a threat to womankind. This was 1913, and as the article reported, already 'the flapper has had a long inning.'

At the roiling turn of the twentieth century, in the U.S. and Britain, the flapper was a troubling adolescent girl, and she generated a crisis of cultural anxiety on both sides of the Atlantic. That anxiety emerged in magazine articles, fiction and theatre; in research by psychologists and physicians; and in manuals addressed to parents and girls themselves, all contributing to an Anglo-American conversation that shifted and evolved for several decades. The adolescent girl, everyone agreed, seemed to be inventing a culture of her own – out of her parents' control – which threatened marriage, the family, the workplace and, not least, propriety. The years between twelve and eighteen, between childhood innocence and womanly sexuality, became the focus of worry, debate and unremitting scrutiny: worry about the girl sloughing off the chrysalis of society's expectations and demands; debate about how to control her passionate spirits, which made her ready to flap her butterfly wings and fly from the past; and scrutiny of this sexy, alluring young being, a mystery to parents, educators, physicians, boys and men. What do we do with our daughters?, parents asked with fear and consternation. And the girls themselves asked, what do we do with ourselves? Who are we? What do we want? What is our future?

The iconic, mythic, post-war flapper has a history. She emerged from a culture obsessed with the adolescent girl: as a problem, a temptation and finally, in the 1920s and beyond, an aspiration. 'We now have a sturdy and athletic, an independent and courageous, pleasure-seeker upon our hands,' the stolid *North American Review* ominously reported in 1906.[12] She was the flapper girl; she became the flapper woman.

About a word

The historian Jane H. Hunter makes a persuasive case that by the end of the nineteenth century, the term 'girls', not 'young ladies', became common usage for adolescent females, preferred by girls themselves. A girl had passed puberty but still had preserved her innocence, individuality and class status. She had freedom in the city streets, yet she was not of the streets. She was a peer and equal of boys, not a refined creature of the parlor.[13]

From my own research, I found ample evidence to support Hunter's conclusion. To convey the spirit of the times, therefore, I use the word 'girl' with no intention to trivialize the experiences and identities of adolescents and young women.

My title 'Lost Girls' alludes to the Lost Boys, Peter Pan's entourage of young adventurers – motherless, fatherless and free. Although sometimes nostalgic for the comfort and protection of the nursery, they celebrated independence; in one sense, they were playing at adulthood, but in another, they were creating a separate world for themselves, and a stage of life that was liminal, unpredictable and fertile with possibility. The Lost Boys achieved the dream of adolescents. Lost Girls did the same as they invented a new image and identity.

These girls, though, did not live in Neverland, but instead in a culture where they were continually warned about the real losses – of men's love, of society's esteem, of their femininity – that they might suffer if they acted upon their secret needs and desires. Some girls, responding to adults who considered them self-indulgent, irresponsible and unwomanly, worried that they might lose their way in the world. Landmarks and guiding stars seemed to disappear, and paths seemed to lead nowhere, or to a dangerous elsewhere. Reinvention seemed reckless; rebellions, many girls realized, do not always end victoriously for those who rebel. *Lost Girls* tells a story of girls challenged and often confused by others' conceptions of who they were, how they were to live and what they risked to lose. It is a story of youth derided and exuberantly fetishized; of maturity, and most definitely ageing, viscerally feared. It is a story of girls evolving into flappers; and a story of women with the everlasting, inexorable desire to be girls.

1 Angelfish

'Strange doings go on secretly in this life of her mind.'
Ida Tarbell, *The Ways of Woman* (1915)

In 1905, when seventy-year-old Mark Twain began to collect a bevy of adolescent girls, whom he called his 'angelfish', he defended his predilection by insisting that he longed for grandchildren. His own daughters were grown – his favourite, Susy, was dead by then – and he was lonely. But grandfathers can have grandsons as well as granddaughters, and Twain, creator of one of literature's most famous adolescents, surely celebrated boys' cheeky energy. There was more, then, to his strange sorority than an elderly man's yearning for grandchildren, more even than nostalgia for his daughters' childhoods. 'As for me,' Twain wrote at the age of 73, 'I collect pets: young girls – girls from ten to sixteen years old; girls who are pretty and sweet and naive and innocent – dear young creatures to whom life is a perfect joy and to whom it has brought no wounds, no bitterness, and few tears.'[1]

Innocent they were, but not as naive as he seemed to think. Certainly they knew that he was a celebrity: that was how it started, when fifteen-year-old Gertrude Natkin saw him leaving Carnegie Hall on 27 December 1905, after a matinee song recital by the German soprano Madame Johanna Gadski. Twain, after all, was instantly recognizable, even before he decided to wear only white. He noticed her, to be sure, saw that she wanted to speak to him, introduced himself and shook her hand. The next day, she wrote to thank him: 'I am very glad I can go up and speak to you now . . . as I think we know each other.' Describing herself as his 'obedient child', she ended her note, 'I am the little girl who loves you.'[2] He responded immediately, calling himself Gertrude's 'oldest & latest conquest'.[3] Their correspondence was playfully flirtatious: he called her his 'little witch'; she called him 'darling'.[4] He sent her a copy of his favourite book, the writings of 'a bewitching little scamp' named Marjorie, who had died just short of her ninth birthday, in Scotland in 1811. 'I have adored Marjorie for six-and-thirty years,' he confessed in an essay. The child, who confided startlingly sophisticated remarks about books, history and religion in her journal, seemed to him 'made out of thunderstorms and sunshine': 'how impulsive she was, how sudden, how tempestuous, how tender, how loving, how sweet, how loyal, how rebellious . . . how innocently bad, how natively good,' he exclaimed.[5] 'May I be your little "Marjorie"?' Gertrude asked coyly.[6] That is how Twain addressed her, in letters filled with what the two called 'blots', or kisses – until 1906, when he was taken aback by her turning sixteen. 'I am almost afraid to send a blot, but I venture it. Bless your heart it comes within an ace of being improper! Now back you go to 14! – then there's no impropriety.'[7] Their correspondence ended, and Twain set his sights on younger girls.

Buoyed by Gertrude's effusive declarations of love, Twain discovered that it was easy to find other young admirers, primarily from among his fellow passengers on holiday trips to Bermuda. By 1908 he had collected ten schoolgirls, dubbed them his 'angelfish', and awarded them membership in his Aquarium Club. In Bermuda, he had special shimmering enamel lapel pins designed for them to wear on their left breast, above the heart. In the spring and summer of 1908, one biographer notes, Twain's letters to his angelfish comprised more than half of his correspondence: one letter sent or received every day.[8] Many contained invitations to the girls to visit him in his palatial house in Redding, Connecticut, which he named Innocence at Home. 'I have built this house largely, indeed almost chiefly, for the comfort & accommodation of the Aquarium,' Twain announced in a mock-serious document that he sent to his angelfish, containing the rules and regulations of the club. The lair of the angelfish was his Billiard Room.[9]

Twain recounted, in an autobiographical entry, how he found his 'jewels'. One morning in Bermuda, as he walked into the breakfast room,

> the first object I saw in that spacious and far-reaching place was a little girl seated solitary at a table for two. I bent down over her and patted her check and said, affectionately and with compassion, 'Why you dear little rascal – do you have to eat your breakfast all by yourself in this desolate way?'

They arranged to meet after breakfast and, he reported, 'were close comrades – inseparables in fact – for eight days'.[10] A friend later told him that the twelve-year-old girl had asked if he was married, and when learning that he was not – his wife had died – said, 'If I were his wife I would never leave his side for a moment; I would stay

Mark Twain and Dorothy Quick, one of Twain's angelfish, 1907.

by him and watch him, and take care of him all the time.' Twain attributed the remark to the girl's 'mother instinct', and willingly submitted, characterizing himself as a 'degraded and willing slave'.[11]

In 1907, on board a ship taking him to England, where he would receive an honorary degree from Oxford, Twain found the sixteen-year-old Frances Nunnally, with whom, he said, he 'grew quite confidential',[12] and who became, however briefly, an angelfish; on the return trip, he befriended nine-year-old Dorothy Quick, who, a newspaper reporter noted, 'guarded him closely during the voyage', sitting on his lap, with her head leaning against his shoulder.[13] He called her 'mon amie', another reporter wrote, and stood on deck with his arm 'thrown paternally around the child's shoulder', at one point giving her 'a fond little hug'.[14]

Twain's collection of girls was well known, inspiring some adult women to press for membership. One came for dinner 'dressed

Innocence at Home, Mark Twain's residence in Connecticut.

for 12 years, & had pink ribbons at the back of her neck & looked about 14 years old'. Impressed, Twain gave her an angelfish pin. 'There's lots of lady-candidates,' he wrote to a young angelfish, 'but I guess we won't let any more in, unless perhaps Billie Burke.'[15] The vivacious and youthful comedienne, 23 at the time, was a favourite actress of Twain's: 'Billie is as good as she is pretty,' he remarked to an angelfish after dining with Burke and a few other Broadway performers.[16] He had met her after a performance of *My Wife*, a play whose May-to-December theme fitted his fantasies, and Burke often visited him at his Manhattan townhouse whenever she was working in the northeast.

During the years that Twain collected his angelfish, he spurned the companionship of his real daughter, Jean, who had been living in medical institutions where her epilepsy could be monitored. In the summer of 1908 Twain's secretary and assistant, Isabel Lyon (the Lioness, he called her, and she called him King), arranged for Jean to live in Gloucester, Massachusetts; she stayed there briefly, unhappily, until she left the country with friends. In 1909 Jean returned to Twain's home, where she drowned in a bathtub, having suffered a seizure.

By the time Jean died, Twain's blatant cavorting with angelfish had been thwarted by his other daughter, Clara. In the summer of 1908 Clara returned from a European concert tour and was appalled by her father's new interest. Rechristening the Redding house Stormfield, she put an end to the angelfishes' visits. The house had lost its innocence, and by that winter Twain began to complain irritably about his declining health and spirits. An odd resurfacing of the angelfish obsession occurred in 1910, just weeks before his death, in letters and notebook entries regarding the fifteen-year-old Helen Allen, a moody young woman who fascinated him. 'She is bright, *smart, alive*, energetic, determined, high-tempered, *intense*,' he wrote; but she was also disappointing, preferring romance literature to poetry, and responding to Twain's witticisms and attempts at banter with 'mute indifference'.[17] More disappointing still, she had a boyfriend, and Twain was jealous: he cautioned Helen to preserve her innocence; he wanted the younger man out of the way.

Twain's obsession with adolescent girls can be explained in part by his exalting of his own teenaged years – years of daring and adventure. His wife, after all, had nicknamed him 'Youth', and his most memorable fictional characters, of course, are the adolescent Huckleberry Finn and Tom Sawyer. Twain focused not on young boys, though, but sexually innocent girls from ages ten to sixteen, with undeveloped boyish bodies and with whom he carried out titillating flirtations. Photographs of Twain and his angelfish show them standing or sitting close to him, their bodies touching his, with his arms around their shoulders or waists. They might be his daughters; or they might be his lovers. His notes about Helen Allen reveal a yearning to be more than protector, mentor and grandfather. Twain regretted ageing, claiming the vigour of a much younger man. 'At 2 o'clock in the morning I feel old and sinful,' he remarked, 'but at 8 o'clock, when I am shaving I feel young and ready to hunt trouble . . . as though I were not over 25 years old.'[18]

At the turn of the twentieth century, the image of a man of Twain's age in the company of an adoring young girl was no anomaly. In literature, such as Jean Webster's novel *Daddy-Long-Legs* of 1912, in cartoons and later in movies, the character of a daddy's girl fulfilled a male fantasy: an older man, usually wealthy, sometimes famous, basked in the attentions of a girl in need of protection and love. Real daughters fed the fantasy. As mothers took on the major role of raising children while their husbands worked in business, daughters learned that fathers were not omnipotent authoritarian figures who must be obeyed, but men who loved to be petted. Daughters read to their fathers, curled up on their laps, nuzzled them. These intimacies stopped short of sex, but fuelled men's desire for the kind of precocious sexuality that pubescent girls represented. Daddy's girls were a seductive substitute. Men exerted their power over the girls – they could bestow, or withdraw, attention and gifts; but girls had power, too: to make an older man feel young and virile and valued, and to serve as adornments.

The popular image of the daddy's girl reflected a prevalent sense of the adolescent female as a sexualized, mysterious being, different from what their mothers had been at the same age, and difficult to control. They were out of their parents' sight more: in school, on bicycles, shopping in towns. Some talked to friends, privately, on the phone. 'Strange doings go on secretly in this life of her mind,'

G. S. Hall, *c.* 1910. His two-volume *Adolescence* (1904) was widely influential.

according to writer and reporter Ida Tarbell, whose early career had included teaching. If a girl's thoughts and desires were revealed, 'they would throw her elders into fits'.[19] Who were these new creatures, parents and educators asked, with urgency and alarm.

Their yearning for an explanation was fed by an assortment of men and women boasting particular expertise in observing or studying adolescent girls. None, however, became as famous for his views – detailed, long-winded and insistent – as the educator and psychologist Granville Stanley Hall.

The expert

G. S. Hall was aged fifty in 1894 when he began to work on the two-volume compendium that would appear, ten years later, as *Adolescence: Its Psychology and its Relation to Physiology, Anthropology, Sociology, Sex, Crime, Religion and Education*. The book promised to reveal everything that could be known about the physical, mental and emotional development of boys and girls as they passed through puberty. Synthesizing a vast number of sources, he filled more than 1,200 pages with charts, tables and data about the body's physical transformation, the development of genitals and the trajectory of psychological and intellectual maturity.

He brought in anthropological studies to make his case that humans recapitulated evolution in their development. He portrayed young people as volatile and intense, moody and passionate, as they weathered the storm and stress of growing into adults. Boys culminated in humanity's highest achievement: the adult male. Girls had different needs, and, Hall asserted, far different potential, intellectually and socially, from boys. His unwieldy, digressive and opinionated tome spoke to an abiding concern among his readers to name and make sense of girls' experience of adolescence, to formulate educational policy and to guide their daughters. Besides the volumes themselves, which sold well and went into a second printing within months of their publication in March 1904, Hall travelled the country speaking on the topic of which he had made himself an acclaimed expert.

Like his former mentor William James, whose *Principles of Psychology* ensured his reputation when it was finally published, also after a ten-year gestation, Hall intended his own first book to stand as testimony to his significance in psychology, a significance to which he had long aspired. Already well known in the field of child study, he had taught at Johns Hopkins University and in 1889 became president of the newly established Clark University, a position that would end badly when financial straits, conflicts with faculty and the founder's loss of confidence undermined his stewardship. During the writing of *Adolescence*, Hall's personal life shattered, as well: in 1890 his wife and eight-year-old daughter died of asphyxiation from a gas leak in a bedroom lighting fixture. Hall, who had been out of town that night, returned to an unthinkable tragedy. Dazed by the loss, he threw himself into his work, needing to be anywhere but at home. His nine-year-old son hardly saw him. Even after Hall remarried in 1899, the focus of his life was his work and reputation.

Coinciding with difficulties at Clark, and the deaths of his wife and daughter, the writing project threw him back into memories of his own adolescence, and intensified feelings of isolation, inadequacy and self-doubt that dogged him throughout his life. His conclusions about adolescence, as one might expect, were shaped by those memories, which made writing the book a time of painful introspection and helps to explain some of his surprising assertions, especially regarding girls.

Hall grew up on a farm in Ashfield, Massachusetts, 'deeply indebted', he said later, to the rural environment in which 'every basal trait' was set, and persisted into adulthood unchanged.[20] Among those traits was a fraught conception of sexuality and his own manhood. 'As a child,' he admitted, 'the only name for a certain part of the body, which I long supposed was its proper and adopted designation, was "the dirty place" for this phrase was applied to nothing else.'[21] At school, he became aware of obscene terms for male genitals, but his classmates' coarse language only exacerbated his disgust. As a young teenager he was so terrified by the possibility of nocturnal emissions and masturbation that he devised some rigging and applied bandages to his body to prevent stimulation. Even after a physician assured him that he was normal, he felt that he was 'secretly and exceptionally corrupt and not quite worthy to associate with girls' – shame that persisted even when he was in university.[22] Dealing with masturbation in *Adolescence*, Hall was less draconian than many of his contemporaries in asserting that masturbation would not cause insanity or physical degradation; still, it had to be avoided, and he advised hard work, loose clothing and cold showers.

The young Hall's self-esteem was not helped by his father, an exacting, impatient man who quashed his son's aspirations towards education and a profession. His mother was understanding and encouraging, but Hall could see that she, too, was cowed by the man she married. 'Of all things in this world,' her son noted, 'she most craved love or the intimate, sympathetic relation she had so long enjoyed with her father,' whom she idolized, even as an adult.[23] His mother's adoration of her father impressed the boy deeply, revived in his musings on adolescent girls, their needs and fantasies about his own role in their lives.

Although he boasted that he was 'always rather a boy's boy and a man's man', for Hall this statement meant not only that he was a rough-and-tumble boy and brawny adult, but that he felt more comfortable socializing with men rather than women.[24] Women unnerved him, possibly because he feared that his own manly identity was compromised by his identification with his spiritual, religious, gentle mother. As a teenager and student at Williams College and Union Theological Seminary, which he attended, unhappily, for a year, he confessed that he never 'called on a young lady or even had more than the most passing acquaintance with one. In this respect, I was, I know, very exceptional among my classmates.'[25]

His very exceptional attitude changed during a trip to Germany when he was 24. There, he said, he met two German girls who revealed to him 'what love really meant and could do . . . There was no engagement and no plans of life together but we were devoted to each other with a *carpe diem* abandon to the pleasure of the passing hour.' Whether he lost his virginity, or simply found himself sexually aroused by a woman for the first time, he suddenly felt that he was a man 'in the full normal sense of that word. Certain old shackles had been shaken off and I . . . acquired a deeper sense of both sin and righteousness and virtue than I had ever attained before.' If sin was temptation to have sex with these women, virtue may well have been the self-control that he had fought so ardently to achieve as a young teenager. The experience, he added, 'made life seem richer and more meaningful. If passion was aroused the power to moderate and control it was also gained and I have never had regret but only a sense of enlargement of soul from it all.'[26]

In 1872 he took a temporary job teaching English and philosophy at Antioch College in Ohio, where he remained for three years. He had previously tutored boys, sometimes establishing his authority by spanking, but at the co-educational college he was startled by the 'select body of mature young ladies who . . . were, on the whole, superior to the men' and 'dominated' the school's atmosphere with a 'strong feminine element' that softened 'the active boy student life that characterized other non-coeducational institutions'.[27] This feminine influence seemed to him then, and emerged in his writings later, as a negative force in shaping strong, competitive, vigorous men.

The girls at Antioch, whom he described as 'mature young ladies', also unsettled Hall by their flirtatiousness, not only towards their male classmates but towards their 28-year-old teacher.[28] One or two, he recalled, 'were prone to make slight advances toward the schoolmaster'. He was tempted, but had been warned by colleagues that it was 'fatal' to respond – 'and I believe,' he said, 'I never did.'[29] Yet he saw how forcefully these girls could stir him, and how easily they could have ruined him.

When the Antioch job ended, Hall once again needed to choose a career path. Inspired by his first German trip, he decided to pursue psychology and to enrol in a graduate programme at Harvard, where he studied with William James. In 1878 Hall earned the first American doctorate in the field. Returning to Germany in 1879, he kept up a correspondence with Harvard colleagues, sharing the progress of his studies and, in a postscript to one of them, mentioning his marriage. He elaborated, just barely, in a letter to James: 'The lady was named Miss Fisher, her home is Cincinnati though she has been living in Europe for four years. She is the sister of a theological classmate & I first saw her when a student in NY.'[30] To James's effusive congratulations, he responded tepidly: 'You fancy marriage has changed me, perhaps. My wife is a sincere Presbyterian, very practical &c.' Marriage, then, was not the life-altering experience that his German flirtations had been, but rather seemed peripheral to what totally consumed him: finding a professional position, and one that would not be hampered by 'how [Harvard President] Eliot will like it, how it will affect my prospects' or whether his philosophical ideas would lead his students astray, which had been a concern at Antioch.[31] When James met up with him in Heidelberg in the summer of 1880, the two men spent hours in fruitful conversation, inspiring James to write on Hall's behalf for a position. The recipient was Daniel Coit Gilman, president of Johns Hopkins, who was looking to make a hire in psychology, and Hall, finally, found a place.

He taught at Johns Hopkins until he was tapped by the wealthy businessman Jonas Gilman Clark to head a university in Worcester, Massachusetts. Hall insisted on its beginning as a graduate-only institution focused on the sciences – physics, chemistry, biology, mathematics and psychology – hoping to mould a new generation of scholars in fields that he believed would be essential for the new century. After accepting the invitation, Hall made a whirlwind tour of European universities, returning with enthusiasm and ideas that he found it increasingly hard to enact. He soon discovered that 73-year-old Clark, a man 'of great reticence' who never articulated his vision for the university, even to the Board of Trustees, refused to disclose just how much ongoing financial support he was willing to bestow on the venture.[32] Clark listened patiently to his faculty's requests for supplies, for example, sent them to Hall, and then forbade Hall to spend any money. The faculty, not surprisingly, saw Hall as the villain in the drama that was playing out on campus, and three years into his tenure, 'a majority of the faculty, after interviewing every member of the board and stating with the greatest fullness their grounds for dissatisfaction, offered their resignations because they "had lost confidence"' in their president.[33]

The uprising rattled him. As aggressive and overbearing as he could be in his writings, Hall was reticent when confronted with conflict. 'If I am not assured of sympathy in my social environment,' he said, 'it is hard for me to speak or to assert myself, and there is also a crust of diffidence that has to be broken before I can come out of my shell.'[34] Sadly, he had few close friends, although he deeply desired that kind of intimacy. Many who knew him, he realized regretfully, saw him as 'somewhat unresponsive sentimentally', a consequence, he thought, of his family's 'atmosphere of repression'. He felt more at ease with students than colleagues: peers too often made him question his abilities.[35] Hall, one colleague said, was 'tragically human . . . with enough sense of weakness, failure, or inward discord in himself to give him insight and make possible his descriptions of naked souls in a death struggle with fear or felt inferiority'.[36] Although he had sympathizers and even admirers among his circle, he was a vulnerable, often lonely man.

He was a man, too, with a secret. When he was 'unknown and away from home', he disclosed in his memoirs, he liked to glimpse 'the raw side of life', such as prize fights, freaks in circus side-shows (he planned to write a memoir about those he had met) and brothels. 'In many American and especially in foreign cities (Paris, where vice was most sophisticated; London, where it was coarsest; Vienna, which I thought the worst of all; Berlin, New York, San Francisco)', he discovered that hotel clerks could tell him about 'the underworld by night', where he could 'catch its psychological flavor . . . In these excursions,' he confessed, 'I have seen some of the most bestial traits of which morbid and depraved human nature is capable, and heard of even worse.'[37] As president of the New England Watch and Ward Society in 1909–10, he gained intimate knowledge of vice among women, knowledge that fed his ideas about sexuality.

Backfisch

Hall and James met from time to time in Hall's home town of Ashfield, where he sometimes stayed on holiday, and James invited him once to Tamworth, in the White Mountains of New Hampshire, where James and his wife had built a home. By 1887 Hall had gained some stature in the psychological community, founding the *Journal of American Psychology*, which he hoped would influence the field by publishing articles about experimental work, to which he was completely committed. Hall, James wrote to one of his British colleagues, the editor of the rival journal *Mind*,

> is a wonderful creature. Never an articulate conception
> comes out of him, but instead of it a sort of palpitating
> influence making all men believe that the way to save their

souls psychologically lies through the infinite assimilation of jaw-breaking german [sic] laboratory-articles. If you try to draw any expressible theoretical conclusion from any of them, he wont [sic] hear it; what you ought to do is to pass on to a lot more of them; and so *in infinitum.*[38]

Hall, James added to his Harvard colleague Hugo Munsterberg, 'hates clearness – clear formulas, clear statements, clear understandings'.[39] When Hall sent his *Adolescence* to the Swiss philosopher Théodore Flournoy, a close friend of James, Flournoy's response echoed that of many other readers: he found the tomes unreadable, 'its style so boring that I had to give it up'.[40] A reviewer in the *Washington Post* called it 'a ponderous work'.[41]

Nevertheless, some who read, skimmed or dipped into it recognized that Hall spoke to their own concerns, especially about the changing behaviour of adolescent girls. Like many of his contemporaries, Hall brought to his depiction of these girls a mixture of fear, scorn and attraction. He feared the power they exerted by their seemingly innocent flirting and coquetry; feared the possibility that they could compete with men intellectually; scorned their aspirations to independence; but was undeniably attracted to their budding sexuality, which emerged in their obsession with fashions, hairstyles and make-up. In dressing up, Hall believed, adolescent girls were practising charms that would serve them as women, making their experimentation much more significant than mere child's play. Indeed, for Hall, adolescence was a stage that a woman never outgrew: she 'lingers in, magnifies and glorifies this culminating stage of life with its all-sided interests, its convertibility of emotions, its enthusiasm, and zest for all that is good, beautiful, true, and heroic'.[42] While he conceded that being an eternal adolescent could make a woman seem fresh and appealing, Hall worried that these eternal adolescents lacked the kind of moral compass that guided men, but instead had a decided predilection 'to ruse and deception'.[43] Still, conflating womanliness with childishness allowed Hall to feel some measure of superiority and control over feminine wiles. Being mired in adolescence, moreover, meant a woman would not attain men's intellectual level.

Hall's vision of an ideal school for girls sounds more like a summer camp or country club than an educational institution. He would put girls in a rural area, on a campus with space for golf and tennis, and a regimen that would allow for regular sleep and good, healthful nutrition. Book learning would not be forced upon them; flowers, gardening, excursions and pets would provide instruction in nature; there would be 'some ideal home building', where girls would be taught 'domesticity' and where 'appeals to tact and taste should be incessant'. 'A purely intellectual man is no doubt biologically a deformity,' he wrote, 'but a purely intellectual woman is far more so.'[44]

Most revealing about Hall's educational scheme is the crucial role of a man who sounds much like Hall himself:

> There should be at least one healthful, wise, large-souled, honorable, married and attractive man, and if possible, several of them. His very presence in an institution for young women gives poise, polarizes the soul, and gives wholesome but long-circuited tension at root no doubt sexual, but all unconsciously so. This mentor should not be more father than brother, though he should combine the best of each, but should add another element. He need not be a doctor, a clergyman, or even a great scholar, but

Charles Dana Gibson, *Girls Hiking and Walking*, 1900.

should be accessible for confidential conferences
even though intimate. He should know the soul of the
adolescent girl and how to prescribe, he would be wise
and fruitful in advice, but especially should be to all a
source of contagion and inspiration for poise and courage
even though religious or medical problems be involved.

The mentor should be 'so poised that impulsive girls can turn their
hearts inside out in his presence and perhaps even weep on his
shoulder'.[45] The mentor should be poised – that is, positioned – to
elicit confidences and to console girls after their emotional outpour-
ings. His poise could also serve as a model for girls' behaviour. Girls,
Hall believed, need to be taught poise, that is, to keep their emotions

in check, and also to hone their natural coquetry and flirtatiousness into socially acceptable behaviour.

Like Twain surrounded by his angelfish, Hall also likened his adolescent girls to fish, referring to the German word for a girl in her early teens: *Backfisch*. *Backfisch*, he wrote,

> means a fresh fish, just caught but unbaked, though fit
> and ready for the process. The naivety of instinctive,
> unconscious childhood, like the glinting sheen of sea hues,
> is still upon the *Backfisch* . . . Her real nature is wild with
> a charming gamey flavor . . . Girls with hair demurely
> braided down their backs, and skirts just beginning to
> lengthen toward their ankles are buds that should not
> blossom for some time, but should be kept as long as
> possible in the green stage.[46]

Although he portrayed his *Backfisch* as childishly naive, they were also coquettes, luring the man who thought he was the power in pursuit of prey. Despite his insistence that girls 'should be kept as long as possible in the green stage', he portrayed their innocence as sexually appealing, with a glinting sheen of wildness shimmering beneath the surface.

The possibility of wildness drove many parents to despair. 'The Girl of the Period,' wrote the British novelist and journalist Eliza Lynn Linton, 'is a creature . . . whose sole idea of life is fun; whose sole aim is unbounded luxury; and whose dress is the chief object of such thought and intellect as she possesses.'[47] Her thought was materialistic, according to Linton, and her intellect negligible. In 1889 one Mrs J. G. Fraser published a piece in the *Congregationalist*, 'Our Lost Girls: A Mother Sadly Regrets that She Can Not Have

THE GIRL OF THE HOUR.

'The Girl of the Hour', happily skating, admired by men and boys, on the cover of *Puck* magazine, 1904.

the Training of Her Daughter'. Girls are lost as soon as they enter their teens, Mrs Fraser complained. Content only when they have visits from their friends, daughters showed little interest in family life. 'Our homes', Mrs Fraser wrote, 'should not be simply boarding houses where our children eat and sleep, but dwelling places where they are to spend most of their time out of school hours,' where they confided in their mothers and looked to them for guidance.[48] But girls took advice from their friends, looked upon their mothers as hopelessly old-fashioned and were no longer willing to see their father as a hero, a paragon of manhood and fount of knowledge.

Parents were troubled with unsettling ideas about their daughters' minds and bodies. Although most girls began to menstruate at around fourteen, rumours had it that the age of menarche was falling, inciting worry about precocious sexuality, a worry fuelled by tabloid magazines depicting girls behaving badly. As Ida Tarbell warned, the deceptively submissive girl who seemed to be 'an obedient creature who loves a pretty frock, wheedles her father, frisks, dances, sleeps twelve hours out of the twenty-four' was harbouring deep mysteries and desires.[49] That girl became society's problem.

2 Daughters Revolt

'Put yourselves in her place, and ask yourselves
how you would like to have no independence, but
be obliged always to live someone else's life, and
carry out only someone else's purposes.'
Alys Pearsall-Smith, 'A Reply from the Daughters' (1894)

The problem was this: middle-class girls coming of age at the turn of the century, teased by freedom, were besieged with contradictory messages about their potential and their future. They were bright and able, according to their teachers. They earned high grades and walked away with prizes. But they heard and read that girls were not as clever as boys, and they did not know what to believe. They engaged in sports, and felt healthier, not weaker, from the exertion. But they heard and read that competitive games were for boys, that exercise and running about would make them nervous and pale. They learned from parents, relatives, newspapers and magazines that controversy swirled around who they were and how they were to live. They learned, as girls, that their futures might not be theirs to shape: they had a particular role to play, a role that had served

The New Woman, *c.* 1896, portrayed with her bicycle, the *Sporting Times* and a golf club on her skirt, is a towering figure in this British illustration.

family life, the economy and social structures for generations. They learned that their God-given and socially prescribed fate was to become wives and mothers. Anxiety about motherhood, particularly intense at this historical moment, inflamed debates about these girls' education, their suitability as wives and the possibility that they would work outside of the home. The prospect of motherhood shaped every facet of their identity, and it made many girls confused, distressed and rebellious.

Even before *Adolescence* was published in 1904, Hall crossed America giving speeches and lectures, making his case that girls needed to fulfil their biological destiny. Girls needed to marry, he insisted. They needed to have children. They needed to raise those children to be strong, healthy and willing to procreate, for the good of the human species. Those prescriptions had been stamped with scientific credibility for many decades before Hall took them up. He got them from Darwin.

Understanding anything about nineteenth-century anxiety urges a return to 1859, with the publication of *On the Origin of Species*. The basis, after all, of Darwin's unsettling ideas about natural selection was reproduction: a species – of flowers, insects, animals – needed to make more of itself to survive competition with others. Without the female of the species producing eggs and without the male fertilizing those eggs, survival was impossible. Most important, the fittest and strongest of a species needed to prevail, passing on their endowments to offspring. For those who believed that the white bourgeoisie marked the pinnacle of human evolution, survival depended on its females to embrace motherhood, become impregnated by the most virile and successful males, and perpetuate that social cohort with numerous offspring. Those offspring needed to be nurtured, their lives protected and the daughters brought up to fulfil their moral, biological and cultural obligation to reproduce. And so it would go, except that by the mid-nineteenth century, and intensifying in the following decades, the survival of the fittest native-born whites seemed threatened in America and Great Britain.

The birth rate among the white middle and upper classes was dropping, while others were fecund: in America, freed slaves, for example, moved off plantations and into cities, where they raised large families; and waves of immigrants from Ireland and Italy, as well as Germans, Scandinavians, Poles and Eastern Europeans – all these groups racially inferior in the eyes of the white middle- and upper-class populations – proliferated. With families of educated, economically successful men and women getting smaller, the prospect for the future was dismal: who would lead the nation, who would provide its models of self-reliance and integrity?

In 1901 Edward Alsworth Ross, a professor at the University of Nebraska, coined the term 'race suicide' for an already prevalent fear. In lectures and articles, the authoritative 35-year-old sociologist reiterated his dire prediction that native-born whites, limiting themselves to two or three children, were at risk of being outnumbered by an 'influx of low-grade aliens' who were engendering families with eight, ten and twelve children.[1] The cause was manifold: for one, he blamed the trend of smaller families on rising economic opportunity and lust for material goods. The expense of raising children, Ross maintained, was seen as an impediment to social mobility and economic security. As intelligent, educated men strived to raise their family's standard of living, they chose to have fewer children. Meanwhile, the poor and uneducated, with no such prospects in sight, put no limit on the number of their offspring. 'A hundred Harvard graduates produced only 68 sons, 46 grandsons, and but 30 great-grandsons,' Ross proclaimed. 'At this rate soon there will be no one to go to Harvard.'[2] A dismal thought, indeed: without Harvard men, the nation would suffer from 'brain famine'.[3]

Besides economic pressures on men, Ross also blamed women for turning away from motherhood – partly because of the physical toll it took on their bodies and the risk of death in childbirth; partly because, availing themselves of higher education, they felt restive. 'Society has put maternity out of fashion,' wrote Eliza Lynn Linton, 'and the nursery is nine times out of ten a place of punishment, not of pleasure, to the modern mother.' For some intellectual women, Linton concluded, 'maternity is looked on as a kind of degradation.'[4] There was a sure link between women's education – especially co-education – and race suicide.

The menace in the classroom

Hall agreed, informing listeners at a National Education Association convention in 1904 that college girls were marrying later and having fewer children than their less-educated cohort; but even more alarming, schoolgirls at every stage were not learning to value grace, charm and their unique capacity for reproduction. 'The rapid feminization of our schools encourages women teachers to give their own masculine traits and ideals free rein,' Hall said. As a result he announced alarmingly that 'a larger percentage of high school girls actually wish they were boys', while boys, encouraged to be gentlemen, were denied their natural tendency to be rowdy and vigorous.[5] 'The school and all institutions should push sex distinctions to its utmost,' Hall announced in another talk about the perils of co-education.[6]

'Concerning the American Girl', an illustration in *Puck*, 1904, shows a clergyman looking with disdain at girls' many activities. His scroll laments the decline of old ideals.

The argument that women were less logical, analytical and creative than men certainly was not unique to Hall, and had been expounded repeatedly in books, articles in the popular press and talks in public forums. Girls' education was a hotly contested topic. In 1873 Dr Edward H. Clarke, a physician and Harvard professor, published *Sex in Education; or, A Fair Chance for the Girls*, which, to the author's surprise, became a best-seller, going into eleven editions. Clarke's mission was to counter the proliferation of co-educational schools, which gave girls access to the same books, ideas and teachings as boys. Endorsed by many educators, parents and especially women with aspirations towards college and career, co-education, Clarke asserted, could threaten the social fabric, making women

'Why Not Go the Limit?', *c.* 1908. The prospect of women
smoking and drinking at a bar was shocking.

unwilling to marry and fulfil their biological destiny of motherhood. Arguments about women's intellectual inferiority were continually disproved by women's achievements, but those arguments continued to be made. Nevertheless Clarke – and Hall, who found Clarke's arguments compelling – focused on girls' bodies rather than their minds, cautioning that girls who taxed their brains would take energy away from their reproductive organs, which needed to be protected from stress.

Clarke took pains to assert that girls were intellectually capable of schoolwork, making him a little more enlightened than some of his peers, but girls engaged in brainwork to their physical detriment. 'The delicate bloom, early but rapidly fading beauty, and singular pallor of American girls and women,' he insisted, 'have almost passed into a proverb. The first observation of a European that lands upon our shores is, that our women are a feeble race . . .'.[7] Speaking at the annual meeting of the British Medical Association in London, Dr Withers Moore, whose ideas made their way across the Atlantic, reported 'the disastrous physical effects of higher education', especially in America, where college for women 'has its warmest supporters'.[8] College girls were pale, fragile and excessively nervous, a result of forcing their blood to nourish their brain instead of their ovaries.

Like Clarke, Hall insisted that a woman's sexuality must be expressed only in her role as a wife, and he noted with alarm women who refused to shape themselves into wives and devoted mothers who would raise healthy, happy children. Women's education, he insisted, needed to be focused on supporting those roles. While acknowledging that women desired fulfilling occupations so as to avoid being 'spoiled by idleness and vacuity of mind which makes them either lazy, phlegmatic, and unambitious, or else restless', he advised that their education 'should not aim to cultivate the thinking powers alone or chiefly'.[9] Instead, a woman should be educated enough to understand her husband's world, but not enough to participate in that world. Girls, to prepare for marriage and motherhood, needed a different setting and curriculum.

Besides making a case for protecting girls' physical needs, Hall endorsed same-sex education, because – possibly remembering his own adolescence – he feared that familiarity with adolescent boys might well breed girls' contempt. Girls, who mature earlier than boys, would become disenchanted with their male classmates' rowdy, immature behaviour. Such a girl, Hall believed, would come to see men as weak, effeminate and sexually unappealing. 'Riper in mind and body than her male classmate', Hall wrote, a girl would decide that a boy 'seems a little too crude and callow to fulfill the ideals of manhood normal to her age which point to older and riper men'.[10] If the girl was to generalize her disillusion to men as a whole, she might come to decide that all of them were 'lax and vapid'.[11] Hall himself did not want to be thought callow or lax, but rather to be one of the 'older and riper men' to whom a girl would be attracted.

Although Hall believed that women are 'weaker in body and mind than men', he maintained that 'they can achieve great things even intellectually', offering the example of Darwin, who did great work even though debilitated by illness.[12] Hall identified menstruation as just such a debility, insisting that intellectual pursuits interfered with regular periods. This assertion, much repeated in the press, was rejected by other experts, such as Mary Putnam Jacobi, a noted physician who argued that girls would do well to learn literature, chemistry, biology and physics. 'Girls', she said, 'are told that it is the part of a man to achieve results in this world, and then to come and lay them at the feet of some woman, whose only exertion should be the generous task of stooping to pick them up.' Rather than live idly, even though 'loved by some successful man', girls 'ought to look forward to something besides marriage'.[13] That use of 'besides' frightened some people: was Jacobi advising that women refuse to marry? Or was she advising that even wives and mothers would be happier having a role outside the home?

Hall was not persuaded by the testimony of the 'splendid spinster presidents' of some women's colleges. Not one of them, he said, asserted that 'the promotion of health' was an important aim. By the time they graduate, they have already matured beyond the age when women in the past started families. 'The body and soul of the girl in the middle twenties,' Hall claimed, 'cries out for love of husband and children.'[14] Most distressingly for champions of motherhood, newspaper and magazine articles displayed tables showing how few women university graduates married. LeBaron Russell Briggs, part-time president of the all-female Radcliffe College and full-time dean of Harvard's all-male Faculty of Arts and Sciences, explained: 'The women who come to college prefer the fortune to which an educated woman has before her in the various professions to a life of dependence.'[15]

In universities and in the world, girls saw models of productive, independent women. Susan B. Anthony, for one, did not suffer from being single and childless. 'She has lived a useful and perfectly unselfish life,' reported one newspaper article,

> but she doesn't know a thing in the world about the serene
> happiness that lies in being housekeeper, cook, chamber-
> maid, nurse, seamstress, hostess and half a dozen other
> things every day in the year till nervous prostration puts
> an end to the complicated business.[16]

Girls saw their mothers exhausted by household responsibilities, even when there were servants to help; they saw infants die – mortality hovered at 30 per cent, even in middle-class households – and they listened doubtfully to ministers' sermons about the glory of motherhood. Whereas religious doctrines underscored a woman's obligation to reproduce, those who were no longer devout questioned, and even openly rebelled against, that command. 'True motherhood is the greatest of the Creative Arts,' enjoined one woman writer. 'The true home is the temple of the soul.'[17] Many girls resisted a future of being confined within that temple with at least four children to raise – the number touted as the minimum needed to avert race suicide. Hall upped that number to six. Mary

Lowe Dickinson, a well-respected educator, gently suggested that motherhood offered a woman the 'chance to recreate and relive herself', and to bestow on a child the 'beauty and knowledge and pleasure and happy opportunities' that she had been denied.[18] But girls, encouraged by their success in school, wanted those opportunities for themselves: opportunities to join clubs, reform efforts or social groups, or even to work.

Hall rang in with a dark characterization of women who refused to embrace their biological destiny. Rather than transmit love to her husband and children, such a woman will funnel her energies into

> the desire for knowledge, or outer achievement . . . Failing to respect herself as a productive organism, she gives vent to personal ambitions; seeks independence; comes to know very plainly what she wants; perhaps becomes intellectually emancipated, and substitutes science for religion or the doctor for the priest.

Most unsettling, she was likely to affect 'mannish ways', seek satisfaction from 'art, science, literature, and reforms' and crave 'stimuli for feelings which have never found their legitimate expression'.[19] Rumours of lesbianism hissed around unmarried women.

Biologist and ardent Darwinian Thomas Henry Huxley, who agreed with Hall about women's excitable, emotional, impressionable nature, more generously proposed that no harm would come from giving women an education. 'Let us have "sweet girl graduates" by all means,' he proclaimed: 'They will be none the less sweet for a little wisdom; and the "golden hair" will not curl less gracefully outside the head by reason of there being brains within.' Huxley was referring to Alfred, Lord Tennyson's poem 'The Princess'

'Wash Day', *c.* 1901. Men feared that the New Woman would emasculate them, as this woman, smoking and wearing britches, threatens to do.

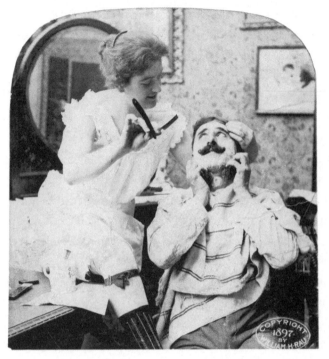

The New Woman, as a barber, frightens her client, c. 1897.

of 1847, which imagined a women's university that gave access to the same knowledge available to men. The defiant woman who proposed this university railed against being treated like a child; but Tennyson, like Huxley, was not threatened. Men, they were certain, would still rule the world.[20]

Anti-feminists shuddered at the thought that women would compete with men in the professions, insisting on the innate inferiority of women, an idea that also found justification in Darwin's work. In 1871 in *The Descent of Man*, he argued that men were superior to women in intelligence, energy and perseverance; and although women were endowed with intuition, perceptiveness and perhaps imagination, they would never reach the level of men, even if they were highly educated. Moreover, their education would have no influence on the evolution of the race. Darwin's own daughters were taught at home.[21]

The British physician, sex researcher and social reformer Havelock Ellis, in *Man and Woman*, his widely read study of sexual difference, embellished Darwin's view: 'Nature has made women more like children in order that they may better understand and care for children.'[22] Although he cited studies that found girls as intelligent as young boys, he maintained that after the age of sixteen 'the intellectual superiority of boys asserts itself'.[23] While women are occupied with bearing and raising children, men 'have roamed the earth, sharpening their aptitudes and energies in perpetual conflict with Nature'. 'It has thus come about', Ellis concluded, 'that the subjugation of Nature by Man has often practically involved the subjugation, physical and mental, of women by men.' Man's conflict with nature had transformed into competition in the business world, no less arduous, no less calling upon man's inherent aggression. Ellis made clear that 'so-called advanced periods . . . are not favourable to the freedom and expansion of women'.[24]

Scientific unions

Ross saw two solutions to the nightmare of race suicide: women needed to 'subordinate the individualist to the motherhood ideal', and the country needed a policy of restrictive immigration to 'shield American stock'.[25] It was this latter idea that led to his dismissal from Stanford University after having taught there for seven years; he objected to allowing Chinese immigrants into California – a stance that Mrs Leland Stanford found deplorable.

Ross found a champion, though, in the vociferous American president Theodore Roosevelt. 'The Nation is in a bad way,' Roosevelt told 400 delegates at the National Congress of Mothers in March 1905,

> if the woman has lost her sense of duty, if she is sunk in vapid self-indulgence or has let her nature be twisted so that she prefers a sterile pseudo-intellectuality to that great and beautiful development of character which comes only to those whose lives know the fullness of duty done, or effort made, and self-sacrifice undergone.

He extolled the virtues of motherhood and effusively praised those who performed 'the first and greatest duty of womanhood, able and willing to bear, and to bring up as they should be brought up, healthy children, sound in body, mind, and character, and numerous enough so that the race shall increase, not decrease'.[26]

Roosevelt's remarks, which he repeated in talks across the country and in his contributions to the *Ladies Home Journal*, proved incendiary. Mothers of large families protested: women already were having too many children to feed, clothe, house and educate properly. Where was he finding a diminishment of the race? Surely not in the slums of New York and Chicago, which were teeming with children. Reformers and activists protested: Roosevelt had no business pushing himself into the nation's bedrooms, and, furthermore, quality, not quantity, mattered. Which was precisely Roosevelt's point. He was concerned not with large immigrant families subsisting in poverty, but with women who walked their dogs, rather than their children, in fine neighbourhoods.

For Roosevelt, and those who agreed with him, fighting race suicide was akin to fighting a war: the project required an exertion of vigorous manhood. And here Roosevelt struck a sensitive nerve. Besides railing against women who failed to do their maternal duty, Roosevelt assailed men who were becoming decadent, effeminate and entirely too civilized to fight for dominance in the racial war. That concern menaced Great Britain, as well, just emerging from the challenges of the Boer War in which soldiers were vastly, shamefully underprepared. They were shorter, weighed less and were weaker overall than troops had been mid-century. Three thousand had to be sent home because of bad teeth. As the war dragged on for three years, the nation had to marshal more than 450,000 troops to overcome 40,000 Boers.[27]

In the popular imagination, one threat to masculinity was masturbation, a more pernicious vice than even drinking and gambling. Hall's condemnation of 'self-abuse', explicitly detailed in his memoirs and in *Adolescence*, influenced Robert Baden-Powell, founder of Britain's Boy Scouts, who admonished scout leaders to be forthright with boys about this vicious behaviour: the result of masturbation, he pronounced, 'is always – mind you, *always* – that the boy after a time becomes weak and nervous and shy, he gets headaches and probably palpitation of the heart, and if he still carries it on too far he very often goes out of his mind and becomes an idiot'. The antidote was self-control: self-restraint, self-discipline and, if those do not work, pouring cold water on one's genitals.[28] Boys needed to save themselves for marriage and procreation, both of which would be undermined by masturbation.

Late Victorian England, notes the historian George Robb, 'was haunted by fears of degeneration . . . In a post-Darwinian world, England's apparent decline was assumed to be essentially biological . . . so that the choice of one's sexual partner became crucial to the nation's future.'[29] Choosing a sexual partner emerged as a central concern of 'eugenics', a term invented in 1883 by Darwin's childless cousin Francis Galton to describe the application of the tenets of evolution to human development: 'what nature does blindly, slowly and ruthlessly,' Galton believed, 'man may do presciently, quickly, and benignly.'[30]

By 1904 eugenics was well-publicized in Britain, the nation's response to a dire need for what it called 'race renewal'. Although eugenists proposed to discourage the reproduction of the unfit – epileptics, the feeble-minded, the mentally ill and alcoholics, for example – their rhetoric often referred to 'racial' inferiority, implying that the fittest were white and native-born. As Leonard Darwin – Charles's fourth son and president of the Eugenics Society beginning in 1911 – put it, the fittest men had the potential to become 'lieutenants and serjeants of industry'.[31] Eugenists identified moral failings as evidence of unfitness, protesting against a social and political system 'which encourages fertility among the lower, less prudent, and less educated classes, at the expense of others'.[32] Social reformers, who wanted to improve living conditions for the poor, were in fact ensuring unchecked procreation of the unfit. Galton, however, insisted that he was not privileging the privileged class: 'The aim of eugenics', he wrote, 'is to represent each class or sect by its best specimens, causing them to contribute more than their proportion to the next generation.'[33] These best specimens should breed with their own class, of course, and not dilute higher-class whites.

The movement quickly spread to the U.S., where the Committee of Eugenics was headed by Alexander Graham Bell, and its members included the president of Stanford, the ichthyologist David Starr Jordan. With scientists at the helm – and with the support of the American Breeders' Association – the committee focused on investigating how much of an individual's ability and potential was due to heredity and how much to environment. At Clark University, Hall established a child study programme to provide just such data and, in addition, information on what racial types could intermarry without detriment or degeneration of the species. One potentially exciting idea, imported from England, was Havelock Ellis's notion of 'eugenic certificates' to be issued by 'a suitably constituted authority to those candidates who chose to apply for them and were able to pass the necessary tests'. No one would be forced to be examined, Ellis said, 'just as no one is compelled to seek a university degree'. Nevertheless, just like someone holding a degree, the certified individual 'would be one of nature's aristo-crats, to whom the future of the race might safely be left without further question'.[34]

Parents were charged with improving the race by raising daugh-ters not just to marry and have children, but to present themselves as suitable mates for certifiably admirable husbands. The ideal woman, according to Galton, was graceful, beautiful, gentle; the ideal man, strong in body and character. These traits were crucial to pass on to one's offspring, more important than anything charities and do-gooders could propose to improve living conditions. 'I am inclined to agree with Francis Galton', Charles Darwin wrote, 'in believing that education and environment produce only a small effect on the mind of anyone, and that most of our qualities are innate.'[35] Biology, and not social reform, would rescue the race from degeneration.

Finding a sexual partner was challenging for young British women at a time when there were hundreds of thousands more women than men, a result of war and emigration. Without a guarantee of marriage, young women did not look forward to a cloistered role as maiden aunt. If they could not marry, they would work, if only they had the education and skills needed to find employment. Rather than making girls desperate for marriage, recognition of a surplus made many desperate for independence.

The revolting maiden

That desire for independence had been forcefully articulated in a much-debated article by Blanche Althea Crackanthorpe, published in January 1894 in the prominent British journal of opinion the *Nineteenth Century*. 'The Revolt of the Daughters' presented the demands of young women for education, opportunities to travel and freedom to partake of such urban pleasures as music halls. Others rang in with their own responses, adding to the list of 'senseless prejudices, meaningless restrictions, and annoying trammels' vested upon young women. Surely, wrote the 22-year-old Lady Kathleen Cuffe in an essay published in March, if a girl could 'follow the natural bent of her mind, she would not be impelled by boredom and discontent into marrying the first person, whether congenial or not, who appeared on her limited horizon'. Cuffe's overriding demand was the freedom to go about without a chaperon. 'No early stroll in the park or afternoon tea-party may be undertaken' unless a girl is accompanied by a brother, parent or 'an unhappy maid or attendant'. Girls wanted only innocent pleasures, not illicit experiences, and one of those pleasures, Cuffe suggested, was having male friends, 'distinguished from flirtation'. If men and women could get to know one another casually, there would be fewer marriages based on 'mistaken impressions'. Some men, however, feared that friendly intimacy would result in fewer marriages, period. A woman's impression of a man's shortcomings might not be mistaken at all. Nevertheless, for Cuffe, casual friendships seemed desirable. 'The so-called revolting maiden only asks for a small amount of liberty,' Cuffe assured readers: 'She does not want anything very startling or very important.'[36] Although Cuffe's views seemed to be those of 'the average girl – not the examination-passing girl with her vast schemes of regenerating mankind' or with some special artistic ability – Cuffe herself hardly conformed to an idealized image of Victorian girlishness. As a child, she rode ponies, climbed trees, tobogganed down the stairs of her family's home and generally led her younger cousins into mischief. As a young woman, she did not want to quash that spirit.

The 27-year-old American Alys Pearsall-Smith, who by the end of 1894 would marry Bertrand Russell, agreed with Cuffe: girls, she said, responding to Crackanthorpe, wanted nothing less than to own their own lives. 'Your daughter wants herself,' she told parents mystified by their child's discontent. 'She belongs to you now, and can only walk in your paths, and enjoy your pleasures, and live your life. She wants to belong to herself. She has paths of her own she is eager to carry out.'[37] The British magazine *The Speaker* tried to soften the outspoken views of Cuffe and Pearsall-Smith, and to reassure its readers: 'The emancipated girl . . . referred to . . . is no argument for emancipation,' an editorial maintained, 'for she is simply an exceptional girl, a person of strong character' and has 'a talent for getting her own way'. Most likely she would end up married, and if she did, the writer jovially suggested, 'she will rule the happy man whom she makes her husband.'[38] Nevertheless, the editorial expressed a worry reprised by many writers, acknowledging 'the ferment which is now assailing youthful feminine brains'.[39] Some parents identified the source of the ferment in high school and university, where girls were encouraged to follow their interests and desires: 'Girls', one editorial maintained, 'are as eager as boys for ideals.'[40] Motherhood was not necessarily one of those ideals, much to the dismay of many parents.

Girls seemed to be choosing suitors with a haughty discernment. As Radcliffe's Briggs noted, 'college women may be more fastidious about whom they marry.'[41] This last remark was electrifying: according to Darwin, the best specimens of manhood and womanhood should produce children. If women could select from among men, they would no doubt reject any who seemed wanting in vigour, intelligence and moral strength. Women's power to choose arose as a new threat for men.

Men needed to prove their vigour, both to themselves and to women. William James responded to this need in 'The Moral Equivalent of War', an essay published in 1910 that promoted his opposition to war, as well as his concern about how men would live a strenuous life. Militarism, James wrote, 'is the great preserver of our ideals of hardihood, and human life with no use for hardihood would be contemptible'. Discipline, daring, physical strength and moral virtue: all these are characteristics of the fighting man, but James searched for an alternative to acting out those traits through killing and violence. 'The duty is incumbent on mankind', he wrote, 'of keeping military characters in stock' and of preventing the proliferation of the 'weaklings and mollycoddles' that Roosevelt so vehemently derided.[42] Strong men, James insisted, could contribute not only to war, but to a peaceful world.

Roosevelt's dream of a nation throbbing with potent manhood necessarily began in adolescence and focused on education. Critics such as Hall and Clarke defended their antipathy to co-education by arguing that girls were distracting and intimidating to boys. Whereas later waves of feminists claimed that same-sex education gave girls a safe space to grow, apart from the tendency of boys to dominate class discussions and win their teachers' favour, many educators at the turn of the century claimed that same-sex education gave boys a space safe from the intimidation of girls.

It was bad enough that girls outnumbered and outperformed their male classmates, but just as harmful, proponents of same-sex schools asserted, was the predominance of women teachers. Just as these unmarried women deformed the minds of their girl students with masculine ideals, these teachers caused boys to become softer and effeminate and, many believed, might lead them to homosexuality. Boys should be taught by men, in schools that built up boys' bodies through robust competitive sports. The classroom and sports field should reek of masculinity, a sure antidote to homosexuality. The Boy Scouts, founded in the UK in 1908 by Robert Baden-Powell and in America in 1910, was one response to this concern: a place where boys could be boys. 'The Wilderness is gone, the Buckskin Man is gone . . . the hardships and privations of pioneer life which did so much to develop sterling manhood are now but a legend in history,' wrote Daniel Beard, whose Sons of Daniel Boone boys' club merged with the newly founded Boy Scouts; 'we must depend upon the Boy Scout Movement to produce the MEN of the future.'[43]

The Scouts' mission was to build boys' bodies and strengthen their sense of duty, loyalty and courage: to make boys 'strong and active and *able* to do the right thing at the right moment, and do it'.[44] Still, scouting involved so much fantasy, special chants and rituals that it seemed more like fun and games than preparation for a manly life. Baden-Powell justified scouts' activities by maintaining that play-acting 'was one of the best means of educating children', developing 'wit and imagination' and incorporating 'lessons of history and morality'. Boys, he wrote, 'are full of romance,

Boy Scouts watching Robert Baden-Powell start a fire in Washington, DC, 1911.
Peter Pan was Baden-Powell's favourite play.

and they love "make-believe"'.[45] Certainly Baden-Powell was full of romance, and brimming with nostalgia for his own carefree childhood; he recommended that boys read the books that had thrilled him: Robert Louis Stevenson's *Treasure Island*, Rudyard Kipling's *Kim* and the Canadian naturalist Ernest Thompson Seton's *Two Little Savages* are all invoked admiringly throughout Baden-Powell's handbook. Although boys were the heroes of these adventure tales, Baden-Powell acknowledged that girls could be scouts too, citing such brave women as Florence Nightingale, journalists Flora Shaw and Mary Kingsley, who famously travelled in Africa, and 'devoted lady missionaries and nurses in all parts of our Empire'.[46]

The women of the future took note and pressed to be included – 6,000 girls signed up to join when the organization began – and in 1910 Baden-Powell and his sister Agnes created the Girl Guides, followed, in 1912, by the USA's Girl Scouts, founded by Juliette Gordon Low. Both organizations pledged to uphold the same values: 'Truth, Loyalty, Helpfulness, Friendliness, Courtesy, Kindness, Obedience, Cheerfulness, Purity, and Thrift.' Considering the mandate of the Boy Scouts to foster manly men, these traits seem oddly feminine: where were discipline, strength and courage? Girls, on the other hand, had been trained since childhood to be helpful, kind and obedient. According to Low, girls had a particular responsibility to promote the scouting values: 'One of the fundamental laws of life', she wrote in the Girl Scouts' handbook, 'is that, in the natural course of things, the influence of women over men is vastly greater than that of men over one another.'[47] Low saw that influence exerted in the home as girls became wives and mothers, charged with caring and nurturing. 'To make others happy is the Scout's first wish,' she said. But sections of the handbook spoke to wider opportunities. Certainly, girls should practise thrift and economy so that they could be better housekeepers; but they might choose to take a job, such as nursing, teaching or clerical work, or to pursue a career. 'Well educated women can make a good income by taking up translating, library work, architecture, and many professions which formerly have been open only to men,' Low advised: 'Try to master one trade so that you will be independent.'[48]

Born of the same impulse to shape the lives of adolescents, both organizations had the same motto: Be Prepared. 'Our country needs women who are prepared,' Low asserted, for a future that portended new roles, new relationships and new definitions of womanhood.[49] For a future far different from their parents' past.

The high school and especially the university graduate had new paths open to her in work that might give her independence. But all girls, no matter whether they went to work, to school or helped out at home, were expected to marry. The Victorian ideal of separate spheres, the angel in the British or American house, the submissive wife and nurturing mother, were deeply cherished images. Faced with the pressures of adulthood, the prospect of reprising their mother's roles and the possibility that they would have to give up their intellectual quests and achievements, girls saw adolescence as a refuge – where they wanted to remain, forever.

3 The Happy Boy

৵

'I'm youth, I'm joy, I'm a little bird
that has broken out of the egg.'
Peter Pan

The quintessential adolescent of the time, who leapt gloriously onto the London stage in 1904 and Broadway in 1905, was Peter Pan, the boy who refused to grow up. Like Mark Twain's Huck Finn, Peter flew to uncharted territory rather than submit to becoming civilized by his family. He gathered around him a community of boys his own age. In many ways, Peter was Hall's 'boy's boy', and the adventure hero that Baden-Powell had so loved. But Peter was an alluring model for adolescent girls, too: from the play's first casting and throughout its history the role was enacted by an adult woman slim enough to pass for an adolescent – an adolescent boy or an adolescent girl. Girls who, like Peter, chafed under their family's proscriptions; girls reluctant to grow up into adult women; girls who refused a future circumscribed by the nursery – they, too, could dream of flying away to Neverland.

In the first British production, the elfin Nina Boucicault was acclaimed in the title role, followed by the lithe American dancer Pauline Chase, who performed as Peter in London from 1906 to 1913. 'Either he must be the whimsical, fairy creature that Nina Boucicault made him, or he must be the lovable tomboy of Pauline Chase,' Peter's creator, the playwright J. M. Barrie, declared. 'There is no other way.'[1] A tomboy, of course, was in fact a girl who behaved like a boy, and by choosing women to play Peter, Barrie underscored the fluidity and ambiguity of his character's gender. As productions of the popular play continued into the next decade Barrie retained control over casting, insisting that Peter – and with few exceptions all of the Lost Boys – be played by slender, appealing young women.

He had in mind, Barrie said, the American actress Maude Adams, his 'dear Maudie', whom he first saw on Broadway in 1896, when she was 24 years old. She was the perfect performer, he told the producer Charles Frohman, for the lead in *The Little Minister*, a sentimental romance that Barrie was adapting for the theatre. Although her role was that of an adult woman, reviews highlighted her 'gay mischievousness, her sudden dashes and spurts of coquetry, her consciousness of her woman's power' and her 'pretty girlish piquancy and grace'.[2] Those qualities, Barrie later told Frohman, inspired *Peter Pan.* In 1903, when Adams visited Barrie in London, he took her walking in Kensington Gardens to show her where the idea of Peter Pan was conceived, and they talked. Whatever they revealed to one another in that and later meetings, they became friends. They felt that they understood one another in ways that others did not. In 1904, when he finished writing the play, Barrie sent her an overview of the characters: Wendy, he said, 'is rather a dear of a girl with ever so many children long before her hair is up

Maude Adams on the set of the Broadway play *Peter Pan*, 1905.

and the boy is Peter Pan in a new world. I should like you to be the boy and the girl and most of the children and the pirate captain.'[3]

Adams was as eager to play Peter as Barrie was to see her in the part, and when she took on the role for the 1905 American production – a role for which Mark Twain's adorable Billie Burke tried out – a *New York Daily Tribune* critic described the 33-year-old actress in ways that echo Hall's assessment of adolescent girls: Adams, the critic wrote, had 'a sprightly presence, indicative of sweetness and mirth, and grace by the allurement of pretty ways'. But the critic seemed unsettled by the casting – and perhaps the conceit of the play itself: 'As an actress, Miss Adams is incarnate mediocrity – for she possesses neither imagination, passion, power, depth of feeling, or formidable intellect, and her faculty of expressive impersonation is extremely limited.' Impersonation, that is, of a male; 'but as a personality she is piquant, interesting and agreeable, and, in such a play . . . she is shown to advantage'.[4] The *New York Times* was more generous: Adams was 'most ingratiatingly simple and sympathetic, true to the fairy idea, true to the child nature, lovely, sweet and wholesome'.[5] Like Chase, she emphasized her own girlishness; at five feet tall and one hundred pounds, she had the petite, undeveloped body of a young adolescent, enhanced by a costume especially designed for her, with a distinctive collar that girls and women eagerly adopted in their own clothing.

Peter Pan was not the first nor last time that Adams took on the role of a male or a cross-dressing female, roles that fed gossip about her sexuality. She played Viola in Shakespeare's *Twelfth Night* and Joan of Arc, a character whom Adams idolized and studied for years. It had long been her dream, she said, to play the heroic martyr who disguised herself as a man to lead an insurrection. Three years after she opened in *Peter Pan*, she starred in *The Jesters*

Pauline Chase, an early portrayer of Peter Pan, 1909.

as a young nobleman who disguises himself to cheer up a lovelorn young woman kept sequestered by her father. One reviewer's choice of pronouns reveals the complications that result when a woman plays a man: Adams, the reviewer wrote,

> with a fine sense of delicate values, gave to the figure
> of Chicot the charm of youth, his spirits, and sympathetic
> sensibility. She was a picture to look upon in a costume
> of cloth and gold, her trim and graceful little figure moving
> lithely and gracefully through the play, her richly pliant
> voice now gently soothing in the tender love passages, now
> manfully defiant when the deed of daring must be done.[6]

Adams gave Chicot the charming attributes of a trim, graceful, tender woman, but a woman who could be 'manfully defiant' and daring if she needed to be. This easy transition between genders struck some viewers as uncomfortable, and they criticized Adams's choices as being unfeminine. 'I play youth, not men,' she shot back, as if youth were a distinct gender category entirely. 'No travesty is ever suggested.'[7]

Rumours began about lesbian relationships: with the eighteen-year-old Mercedes de Acosta, a socialite whose escapades fuelled gossip columns and who appeared backstage at several performances of *Peter Pan*; and with other actresses, including Lillie Florence, who was in the same cast as Adams in *The Masked Ball* in 1892. At the time she played Peter, she took on a secretary, Louise Boynton, who continued as her live-in companion until Boynton's death in 1951. Two years later, Adams was buried beside her. Self-protective and shy, she rebuffed male admirers and travelled only with her mother or women friends. Her producer tried to protect her from gossip, and Adams took pains to deflect the public's assumptions about her private life.

Adams and Barrie saw each other as kindred spirits: for all their acclaim, they felt insecure. For all their fame, they felt like outsiders. Adams often retreated to a country house, and later a convent, in upstate New York; Barrie to the country, where he surrounded himself with the boys who really had inspired his Peter Pan stories.

Sir James M. Barrie, *c.* 1904, the author of *Peter Pan*.

Meeting Barrie, Adams said, was 'a joy'.[8] Friendship with Adams, Barrie claimed, served as inspiration for many more plays. 'What Every Woman Knows', he said, was written because 'there was a Maude Adams in the world. I could see her dancing through every page of my manuscript.' She intuitively understood his characters, he said. 'She really needs no direction. I love to write for her and see her in my work.'[9]

Robert Baden-Powell saw the play repeatedly in London, as he worked out his plans for the Boy Scout movement and his handbook, *Scouting for Boys*. Like Peter – for whom he later named his son – Baden-Powell longed for eternal boyhood, living in the company of other boys, revelling in a life of adventure, carefree and resourceful and independent of parents. He called himself a 'boy-man', a term, one biographer suggested, 'corresponding to the split between his two readerships, of boys playing at men, of men playing at being boys'.[10] Like Barrie, he idealized motherhood: 'a really good manly fellow', he wrote, must be a good son. 'There is only one pain greater than that of losing your mother, and that is the pain your mother would suffer if she lost you.' Not by death, he added, but by 'your own misdeeds'.[11]

Across the Atlantic, Baden-Powell's contemporary, another celebrant of adolescent boys, saw Adams's Peter Pan soon after the play opened on Broadway in November 1905. Mark Twain praised the play with his customary enthusiasm, gushing that

> all the implacable rules of the drama are violated, yet the result is a play which is without a defect . . . It is a fairy play. There isn't a thing in it which could ever happen in real life. That is as it should be. It is consistently beautiful, sweet, clean, fascinating, satisfying, charming, and impossible

from beginning to end. It breaks all the rules of real life drama, but preserves intact all the rules of fairyland, and the result is altogether contenting to the spirit.

'The longing of my heart', the seventy-year-old Twain added, 'is a fairy portrait of myself: I want to be pretty; I want to eliminate facts and fill up the gap with charms.'[12] Twain saw in Peter the adolescent he so fervently wished to be, eternally.

What Twain saw as a fairy play, other audience members recognized as both a fantasy for children and a caricature of English domestic life. Peter ran away from his parents the day he was born, he tells Wendy, because he heard them talking about what he was to be when he became a man. Refusing to grow up, he lives with a group of motherless boys – boys who had been cared for by distracted nannies. When they fell out of their prams as infants, Peter swooped them up to Never Never Land. But Peter, like all the males in the play, and like its author James Barrie, has a secret longing for a mother's love and nurturing, and he surreptitiously sits on the windowsill outside the nursery where Mrs Darling reads to her three children, Wendy, John and Michael. One day, as he is leaving, his shadow becomes caught in the window as it is being shut and tears off. As the play begins, Peter has come to retrieve it. Wendy awakens, and soon she and her brothers are caught up in the fantasy of Peter's life. It takes little persuasion for the children to decide to fly away with him.

Despite its apparently serene domesticity, the Darling household betrays some tensions as prevalent in Edwardian England as they were in America. The Darlings live in 'a rather depressed street in Bloomsbury', where the nursery would seem like 'a shabby little room' had Mrs Darling not decorated it cheerfully with her own handiwork. Her wedding gown, for example, has been torn up and sewn into coverlets for the beds.[13] Mr Darling represents the absent father, who leaves the running of the household and raising of children to his wife while he focuses all of his energies on his work and career. As the cultural historian Claudia Nelson notes, 'not only did fatherhood end where motherhood began (that is, at the moment of conception), but this limitation turned the father into the mother's child within the family context. If he were to be a concerned parent, she would first have to be his teacher.'[14] Mr Darling has a job in the city, 'where he sits on a stool all day, as fixed as a postage stamp', indistinguishable from his work colleagues. At home, Barrie adds, 'the way to gratify him is to say that he has a distinct personality.'[15] Mr Darling is so concerned with finances that he calculates how much it costs to raise a child before he will accede to his wife's desire to have more children after Wendy is born. But though Mr Darling inhabits the business world, Barrie presents him as weak-willed and petulant. He behaves childishly, refusing to take his medicine, for example, instead pouring it into the food bowl of the family's dog – and children's nursemaid – Nana. The Darlings have a dog for a nurse because it is cheaper than a woman. In any case, servants were becoming increasingly difficult to find, and Nana, a Newfoundland whose kennel resides in the nursery, seems competent enough.

Mrs Darling treats her husband like one of her children, mollifying him when he is distressed, but punishing him when he angrily banishes Nana from the nursery. She relegates him to the doghouse, from which he sallies forth to business and social events.

Mrs Darling has trained Nana to oversee much of the children's care – even walking them to school and making their beds – but she herself reads them nightly stories, and once they are asleep spends each evening sitting by them, tidying up their minds. 'If Wendy and the boys would keep awake,' Barrie wrote,

> they might see her repacking into their proper places the many articles of the mind that have strayed during the day, lingering humorously over some of their contents, wondering where on earth they picked this thing up, making discoveries sweet and not so sweet . . .

She hides naughty thoughts in the bottom drawers, so that the children awaken with only pretty, if banal, ideas to start the day.[16]

'Tidying children's minds' – a mother's efforts at moral guidance – is a daunting task when ideas fly in from sources beyond her control. She cannot, for example, counteract Peter's influence, a frustration she shares with other mothers facing peer relationships of which they disapprove. Although Barrie portrays Mrs Darling as lovely, intelligent and caring, neither motherhood nor marriage to a shallow man gives her much to do. Like children, many mothers chafe against being confined to the nursery. 'All I remember about my mother', a Lost Boy, Nibs, tells his comrades, 'is that she often said to father, "Oh, how I wish I had a cheque-book of my own!"'[17] Control over her own money would be a move towards independence, but women like Mrs Darling are dependent on their husbands. With this model of her future before her, Wendy is only too glad to fly from the nursery.

Her new role, though, is quickly, and disappointingly, defined: 'What we need is just a nice motherly person,' one of the boys tells Wendy immediately after she arrives in Neverland. 'Oh dear,' she replies with a hint of dismay, 'I feel that is just exactly what I am.'[18] Although she hoped for a thrilling experience, Wendy's adventure consists of mothering: reading to the boys, darning their socks and caring for them, and especially for Peter, when he returns from his exploits. When she becomes involved in his adventures, she is the damsel in distress, in need of rescuing. Peter's freedom, restlessness and impetuous drive stand in stark contrast to Wendy's domesticity; Peter takes risks, overcomes obstacles, displays his strengths, while Wendy sews. Wendy's role as mother, however, does not include being Peter's wife. Repeatedly she asks, 'What are your exact feelings for me, Peter?' He repeatedly replies, 'Those of a devoted son, Wendy.'[19] That is not the answer Wendy wants: she is attracted to Peter, as is his feisty fairy Tinker Bell and the Native American princess Tiger Lily. In the earliest draft of his play, Barrie made it clear that the three females 'would prefer a more adult relationship with the eternal boy', desires that were tamped down as he revised and reoriented the play towards children.[20]

Barrie portrayed a celebration of rebelliousness along with a theme that seemed contradictory: a child's deep yearning to be mothered. The eternal boy is fixed on finding a mother. He once tried to return to his own, he tells Wendy, and discovered that his mother had barred the window; a new son was sleeping in Peter's bed. Wendy and her brothers are shocked: 'Are you sure mothers are like that?' she asks incredulously. John, shaken, wants to go home immediately, before he, too, is forgotten.[21] Their departure, though, is delayed when they are captured by the pirate Captain Hook. He wants a mother, too, for himself and his crew. Hook, a cruel, egotistical man usually played by the same actor as Mr Darling, is foiled by Peter, who stages a bold rescue. 'I'm youth,' he crows, triumphantly, 'I'm joy, I'm a little bird that has broken out of the egg.'[22]

The Darling children return to a joyous mother, and offstage, the Lost Boys are reunited with their own mothers. In a scene dropped from his production draft, Barrie satirized that reunion by requiring the boys' twenty mothers to prove their competency by performing a few feats: displaying an emotional reaction to baby clothes, kissing their sleeping children without awakening them and insisting that their own chosen child is the prettiest.[23] Peter's mother is not among the bevy who come to find their sons, but when Mrs Darling offers to adopt him, he refuses. 'I don't want to go to school and learn solemn things,' he proclaims. 'No one is going to catch me, lady, and make me a man.'[24]

One Washington, DC, viewer concluded unequivocally that the play was a morality tale exalting motherhood.

> When the pirate tests the patriotism of these children, they
> each turn to the other and ask: 'What would your mother
> tell you to do?' And so, too, in the hearts of men this early
> motherly advice often serves them in time of need.[25]

Motherly advice, though, was precisely what men were fleeing when they identified with adventurers, cowboys and explorers; and what Peter rejects when he spurns Mrs Darling's invitation of adoption.

Barrie's boys

Despite Barrie's claim that the play was inspired by Maude Adams, the character of Peter appeared much earlier in his work, in a tale called *The Little White Bird*, created over many years before it was published in 1902, and which he invented as entertainment for the sons of Sylvia and Arthur Llewelyn Davies. The story both chronicles Barrie's relationship with the family and reveals his own feelings about boyhood, manhood and mothers, including his own, Margaret

Ogilvy. Margaret's mother died when she was eight, leaving her to become a substitute mother to her younger brother, and to take on many household chores. Margaret told sunlit stories of her girlhood, romanticizing her past, and leaving her son with an image that deeply impressed him, but an image starkly contradicted by his own experience of her mothering.

Margaret Ogilvy was a puritanical, demanding woman who clearly had favourites among her ten children. James was not that; David, seven years older, was. But just before his fourteenth birthday, David died after a skating accident, and Margaret went into lifelong mourning for the tall, handsome adolescent with a golden future. Try as he might, six-year-old James could not console her. He tried to make her laugh, he tried to make her love him, but instead, she sent him to live with another older brother. For his whole life, Barrie was haunted by David frozen in adolescence, with the magical power to torture his mother, and Barrie himself, because he never could grow up. In an early note, he referred to the play as '"The Happy Boy": Boy who can't grow up – runs away from pain & death.'[26]

For Barrie, boyhood and manhood were tragically entangled with love and loss. If he could only revise his own boyhood, he might find the love he so desperately desired, and so he returned to a nostalgic fantasy of what that boyhood might yield for him. 'I fancy I try to create an artificial world to myself,' he once wrote to a friend, 'because the one I really inhabit, and the only one I could do any good in, becomes too somber. How doggedly my pen searches for gaiety.'[27] In his fiction and plays, he created iconic boys, even if they were grown men. 'Poor Tommy!' he wrote of the protagonist of his autobiographical novel *Tommy and Grizel*, 'he was still a boy, trying sometimes, as now, to be a man, [but] always when he looked round he ran back to his boyhood as if he saw it holding out its arms to him and inviting him to come back and play.'[28] Physically, Barrie looked like a young boy even while others his age were growing into men. At seventeen, a biographer wrote, he had stopped growing at five feet and had not yet begun to shave.[29] It was no wonder that the slender adolescent was taken to be much younger than he was; and he was shy, as well, uncomfortable when his classmates talked about women and sex, uncomfortable when he had to socialize with girls. When he was in his twenties, he lamented that young women hardly noticed him. He wished he had grown to over six feet: 'it would have made a great difference in my life,' he wrote. His 'sorrowful ambition' was 'to become a favorite of the ladies . . . The things I could have said to them if my legs had been longer.'[30] He missed the 'flirting days of boyhood', he confided in his notebooks. He never had 'contact with a woman' and wondered if he were even capable of 'genuine deep feeling'.[31] Yet he yearned for a woman's attention, and for love. He developed crushes on young actresses, and in 1894, when he was 34, one of those actresses, Mary Ansell, agreed to marry him after she had nursed him, in motherly fashion, through a serious illness. The future did not bode well: 'Morning after engagement, a startling thing to waken up & remember you're tied for life,' he wrote in his notebook. 'Our love has brought me nothing but misery,' he added days before the wedding.[32]

The marriage was difficult, frustrating for both parties. Mary poured her affections into her cherished St Bernard dogs, who gave her the love and attention she never got from her husband. She regretted 'silent meals . . . When the mind of your man is elsewhere, lord knows where, but nowhere in your direction.'[33] And she had affairs. Barrie fell in love with his fictional adolescents, and with Sylvia Llewelyn Davies and her five very real sons. 'You are good at boys,' Barrie once wrote to Sylvia, 'and this you know is the age of specialists. And you were very very nearly being a boy yourself.'[34] One biographer sees Sylvia transformed into Tommy's 'boyish' love interest in *Tommy and Grizel*. 'There were times when she looked like a boy,' Barrie wrote. 'Her almost gallant bearing, the poise of her head, her noble frankness, they all had something in them of a princely boy who had never known fear.'[35] But for Barrie, Sylvia was also motherhood incarnate, the mother he wished he had, although one of her sons offered a different view. Sylvia, he recalled, 'wore her children as other women wore pearls or fox-furs. They were beautiful children, but beautiful as a background to her beauty.'[36] Still, to Barrie, her mothering seemed exemplary, and her talent for decorating, and her love for her sons, found their way into the character of Mrs Darling. With Sylvia as a model, he discarded an earlier note: 'Important the mother treated from child's point of view – how mother scolds, wheedles, &c.'[37] Instead, it was Mr Darling who was presented as if through a child's eyes, as a fool.

The Barries had no children, although Mary desperately wanted them. 'J.M.'s tragedy', Mary wrote to one of Barrie's biographers, 'was that he knew that as a man he was a failure and that love in its fullest sense could never be felt by him or experienced.'[38] Barrie wanted to be not so much a father as a playmate to boys who would allow him to recall, and retreat into, his idealized childhood. George, Sylvia's oldest, was the first to elicit the Peter Pan stories, and Michael – 'the cleverest of us, the most original, the potential genius', one brother recalled – was Barrie's favourite.[39] He looked like Sylvia, and it was obvious to everyone that Barrie was besotted with him: 'He has given his heart to Michael,' a friend observed.[40] Barrie's affection for George and Michael, recalled another brother, had 'a dash of the paternal, a lot of the maternal, and much, too, of the lover',[41] allowing that for Barrie, loving was chaste. His relationship with Sylvia and her sons intensified after Barrie's wife divorced him in 1909, after fifteen years of marriage. Mary would go on to marry her current lover; Barrie never married again. He was enough of a celebrity that his divorce made newspaper headlines, with the rumour that he intended to marry the young actress Pauline Chase, another Peter Pan, who had been seen in the couple's company so often that she was assumed to be like an adopted daughter. But Barrie preferred to devote himself wholeheartedly to the Llewelyn Davies family; and that devotion solidified after Sylvia and her husband died when the boys were still young, and Barrie insinuated himself into their lives as their guardian.

Open and carefree in the company of his boys, he was taciturn among adults, especially adult women, so intimidating as to seem sinister. But not to the actresses who embodied his hero, actresses that played the part of a boy. By the time *Peter Pan* debuted, Wendy, the surrogate and future mother, was not an appealing role model for girls who were growing up amid controversies about their abilities, education and future. Peter, a free spirit played by a young woman, was. *Peter Pan* laid before viewers the question of whose role was the more enviable: the girl who played mother, who would grow up to be ensconced in a nursery, who had no cheque-book of her own – or the girl who played a boy? To travel the world like Peter Pan: that was the dream one twelve-year-old girl confided to her diary, just before going to a barber shop and getting her hair cut, 'just like a boy's'.[42]

The boyish girl

Barrie had an ancillary family to the Llewelyn Davies boys: their girl cousins Angela, Jeanne and Daphne du Maurier, daughters of the actor Gerald du Maurier, Barrie's favourite male lead and his choice for Mr Darling and Captain Hook. Divorced, with Arthur and Sylvia dead, Barrie had ample time for children. He was the girls' 'Uncle Jim', spending hours in their nursery, and directing their amateur productions of *Peter Pan*. Daphne was Peter. She and her sisters adored and envied their boy cousins, and Gerald fed their desire to be tomboys by encouraging them to read adventure stories and to act out daring, swashbuckling characters facing mutiny, shipwreck, plague and revolution. The sisters knew, also, that Gerald had hoped for a son to carry on the family name; Daphne, more than the other two girls, wished she could have been that boy. In fact, as she grew up, she came to believe that she really was a boy. Although outwardly a girl, she claimed that her real identity as a boy was 'locked up in a box': 'Always being a little boy. And growing up with a boy's mind and a boy's heart.'[43] Gerald, judging by a poem he wrote when Daphne was a young adolescent, appears to have noticed that this daughter was different from his other children:

> . . . sometimes in the silence of the night
> I wake and think perhaps my darling's right
> And that she should have been,
> And, if I'd had my way,
> She would have been, a boy.[44]

Seeing how her father became transformed when he appeared in costume, Daphne dressed in boys' clothing. At the age of thirteen, she invented 'a splendid new character', her alter ego, 'namely one Eric Avon, captain of cricket' at the School House dormitory of the Rugby School. 'There were no psychological depths to Eric Avon,' Daphne wrote later, in a memoir, but she admitted that his character 'remained in my unconscious', inspiring the narrator, 'first person singular, masculine gender' in five of her novels. For two years, until she was fifteen, Eric dominated Daphne's imagination. Why she picked Eric Avon 'and not an imaginary Peggy Avon' seemed a mystery to her. Surely she was influenced by the athletic, impetuous boys in such books as Thomas Hughes's *Tom Brown's School Days*, set at the Rugby School, and John Finnemore's *Teddy Lester* series. She read novels aimed at girls as well, and said they were 'equally enjoyed', but they did not make as much of an impact on her. She might well have modelled herself after Peggy, the protagonist of Angela Brazil's *A Terrible Tomboy*, who celebrated the qualities of boyhood just as much as Daphne did.[45]

Like many heroines of girls' fiction, Peggy was not raised by her mother, who had died, but by her father and his younger sister, who encouraged Peggy's 'pluck and spirit'. As the narrator notes indulgently,

> poor Peggy really did not mean to be naughty; she was so
> eager, so active, so full of overflowing and impetuous life,
> with such restless daring and abounding energy, that in
> the excitement of the moment her wild spirits were apt to
> carry her away simply because she never stopped to think
> of consequences.[46]

Her town's spiritual leader also looks kindly on the girl, advising that she enjoy her freedom. 'Don't prune her too hard,' he said, 'for it is sometimes the side-shoots that bear the best flowers, after all.' Harshness, her father and Aunt Helen agree, would only make her heart 'sullen and obstinate'.[47] Peggy has an older sister, Lillian, a more conventional girl, and an eight-year-old brother, Bobby, whose nature is so gentle that he is sometimes taken for a girl. Aunt Helen joked that the two 'must have got changed, and that Peggy should have been the boy and Bobby the girl'; after all, Peggy 'had the most of the enterprising spirit which is generally thought a characteristic of the masculine mind'. For her part, Peggy would have preferred to be a boy, but she hated the word 'tomboy, by which people meant "a horrid, rough sort of creature who isn't fit to be either a boy or a girl"'. Would Joan of Arc or the famous lighthouse-keeper's daughter Grace Darling, who rescued shipwrecked sailors, be called a tomboy? Peggy bristled at chores such as darning socks, and she looked with dismay at a future of housewifely duties. 'Why can't I climb trees and jump fences, and enjoy myself like boys do, and yet be a thorough girl all the same?'[48]

Like Daphne, Peggy read novels meant for boys, such as *Treasure Island*, which enthralled her; pirates, sailors, dangerous escapes and wild thrills made her almost weep with disappointment that she was not a boy. And if not a boy, then a foundling or an orphan: either seemed potentially liberating and romantically adventure-some. At the end of the novel, the narrator assures readers that Peggy will not lose her spirit and spunk, but 'will keep that most priceless of possessions, the heart of a little child'.[49] But harbouring a child's heart in a woman's body was not what Peggy, or Daphne du Maurier, or other spirited adolescent girls, wanted.

In the first decades of the twentieth century, 85 girls' series were published in the U.S. featuring adventurous heroines.[50] These books were far different from moralizing, sentimental tales, such as the

What Katy Did series, published beginning in 1872, written by Sarah Chauncey Woolsey under the pen name of Susan Coolidge. Katy Carr is twelve, the oldest of four siblings, and lives with her father, a busy physician, and his sister, Aunt Izzie. Dr Carr encourages his children in rough and tumble play, much to the consternation of Izzie, who wishes they would be clean, quiet and obedient. Katy is a tomboy, 'fond of building castles in the air, and dreaming of the time when something she had done would make her famous, so that everybody would hear of her, and want to know her'.[51] When asked about her future, she says she wants to save people's lives like Florence Nightingale, lead a crusade like Joan of Arc or become a famous artist. But her dreams are dashed: disobeying her aunt, she takes a bold ride on a swing, which breaks, injuring her severely. During her long, hard recovery, repentant Katy has a chance to reconsider her behaviour, and she emerges transformed into a good, caring, nurturing girl.

Later girls' series, though, had no use for punished tomboys. Instead, their intrepid girl characters were modelled on those from such series as the Rover Boys, set in an American military academy, and the prolific Tom Swift tales. Both series were published, and most of the books written, by Edward Stratemeyer, who came to dominate adolescent literature for decades – offering, for example, the hugely popular Nancy Drew series in the 1930s. Other publishers, too, recognizing the buying power of adolescent readers, produced a spate of books featuring independent, active girls whose lives were not dictated by adults, such as Evelyn Raymond's Dorothy Chester books, centred on young Dorothy, who was left as a foundling on the doorstep of a couple, who raise her on a farm in the Hudson Highlands. A wealthy friend takes an interest in Dorothy's education, giving her the advantage of private schooling and travel. In *Dorothy's Travels*, published in 1908, the girl sets out with her best friend and a teacher, headed for New York City, and then Nova Scotia for the summer. The book incorporated details that would recur in other series: an adopted girl, a benefactor and a companion who shared in adventures outside of parental oversight.

The Stratemeyer Syndicate created the pseudonym of Laura Lee Hope for the *Bobbsey Twins* series, which first appeared in 1904 and ran for 72 volumes, and the equally popular *Outdoor Girls* series, which debuted in 1913. The Outdoor Girls were four adolescents living in upstate New York: temperamental Mollie (her mother is French, accounting for Mollie's volatile moods), who is called Billy by her friends; Betty, a sixteen-year-old whose decisiveness and practicality earns her the epithet 'Little Captain'; Amy, the shyest of the four, who has just been told that she was adopted; and Grace, tall and slender, whose figure, the others note, was perfect for 'the newer style that seems to forbid the existence of hips'.[52]

'I detest monotony,' one girl exclaims in the first pages of the first volume, and as the school year draws to a close, the friends decide to form a Camping and Tramping Club. They plan to hike 200 miles over two weeks, spending nights in the homes of relatives along the way. A teacher encourages their walking – physical activity is good for health, she says – and their parents encourage their independence. At the time the book was published, exercise for adolescent girls was controversial: although health reformers hailed physical education as a positive step to developing strong bodies, some doctors warned that girls would develop male characteristics, such as a flat chest and facial hair, if they played the same sports as boys or otherwise taxed their developing bodies. In the *Outdoor Girls* novels, educators' and parents' encouragement represented a definite stand on the issue.

Of course, the girls must have proper outfits, buying sturdy boots, cute caps and suits of olive drab, with skirts short enough for movement, and – to the girls' delight – pockets. Several times during their trek, they are mistaken for suffragists: 'Are you a "Votes for Women" crowd?' one person asks. Along the way, the girls encounter a few problems, which they handle adroitly: they find a broken rail on a train track and worry about a derailment, but soon find a flagman to report the problem. They come upon a little lost girl who claims she has two mothers, and there is some consternation among the girls about that absurd story until they find out that one of the so-called mothers is the girl's aunt. During a rainstorm, they take shelter on the porch of a house that, they discover, is completely empty. Someone surely lives in the house, though, and when Amy notices a man's hat hanging on the hat rack, they surmise that the inhabitants are a couple. But Grace suggests another possibility: 'I've often heard of a lone woman's borrowing a man's hat – when she didn't have – didn't want, or couldn't get a man.'[53] No one responds to Grace's strange remark, which implies that a woman, alone in a house, might hang a man's hat in sight of the front door to warn tramps or thieves. But Grace implies, also, that a woman who 'didn't want' a man might dress in men's clothing herself. As night falls, the girls wonder what to do, and Grace remarks that they might go out in the rain if they were boys. 'I won't admit that we can't do it because we are *not* boys,' Betty retorts.[54] Still, they decide to help themselves to food and stay overnight. The Outdoor Girls' adventure ends happily, and continues in many other volumes in the series.

These books celebrated the freedom of the adolescent girl, a freedom that real girls did not want to give up. 'I "ran wild" until my 16th birthday,' wrote Frances Willard, who became a temperance campaigner and ardent bicycler as an adult. At sixteen, she was made to wear 'hampering long skirts . . . with their accompanying corset and high heels; my hair was clubbed up with pins,' she remembered, and her wild spirit was tamped.[55] Edwardian girls' fiction exulted over girls' wild spirits. As the literary scholar Sally Mitchell notes, in these stories

> neat, clean, gentle, and obedient girls are not often likeable. When the initial description mentioned a girl's untidiness and careless dress, readers know at once that she would be jolly, wholesome and active. A generation earlier the same terms had served as warning of a moral flaw.[56]

But by the early twentieth century, those tales of self-sacrifice and duty had given way to tales of adventure that – like Peter Pan – laid before modern girls the temptation of wildness.

4 Private Lives

&

'Until I was eighteen I did not know the origin of babies.'
The Mosher Survey (1894)

Who is the modern girl? That was the question asked with urgency and consternation as early as the 1890s, and repeatedly into the 1920s. 'In the club and periodicals, at the dinner-table, and on the platform, what girls were, are, will be, and should be is the constant question,' noted the British novelist, essayist and gadfly Sarah Grand.[1] The answer, Grand said, 'is easy enough. Consider them, respect the needs of their nature, and do not require them to conform to the exigencies of the day before yesterday.'[2] That advice, for many parents, was hard to accept: the day before yesterday felt serene and secure. Girls would grow up quietly at home, submissive to their parents and, eventually, to their husbands. They would become nurturing mothers, raising a new generation of daughters in their own image, and of manly sons, like their fathers and husbands.

But in 1894, when Grand shared her advice, parents already felt assailed by noisy, contentious views, not the least of which concerned sex. What should girls be told about menstruation, reproduction, their newly excited attraction to boys and some disturbing topics: prostitution, for one, and masturbation? How, parents wondered with consternation, could they preserve their daughters' innocence and counter the gossip and misinformation that girls would hear from their friends? 'The period of the greatest danger of sex perversion in the life of the ordinary girl', announced one parental advisor, 'is at the beginning of adolescence.'[3]

Parenting manuals, often written by medical doctors, placed great responsibility on mothers for making sure their daughters were aware of the temptations that lay before them, as well as of the glories of motherhood, which invariably were presented as a girl's highest achievement. Mothers were advised to forge close relationships with their daughters, make themselves available for confidences even if their children were away at school and dissuade their daughters from sharing their feelings with or seeking advice from peers, especially about anything that had to do with sexuality. Ida Tarbell spoke for many parents who were frustrated because they could not oversee their daughters' social lives as closely as they wanted to. 'We have removed largely from boys and girls the protecting social devices by which we once guided their relations and choices,' Tarbell wrote. 'They go and come freely and, as might be expected, marry with less sense of the seriousness of their undertaking. More mistakes are probably made, and where they turn out to be very bad mistakes there is nothing for it but divorce.'[4] Divorce was scandalous, to be sure, but even more horrifying was the fate of an unmarried mother.

Although there were many sources to inform a mother's frank conversations with her daughter, and a few books addressed to girls themselves, many girls were shocked by their first experience of menstruation, and many women married without any hint of what to expect about sex with their husbands. From 1892 to 1920 the medical researcher Clelia Duel Mosher collected questionnaires from American women who had been adolescents in the last quarter of the century. Her respondents were middle-class wives, some who had a college education, some married for a year or two, others for decades. Mosher asked them for intimate details about their private lives: how long had they been married, did they sleep with or apart from their husbands, how often did they have intercourse and what, in their opinion, was the purpose of sex in marriage? She also asked what they had known about 'sexual physiology' before they were married, and if they had such knowledge, where they obtained it.

The overwhelming number of respondents admitted no knowledge at all. 'I was so innocent of the matter', one woman reported, 'that until I was eighteen I did not know the origin of babies.'[5] One woman's mother, a physician, refused to answer her questions, telling her daughter that she could read books about it when she was older. Another respondent, who had heard shocking details from a classmate, spent several sleepless nights before going to her mother, who, she said, 'did not help much'. She got information from a married cousin, just before her wedding.[6] In 1920 a woman who described herself as a 'very active out-of-door girl', with a bachelor's degree from Stanford, had only rudimentary knowledge of sexual physiology, drawn from inferences she gleaned from 'hearing and reading'.[7] Although she attributed her lack of knowledge to her mother's death when she was a child, other women testified that mothers were hardly enlightening about a subject they felt embarrassed to discuss.

Some women got information from relatives or close friends; others from books, sometimes written by clergymen, but more

Clelia Duel Mosher, who surveyed women's sexual experiences.

often by physicians or educators. The obstetrician and gynae-
cologist Alice B. Stockham's *Tokology: A Book for Every Woman*,
published in 1886, was mentioned by a few of Mosher's respondents. From Stockham, they learned more about what to expect
from pregnancy and how to care for an infant than how conception
actually occurred. Stockham's focus reflected her conviction that
motherhood 'is the central fact of human life', and certainly of a
woman's destiny.[8] Only one chapter, on chastity, dealt with marital
sex, leaving much to the reader's imagination. Stockham was interested in helping women avoid pregnancy, for which she advocated
continence, advising the husband to 'attain the same self-control he
practiced during courtship'. Countering the popular assumption
that men needed to act upon their strong, innate sexual desires, she

argued that men, in fact, 'reverence the maternal in women, and if taught that continence serves the best interests of motherhood and posterity, will cheerfully accord their lives with it'.[9] Stockham's views were shaped in part by her experiences as an obstetrician, observing the toll on women – and their children – of closely spaced pregnancies. But she also reflected a more widely held view that 'control of appetite' – for sex, food, alcohol or stimulants – is an important attribute of a highly civilized society.[10]

Stockham's views on continence were not echoed by those among Mosher's respondents who celebrated married love. When asked what reasons besides reproduction warrant intercourse, many women agreed with the respondent who thought intercourse was 'an expression of true and passionate love' that reflected 'the personal feeling and desires and health' of both partners.[11] Intercourse, another woman said, offered 'a sense of intimacy not to be had in any other way' and 'serves as a bond above even physical pleasure'.[12] Many respondents, though, saw reproduction as the primary purpose of marital sex, and reported little pleasure from it; they would likely convey those feelings, even if covertly, to their daughters.

A few years after *Tokology*, Stockham published a shorter book addressed specifically to adolescents, *Creative Life: A Special Letter to Young Girls*, which detailed female anatomy, menstruation and, in greater detail than *Tokology*, the process of impregnation. Boldly, she acknowledged that '*Sex-sense*, or *passion*, is a sign of maturity.'[13] Stockham focused much attention on menstruation, believing that informed adolescents were far less likely to suffer cramps than girls who were ignorant of the process. She condemned wearing corsets, encouraged all girls to exercise vigorously and asserted that girls in school, focused on productive studies, experienced less menstrual discomfort than those who stayed at home. Even though she endorsed higher education for women, she insisted that the 'natural desire of every girl as she matures is to become a mother. The maternal instinct is deeply graven in her soul.'[14] That message was underscored by other advice books as well.

Like Stockham, Isabelle Smart, also a physician, saw motherhood as a girl's highest achievement, on which the future of humanity depended: 'only a great mother can produce a great man,' she asserted.[15] Although she addressed mothers, her book easily could be handed to daughters to read on their own, the better to avoid awkward conversations. Smart offered an overview of girls' anatomy and changes at puberty, assuring girls that although their ovaries and uteruses were readying for a child, pregnancy could occur only when an egg met the life-giving cell from a man. How that happened was left vague. Nor did she connect conception to girls' sexual excitement, but she did make the point that those feelings could well lead girls astray: 'woman is more sensitive than man and more easily excited and less likely to stop to reason.'[16] Boys, subject to more temptations than girls, needed to be kept in check. 'You will find yourself much in need of self-control when you feel for the first time the stirrings of your emotional nature,' Smart cautioned her readers. Girls needed to be 'exceedingly careful'.[17] Like other writers, Smart explicitly dramatized the perils of masturbation; 'unusual excitement' of the genitals 'can only be accompanied by serious results', including 'marks upon the face', making a girl's vile habit visible to everyone.[18]

The physician John Cowan, whose *The Science of a New Life* (1869) also was mentioned by Mosher's respondents as a source of edification about sex, condemned masturbation with equal vehemence. In both boys and girls, he maintained, masturbation causes headache, dyspepsia, epilepsy, heart palpitations, impotency, hysteria, paralysis and insanity, among other debilities.[19] He advised self-control, even in sexual relations within marriage, agreeing with Stockham that continence was a habit to be cultivated. He recommended that couples abstain from sex during pregnancy until the woman's first menstruation after weaning. To that span of at least 21 months, Cowan added another year to fifteen months, which meant that no intercourse would occur for around three years. Cowan insisted that women needed the time to recover their strength after childbirth and nursing (he roundly condemned women who did not want to or could not nurse), and men could prove, by their continence, that they recognized their responsibility to protect their wives and infants. Like Stockham, he believed that continence was a sign of advanced civilization. Indeed, he blamed parents' 'excessive amativeness' as a cause of masturbation among their offspring.[20]

Cowan offered graphic (and illustrated) chapters on the anatomy and physiology of male and female sex organs, along with recommendations about qualities men and women should look for and avoid in a spouse. Men should absolutely shun women with small waists; and women should shun men who use alcohol and tobacco. Advertisements were a perfectly acceptable means of finding a mate, he said, and once a likely candidate appeared, he advised hiring a phrenologist to conduct an examination.

Despite his view that women should learn 'details of every household duty', he put forth views about girls' educations and futures that were far advanced for 1869, when his book first appeared.[21] He believed that 'the rights that women should strive for, obtain, and exercise' included suffrage; the right 'to own, possess, and manage property'; 'the right to share in the management of government and of the country, local and general'; the right to adopt any employment in life for which her capabilities adapt her – with equal pay for equal work; the right to the same educational opportunities as a man; and 'certainly not the least – the right to her own person'. He recognized parents' concerns about what to do with their daughters, but thought the answer was not 'Get them married.' With a larger population of women than men in the UK and the U.S., he realized that many women would not find husbands. 'Equally with boys', therefore, a girl 'should be started in life with the purpose of acquiring and cultivating the qualities necessary to the trade or profession she is to adopt'.[22]

Parents could find encouragement for allowing girls to be tomboys, go to co-educational schools and have boys as friends, but such advice usually drew the line at girls expressing their sexuality. William Arch McKeever, a popular writer on raising adolescents, admitted that when she reached puberty 'the ordinary girl is involved in a great deal of mystery about her own life', especially regarding sex. 'The training of a girl in regard to her sex life', he wrote, 'amounts to a course of training in secret thought habits.'[23] Like many of his readers, McKeever worried that girls would succumb to such temptations as public dance halls, which he roundly condemned as 'one of the chief contributing causes of the downfall of young girls'. Unlike church dances, public halls, both because of their clientele and the kinds of dances they allowed, drew participants 'toward the border line of sensuality'.[24]

Advice manuals addressed to young women sympathized with their discontent, but attempted to calm their rebelliousness. The American clergyman Beverley Ellison Warner observed that the adolescent girl 'not infrequently grows mutinous', but deftly conceals her feelings: 'she fastens innocent eyes upon the wide face of counsel and with a demure and absorbed attention that would deceive the very elect, appears to listen.'[25] All the while, she believes any man is 'self-deceived as to think he knows anything about her at all'.[26] Warner portrayed adolescent girls as bristling under 'perpetual orders to do this or that thing, which she cannot co-ordinate with her ideas of life . . . The word "Don't" is constantly ringing in her ears.'[27] But Warner added to those prohibitions by warning girls that affecting 'manly habits' undermines their attractiveness to men, while playing up their femininity makes them appealing.[28] Surely girls could pursue intellectual interests to enrich their lives and make them better wives and mothers.

For all his apparent sympathy for girls striving for independence, Warner saw them as vulnerable to many bad influences: 'the decadent theatre, the problem novel, the very billboards which flaunt their immodest pictures', all of which 'have brushed away' their innocence.[29] In the progressive British quarterly the *Westminster Review*, eighteen-year-old Gertrude Hemery protested views such as Warner's: keeping young girls from knowledge about life – meaning sex and marriage – is 'mere false delicacy'. Let them go and see plays like Sir Arthur Wing Pinero's *The Second Mrs Tanqueray*, a drama about a woman with a notorious sexual past, or read Sarah Grand's controversial *The Heavenly Twins*. 'Speaking from my own experience,' Hemery wrote, 'I think I may venture to assert that any young girl who takes the moulding of her life into her own hands, and asserts her right as an individual to the exercise of individual thought and action, will never have occasion to regret the step.'[30] So-called problem plays and novels came to fuel many girls' imaginings about how to shape their future.

Every second novel

Sarah Grand, the pen name of Frances Elizabeth Bellenden McFall, emerged as one of the most important, and controversial, feminist voices at the turn of the century, a model for independent women and a defender of modern girls. Born in Ireland in 1854, at the age of seventeen she married a 39-year-old army surgeon, a widower with two young sons. Within a year of their marriage, she had a baby and was settled in India, where her husband was stationed; they returned to England once he retired from the military. After she privately published a novel in 1888, she left her family, moved to Bath in the west of England, changed her name to Madame Sarah Grand, and devoted herself to writing. Her novel *The Heavenly Twins* catapulted her to notoriety in America and the UK when it was published in 1893, and repeatedly reprinted for the next thirty years. Grand's opinions on marriage, sex and men were sought by journals such as the *North American Review*, where she published a spate of essays. In one, published in 1894, she coined the epithet 'New Woman', which came to apply not only to suffragists, college graduates and so-called 'bachelorettes', but to girls who were facing their future. Grand saw clearly that reverence for women masked fear and prejudice. 'There used to be a great deal of sentimentality expended on the subject of the Women's Sphere,' she wrote; 'but, by a curious contradiction, beneath all the sentimentality one could detect a certain contempt for the position. It was evidently considered an inferior position – or rather, the position of an inferior.'[31]

'Every second novel which one takes up this year is concerned with the New Woman – whether in exaltation or derision of her,' reported the London *Times*.[32] And not only novels, but theatre, as well:

the New Woman became the central figure in plays by George Bernard Shaw, Arthur Wing Pinero, Elizabeth Robins and many other playwrights, most notably Sydney Grundy, who satirized 'The New Woman' in a brisk, timely comedy. 'Oh, this eternal babble of the sexes!' one male character cries. 'Why can't a woman be content to be a woman? What does she want to make a beastly man of herself for?'[33] Grundy created what would become stock characters in the proliferation of plays about New Women: mannish, cigarette-smoking feminists, including an authoritarian woman doctor; submissive, womanly women; yearning wives who search for true love, not necessarily with their husbands; and befuddled – sometimes effeminate – men, who fear that women's calls for equality means 'girls should be boys, and maids should be young men . . . They have invented a new gender.'[34]

Grundy's characters expressed widely debated views: that New Women are a regrettable result of educating girls; that these women are intent on 'making a public exhibition of the Decay of Man';[35] that tomboys, however appealing they might seem to men, are really empty headed; and that the campaign for equality is only a temporary glitch in the status quo. 'Do you deny that Woman has arrived, Man has departed?' one woman asks another. 'I don't wonder at it,' her companion replies. 'But Man has an awkward habit of coming back again.'[36] *The Times* echoed that sentiment, sanguine about the current upheaval of 'revolted daughters and new women', dismissing it as nothing more than 'fleeting bubbles on the stream of contemporary life' that surely would not affect 'the young lady in short skirts', who supposedly saw 'remarkably little without the knowledge and consent of her parents'.[37] But girls were not cut off from the stream of life, nor from the debate about the women they might become.

A girl had choices, Grand insisted, to decide

> which she would rather be, the gentle namby-pamby, of
> little consequence, never at ease, incapable of independent
> action, unfitted for liberty, a dependent and a parasite from
> the cradle to the grave, or that nobler girl who is not the
> less tender because she is self-reliant, nor the less womanly
> because she has the power to resent insult and imposition.[38]

Grand railed against the imposition of marriage to degenerate men – men who had contracted syphilis, for example, or who frequented prostitutes, about whom she learned in detail from her husband, who had provided medical treatment to prostitutes in England. *The Heavenly Twins* focused on three women: one who died after being infected with syphilis by her husband; another who refused to have sex with her husband once she learned details about his sexual past; and the third who chose marriage with a man twenty years older, on the condition that she had freedom to live her own life. That freedom included taking lovers and, when the spirit moved her, dressing like a man.

Husbands who infected their wives were an extreme example of men's prevailing, and increasing, decadence. 'From the modern girl's point of view,' Grand said, 'the man of the moment is not of much account.' Spurred by publicity over race suicide, girls looked to marry strong, virile men; instead they found flabby, weak con-tenders for their affections. The more intimately a young woman came to know a man, the more likely she was to find him 'a common creature, of no ideals, deficient in breadth and depth, and only of a boundless assurance'; he became a subject, Grand observed, 'both for contempt and pity'.[39] Some politicians even suggested that men needed to fight another war to build their strength. To accusations that women wanted to become men, or take their place in the world, Grand argued that only men's conceit and arrogance made them see themselves as enviable models:

> that she should be content to develop the good material which she finds in herself and be only dissatisfied with the poor quality of that which is being offered to her in man, her mate, must appear to him to be a thing as monstrous as it is unaccountable.[40]

Morally immature, increasingly effeminate, men needed to be taught responsibility, to understand that liberty does not mean licence.

Men's derision about daughters' revolts and New Women's demands reflected their desperate attempt to secure their place in the entrenched social order. Often, they expressed horror that women were entering the professions, where they earned their own income; professional women meant empty nurseries, and that meant race suicide. But railing against working women brought up the problem of a female surplus, caused in part by emigration by men to British colonies, partly by war casualties, leaving men to grope for solutions for how such women could lead productive lives. 'In the midst of this,' Grand wrote, 'a cry is heard that the physique of the race is deteriorating. Bang goes the population-difficulty door, and now there is some really beautiful talk about health and virtue.' A healthy and virtuous society, these men assert meaningfully, is a woman's responsibility to impart to her children – returning to the desolate image of empty nurseries.[41]

Sarah Grand shared the literary limelight with another influential British writer, George Egerton, the nom de plume of Mary

Chavelita Dunne Bright. In 1887, when she was 28, the Australian-born Dunne made the rash, regrettable decision to elope to Norway with a friend of her father. Henry Higginson, as it turned out, was a bigamist, but he promised Dunne that he would not blight her life: he was quite ill, about to die, and by 1889 she was a widow. Norway proved a revelation for Dunne: she discovered Ibsen, Strindberg, Nietzsche and Knut Hamsun, with whom, she said, she fell instantly in love, and whose novel *Hunger* she later translated.[42] After leaving Norway for Britain, she married George Egerton Clairmonte, from whom she took her professional moniker, and set herself to supporting them both through her writing. She sent her early stories to Thomas Gill, who wrote a literary column, in hopes of being published in his newspaper. Like many of her first readers, he thought the 'virile sketches', so sensuous and possibly scandalous, were written by a man.[43] When she corrected his assumption, he offered his help in finding a publisher, suggesting the spirited firm of John Lane, whose authors included Henry James, George Moore and Max Beerbohm. *Keynotes* was published in 1893, followed by *Discords* a year later. Suddenly, Egerton was famous and, for some readers, infamous. She was not surprised.

A few years before, she had been amused by London audiences' shock over Ibsen's *Ghosts*. 'I am afraid my sensibilities are blunted,' she wrote to her father,

> considering that every little hospital nurse knows of the existence of syphilis, every married woman and a large number of the unmarried ones, and that every day's paper has a 'horror' of some kind or other . . . It is all humbug, part of the most positive British doctrine of commit adultery, seduce any woman you can, in fact sin as you please but don't be found out.[44]

If some reviewers found her work shamelessly erotic, she was gratified by letters she got from women readers confessing that they identified with her characters and 'are glad to see their sensations made matters of record'.[45]

Like Sarah Grand, she focused on women's lives, desires and frustrations. One of the most talked-about stories in *Keynotes* was 'A Cross Line', whose protagonist, a married woman, revels in her sexuality. She recognizes an 'untamed spirit' within her that fuels her erotic daydreams; she smokes; she is so tanned from being out-doors – she loves fishing – that she appears to be a gypsy; and she admits to a 'restless craving for sun and love and motion'.[46] When her husband remarks that 'being married to you is like chumming with a chap!' she replies flirtatiously: 'Perhaps I was a man last time, and some hereditary memories are cropping up in this incarna-tion!'[47] But their relationship is hardly chummy: sitting on his lap, running her fingers through his hair, biting his ear, she seduces him until he is aroused, his eyes dilated, his skin blushed, and he picks her up and carries her to her bedroom. Still, despite her passionate nature, when she has a chance to run off with a lover, she chooses 'monotonous country life', with her husband. If not for affection, she confesses to the man who pursues her, 'we women would master the world . . . At heart we care nothing for laws, nothing for systems,' but 'this untameableness of ours is corrected by our affec-tions. We forge our own chains in a moment of softness' and must wear them with grace.[48] The idea that women harboured thrill-ing, secret fantasies sparked recognition in many readers; *Keynotes* became a best-seller; *Discords*, less critically acclaimed, went into four editions.

Discords contained the disturbing 'Virgin Soil', focusing on the frustrations and anger of a young woman who, at seventeen, was married off by her mother with no knowledge about sex. Five years later, she returns home, gaunt and desperately unhappy. Her husband has gone off with a mistress, she informs her shocked mother, and not for the first time. She says she's leaving him, and blames her mother for keeping her ignorant about the sex act itself, and about a husband's power. Marriage, she realizes, is based on inequality: the husband can demand sex from his wife as his right, but considers sex from a mistress 'as a favor' to be rewarded with money and gifts. Marriage seems to her no different from 'a legal prostitution, a nightly degradation, a hateful yoke under which [women] age, mere bearers of children conceived in a sense of duty, not love'. She refuses to blame herself for her husband's philandering, claiming that men need to be responsible for their own sins. But she does blame her unhappiness on her mother:

> I say it is your fault, because you reared me a fool, an
> idiot, ignorant of everything I ought to have known,
> everything that concerned me and the life I was bound to
> lead as a wife; my physical needs, my coming passion, the
> very meaning of my sex, my wifehood and motherhood to
> follow. You gave me not one weapon in my hand to defend
> myself against the possible attacks of man at his worst
> . . . You delivered me body and soul into his hands
> without preparing me in any way for the ordeal I was
> to go through.[49]

Like many other young women, Egerton's dismayed character entered into marriage with illusions that were soon shattered; powerless and degraded, she looked forward to a sad future.

Women who did

Katy Carr, a girl punished for her daring in Susan Coolidge's *What Katy Did*, became, twenty years later, a woman punished for daring in Grant Allen's incendiary novel *The Woman Who Did* (1895), which went into nineteen editions in its first year and was translated into French, German and Swedish. Allen, born in Ontario, Canada, in 1848, grew up in the U.S., France and England, where he later settled. At the age of twenty, he married a woman three years older, who had been either a prostitute or a woman abandoned by a lover. Ill with tuberculosis when they married, she died three years later; Grant remarried and had one son. A prolific writer, his work included essays, especially on science and eugenics, novels, science fiction and detective stories. He published two novels under the pseudonym of Olive Pratt Rayner, a name chosen, he said, to make his first-person female narrators seem more believable.

As a disciple of Herbert Spencer and a hearty supporter of eugenics, Allen proposed a scheme for ideal marriages, in which women would serve as 'eugenic gatekeepers'. Once they were educated and financially independent, he believed, 'marriage would have no economic function and prostitution would vanish . . . Illicit sex being no longer on the market, and men's sexual appetite being the stronger, almost every woman would receive marriage offers and so be able to blackmail men into virtue.' Men were obligated to make themselves strong and virile, thereby to pass on their attributes to their offspring. Women could easily reject inferior males, 'so the unfit men – the immoral, the diseased, the stupid – would gradually be eliminated'.[50] Yet although Allen said that he recognized women's power to make an advantageous marriage on their own terms, or to reject marriage completely, the fate of his heroine in

Grant Allen, author of the scandalous novel *The Woman Who Did* (1895).

The Woman Who Did seemed to contradict, rather than celebrate, his vision of liberated womanhood. 'Of all the vicious writers in the English language,' the critic Jeannette Gilder lamented, 'I think that Grant Allen is the most vicious.' Even more than George Egerton, whose *Keynotes* and *Discords*, Gilder said, 'have hardened the public mind and twisted the public morals'.[51]

The protagonist of Allen's morality tale is Herminia Barton, immediately identified as a New Woman by the 'curious oriental-looking navy-blue robe' that falls gently

> in natural folds and set off to the utmost the lissome
> grace of her rounded figure. It was a sort of sleeveless sack,
> embroidered in front with arabesques in gold thread, and

fastened obliquely two inches below the waist with a belt
of gilt braid and a clasp of Moorish jewel-work. Beneath it,
a bodice of darker silk showed at the arms and neck, with
loose sleeves in keeping.

The outfit was novel, and charming 'in the way it permitted the
utmost liberty and variety of movement to the lithe limbs of its
wearer'.[52] The looseness, embroidery, gold thread and Moorish clasp
convey Herminia's exoticism; the soft 'natural' folds of the robe make
it clear that she is not wearing a corset, a sure sign of new womanhood. And even more than her striking outfit, her face was 'frank
and fearless', reflecting a 'perfect air of untrammelled liberty'.[53]

At a party, Herminia meets Alan Merrick, a barrister over thirty
who is ready for marriage. He notices her immediately, and in the
course of their conversation she tells him that she had attended
Girton College at Cambridge, the first British women's college, but
left without taking the final examination. 'I didn't care for the life,'
she tells Alan.

> I thought it cramping. You see, if we women are ever to
> be free in the world, we must have in the end a freeman's
> education. But the education at Girton made only a pre-
> tence of freedom. At heart, our girls were as enslaved to
> conventions as any girls elsewhere. The whole object of the
> training was to see just how far you could manage to push
> a woman's education without the faintest danger of her
> emancipation.

Alan agrees that women students at Somerville, Oxford's analogue
to Girton, did not participate as fully in student life – sports,

socializing – as the men did, even though they earnestly pursued their studies. 'They're trying hard enough to develop us intellectually,' Herminia says, 'but morally and socially they want to mew us up just as close as ever.'[54] Allen's contemporaries were well aware of the connotations of a Girton education. 'The "Girton Girl"', the Victorian scholar Chris Willis notes, 'became a cultural stereotype, being the subject of many news stories, articles, cartoons and novels . . . invariably referred to as a "girl" rather than a woman, although university educated men of her age were referred to as "Varsity *men*".'[55]

Herminia aspires to be financially independent, and she repeatedly resists Alan's pleas to marry him. She simply does not see why they need to legitimize their love by marrying. Instead, they have an affair, she becomes pregnant and they go to Italy for her confinement. Although she is uneasy about the deception, they register at a lodging as Mr and Mrs Merrick. Herminia defies her own father and Alan's in her stalwart refusal to marry. Neither has a mother.

In Perugia, Alan contracts typhoid fever and dies. When his father finally arrives, he is incensed that his son and Herminia had not married, and tries, but fails, to evict her from their rooms. Knowing that Herminia is living in precarious financial circumstances because Alan's will was not executed, Dr Merrick offers her £50. But Herminia, determined to be independent, refuses. After her daughter, the aptly named Dolores, is born, they return to England, but can secure lodging only if she claims to be Mrs Barton. Gradually she finds work as a journalist and writes a 'blankly pessimistic' novel that 'embodied the experiences and beliefs and sentiments of a martyred woman'.[56] The novel is largely ignored, garnering only one review, and Herminia struggles to eke out a living for herself and Dolly.

Herminia is convinced that she can raise her daughter alone to become an independent woman, with more opportunities than she herself had. But Dolly, who grows to be stunningly beautiful, shares none of her mother's attitudes. She resents Herminia for not marrying and giving her legitimacy, and for bringing her up in poverty. She loves beautiful things and covets wealth. Herminia is bitterly disappointed. When Dolly tells her that she will not marry her ardent suitor until her mother is dead, Herminia commits suicide.

Many readers condemned the self-righteous Herminia as a prig, some criticized Allen for killing off his protagonists instead of having them live together, and others damned him for promoting libertinism rather than liberty, and for insisting that Herminia be a martyr. Allen defended himself, telling an interviewer that he meant his novel to

> get at women, and especially young women, who are still
> plastic and may yet be susceptible to influence. I want to
> say to these: 'Your purity, of which you make so much,
> is an artificial product, which can only be kept up at the
> expense of unspeakable misery to thousands of other
> women who are sacrificed on your account.'

He condemned Dolly, not Herminia: it was Dolly who wanted to present herself as one of the 'good, marketable commodities for men who want to buy'. Every man and woman, Allen said, 'ought naturally to form a union of affection at the moment when such unions are possible. If this were the rule we should have neither celibacy nor the social evil' of prostitution, including what Allen deemed to be prostitution within marriage.[57]

Allen followed his scandalous novel with stories featuring women detectives who both solved mysteries and sailed happily into a contented future. Two years after publishing *The Woman Who Did*, Allen returned as Olive Pratt Rayner in *The Type-writer Girl*, featuring another young woman educated at Girton. Juliet Appleton has just been orphaned when her father, an American-born naturalized British citizen and colonel in the British Army, dies. Because he had refused to carry out orders to which he was opposed, he was denied a pension, leaving Juliet without any financial support. Like many New Women protagonists, Juliet is motherless: her mother, from a famous Anglo-Indian family, apparently died in childbirth. Although Juliet has a Girton education, instead of becoming a teacher, which would be an expected profession, she decides to become a typewriter girl, manipulating a new technology in a male-dominated world of business.

She gets a job at a law firm, where she feels suffocated, and quits, briefly joining an anarchist community, which she soon leaves, uncommitted to its ideology. She lands a job at a publishing house, where her boss, Mr Blank, falls in love with her, and she with him. Along the way, she meets a delicate, wealthy girl, Michaela, who befriends her, and she discovers that her boss, whom she calls Romeo, has been engaged to Michaela for the past five years. Although he wants to break his engagement, claiming that Juliet – intelligent, feisty, interesting – is a better match for him than Michaela, Juliet insists that he honour his promise, and she goes off to get a job at another office. Although Juliet does not end up marrying Romeo, Allen portrays her as independent and optimistic about her future. On her trusty bicycle, she is bright and energetic, a far more appealing character than the 'womanly woman' represented by Michaela.

Allen realized that Juliet was an exception; most young women struggled with the tensions between wanting to be independent and yearning to marry. In *Miss Cayley's Adventures*, the intrepid detective Lois (not surprisingly a Girton girl) refuses to marry her suitor because he is wealthy and she, penniless, feels she would stand in the way of his future. Alone in her room, she breaks down in tears. 'It's all very well being modern,' she thinks, 'but my experience is that, when it comes to the man one loves – well, the Middle Ages are still horribly strong within us.'[58] Within young women, and also within confused young men.

The Scottish writer Alice Mona Alison, known by the nom de plume of Mona Caird, tackled the confusion in 'The Yellow Drawing Room', in which the narrator, Mr St Vincent, meets the unconventional Vanora, who has painted her drawing room bright yellow, shocking her friends. 'The true woman', St Vincent reflects, 'is retiring, unobtrusive, indistinguishable even until you know her very well, and then she is very much like what every other woman would be under the same conditions.'[59] True women were quiet and predictable, but Vanora was dazzling, with her 'glistening, golden hair', 'eyes like the sea' and a 'robust, erect, pliant, firmly knit' figure. 'She was vital, not galvanic.'[60] But her electrifying presence frightened St Vincent. He respected women's power, but believed unwaveringly that they needed to exercise that power in their rightful sphere, the home. 'If only women realized where their true power lay, and how mighty was that power, they would never seek to snatch it in directions where they are inevitably weak, and – if I must say it – inevitably ridiculous.' But Vanora reports that her father never taught her to circumscribe her life to fit any sphere, 'and in my case', she added, 'instinct seems at fault'.[61] St Vincent, enraptured by Vanora, tries valiantly to get her to submit to him, 'and to be a woman in the old sweet sense': 'I longed to make her yield to me; to love me with a lowly up-looking love. I have a burning desire to subdue her.'[62] But Vanora rejects his vision: she wants to own her destiny. 'When you describe your doctrines,' she tells St Vincent, 'I seem to see the doors of a dark prison opening out of the sunshine.'[63]

Like eighteen-year-old Gertrude Hemery, young women glimpsed a sunlit future, despite their parents' worries, suitors' old-fashioned ideas and their own trepidations. It took Anne Morgan, the strong-willed daughter of financier J. P. Morgan, thirty years to break away from her father's domination, but when she did, she found kindred spirits among a group of artistic, independent women dubbed 'the Bachelorettes'. To the theatrical agent Elisabeth Marbury, who was Anne's lover, the young woman seemed 'young for her age . . . There was something pathetic about this splendid girl, full of vitality and eagerness, yet who, as the youngest of a large family, had never been allowed to grow up. Her environment had always been conservative.'[64] She was her father's travelling companion and hostess throughout young adulthood, bristling at his patriarchal views and derision of New Women. 'Her mind', Marbury said, 'was ready for the spark plugs to be adjusted. Her moment of mental expansion had dawned.'[65] By the early 1900s, with novels, stories and plays offering a new plot for women's experiences, the light that dawned for Anne Morgan illuminated the lives of many of her contemporaries. It was time, they decided, to break away from the past.

5 Bodies in Motion

ᘐ

'On with the dance! Let joy be unrefined!'
Atlanta Constitution, 12 January 1913

As the twentieth century dawned, adolescent girls found two new venues where they could exert their independence, trouble their parents and see the notoriously subversive New Woman in action: movie theatres and dance halls. Both exploded on the landscape of cities and small towns throughout the u.s. and Britain, attracting patrons of all ages and classes. Crowding in theatre lobbies awaiting the start of a show, sitting in the dark watching flickering images and strutting to ragtime on a crowded dance floor: each entertainment offered a chance to mingle in a social setting apart from school, the workplace and family. Working girls met students, rich met poor, sexually experienced young women met those who were romantically naive. They saw how other girls dressed and behaved; sometimes they were shocked or shaken, or even frightened. Each entertainment had a thrilling potential to disrupt and corrupt.

Unlike plays or concerts, movies were cheap – ticket prices in the U.S. were 5 cents in the ever-popular nickelodeons, and 10 cents for adults in other movie houses. In the UK, seats could be had for as little as a penny. Because showing movies was cheaper than mounting a play, stage theatres transformed themselves into the more lucrative movie houses. By 1909 the *New York Times* reported a 'Nation-wide Wave of Moving Pictures' that had grown during the past five years: 'their glaring signs, strident music, and brightly lighted portals have been multiplied by thousands with a rapidity almost magical.'[1] Features were short, generally under fifteen minutes long, and a typical show included a drama, a slapstick comedy and a western. Sentimental dramas were staples of the early days of movies, but it soon became clear that audiences wanted action, pathos, crime and love stories with happy endings.

Westerns were hugely popular with young women, many of whom had read stories like the *Outdoor Girls* books, whose protagonists had adventures on their tramps through the woods. They could imagine themselves in the wide-open spaces of the American frontier, conquering the challenges of the terrain, outlaws and hardscrabble ranch life. They could imagine themselves on horseback, the wind in their hair, riding, maybe, into the arms of a virile cowboy, or tending gently to his wounds. By 1911 many westerns were shot on location, giving city and small-town girls a sweeping view of deserts and mountains. With plots that focused largely on good battling evil, the female lead stood as the triumphant moral centre: strong but feminine, unyielding yet nurturing.

Even more popular were adventure serials featuring an attractive young woman escaping danger and outwitting malicious men through courage, daring and ingenuity. The film historian Shelley Stamp notes the repetitive plots of most serials: a young woman is

Cowgirl, Newton, Kansas, 1908.

thrust into an independent life when her father or male guardian dies. She embraces that independence, though, by refusing to marry, and insisting on following her own dreams and ambitions. And in each episode she must overcome a new obstacle. The final instalment, nevertheless, often finds the heroine safe in the arms of her suitor, with marriage in her future.[2] As much as the serials celebrated young women's freedom, they also endorsed the cherished notion that a woman's greatest happiness and highest achievement came by marrying.

Each series introduced viewers to characters played by charming, spunky actresses who performed their own stunts, whom they followed week after week, through dozens of episodes, ensuring a loyal repeat audience. In an innovative marketing strategy, some producers arranged for story instalments to be published simultaneously in women's monthly magazines and hundreds of newspapers, which also ran articles about particular stars, as well as enticing movie advertisements.

The Girl Spy, in 1909, soon was followed by a spate of others, including *The Girl Detective*, *The Adventures of Kathlyn*, *The Trey o' Hearts*, *The Hazards of Helen*, *The Exploits of Elaine* and *Zudora*, in which a girl detective battles supernatural forces. Producers publicized the risk-taking of their featured actresses, such as the intrepid Florence La Badie, the heroine of *The Million Dollar Mystery* (1914); Kathlyn Williams, who boasted having flown in a plane; and Pearl White, a former trapeze artist, whose career catapulted with *The Perils of Pauline* (1914), a cliff-hanger series that followed the travails of an orphan on the run because a greedy man wants to kill her and benefit from her inheritance. 'Pearl White sure has to do some strenuous work in this series,' a reviewer commented, and she 'is entirely praiseworthy'.[3] In one episode of the enormously popular *What Happened to Mary* (1912), the heroine escapes from a seventh-floor bedroom by lowering herself down a rope made of bed sheets. 'I just wanted to see if I had the courage to do it,' actress Mary Fuller told an interviewer, 'but, oh, I *was* frightened when swinging on the rope and looking far down to the pavement and spiked fence and sea of faces watching. I hope the picture gives my audiences the thrill it gave me.'[4]

To meet the public's apparently insatiable demand, movies were shown in various public places besides theatres, including village halls, churches, schools and even in tents. Nickelodeons and makeshift theatres offered no amenities: most of the time, seats were hard, ventilation was poor and the audience sometimes unruly. But all that hardly mattered. The movies were enrapturing, transporting and cheap delights, even in the movie palaces that began replacing nickelodeons around 1910. 'Marble, beveled glass, polished oak and

Scene from the movie *The Perils of Pauline* (1914).

walnut, dazzling electric lights, lavish carpeting and huge mirrors' created an opulent venue, notes the movie historian Eileen Bowser.[5] A welcoming staff that included a manager and ushers made patrons feel valued; and there were restrooms, no less luxurious than the auditorium. Lobbies became commodious, a place to buy tickets, meet friends, exchange gossip and show off dresses, hats, shoes and make-up. As Shelley Stamp discovered, for some women, 'putting oneself on display' became 'the chief feature of attending the show'.[6] They watched one another as attentively as they watched performers on screen.

In 1910 in the u.s., more than 7,500 picture houses and 2,500 vaudeville theatres attracted more than five million viewers daily, most of them women – young women meeting friends, working women on their lunch hours, mothers with children, shoppers taking a break – and children of all ages, who would pop in after school and stay in the theatre until bedtime. In the uk, by 1916, more than a billion tickets were sold each year. Between 4,000 and

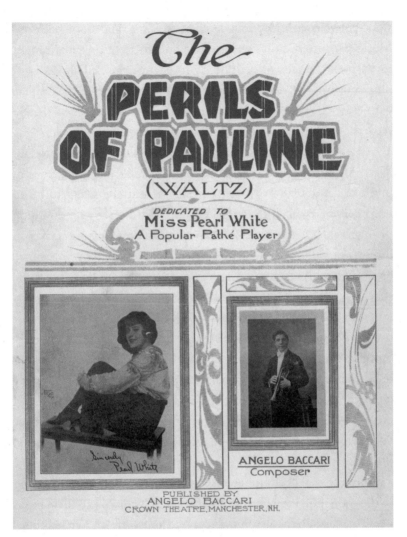

Sheet music for 'The *Perils of Pauline* Waltz'.

5,000 cinemas each accommodated between 100 and 4,000 patrons.[7] Music-hall proprietors, seeing their audiences shrink alarmingly, toyed with the idea of petitioning to change the British law banning stage theatres from opening on Sundays, in order to compete with cinemas that were not subject to the law. The cost of a theatre staff, though, made the proposition economically untenable.

As moviegoing burgeoned, so, inevitably, did suspicions. Watching moving pictures in the dark seemed, on the face of it, immoral, and by 1910 parents, teachers and the usual cadre of reformers marshalled their opposition. 'There can be no doubting the firm and lasting hold this inexpensive and moving drama has on its gigantic public or the need of keeping its influence wholesome,' one writer warned in *Harper's Weekly*.[8] Widely publicized was the shocking disclosure that some boys brought up on charges of theft said they got their ideas from movie plots. But movies seemed most threatening to the innocence of girls. Chicago's Children's Society brought up the chilling fact that men could sit next to children in the dark. Segregation of the sexes was the solution, the Society insisted, along with showing movies with the lights on. To find evidence of wrongdoing, the Society questioned forty girls, whose testimony, although never publicly revealed, apparently supported the group's fears.[9]

Those fears ranged from whispered remarks and furtive touching to the more horrifying possibility that girls would be abducted into white slavery. Between 1900 and 1915 thousands of articles about white slavery appeared in American newspapers and magazines, making it one of the most prominent causes for social reformers, as the British suffrage leader Emmeline Pankhurst noticed when she toured the country in 1913.[10] In Britain, where prostitution was not illegal, the threat of white slavery was barely noted.

In the u.s., however, like all other reform issues, this one energized public debate: some believed that public places of any kind
– parks, dance halls and movie theatres – were 'breeding places
of vice';[11] others laid the blame on flirtatious young women, no
matter where they happened to be; and still others saw the cause
as economic. 'All this vice is a reflex of social conditions of poor
housing and poor wages,' claimed Howard A. Kelly, a professor at
Johns Hopkins University, speaking at the International Congress
of Hygiene and Demography in Washington, DC. 'It is not due
to the inherent profligacy of women', he asserted confidently; the
white slave 'is nearly always coaxed, drugged or cajoled into her
life of shame'. But the threat was real, and widespread. 'White
slavery', Kelly said, 'is the worst plague spot on the social body
to-day. It is a worse scourge than cancer and all infectious diseases
put together.'[12] Emma Goldman, however, drew a cynical conclusion: 'Whenever the public mind is to be distracted from some
great social wrong' – poor housing and poor wages – 'the reformers
always raise a hullabaloo over some side issue.' White slavery occupied the minds of reformers and, Goldman pointed out, the fear of
it created high-paying jobs for political appointees who benefited
from inflaming national hysteria.[13] Nevertheless, that hysteria contributed to the public's suspicions about the deleterious impact of
movie theatres.

Other reformers objected to content – including movies that
depicted the evils of white slavery. Censorship was the answer,
with civic boards and church committees formed 'to eliminate
inspiration to ill-doing, and to encourage good impulses and the
spread of useful knowledge'.[14] Censors were alert to depictions of
crimes, excessive violence and lawlessness that were not met with
sufficient retribution – behaviour, censors believed, that threatened

the welfare of the community. The result of censors' efforts was a hotchpotch of overseers, from local police to a self-proclaimed National Board of Censorship, based in New York, which had no legal power to enforce its decisions. Movie-makers willingly submitted their pictures to the National Board and produced movies they considered inoffensive, hoping for approval that reassured theatre proprietors and audiences. Some enterprising theatre-owners, though, realized that censorship could be a boon to business. 'Adults Only' signs began to appear in front of theatres, no matter what the movie's content, doubling attendance and inspiring owners to increase admission prices.

A similar quandary existed in the UK, where films were rated A, suitable for adults, and U, suitable for everyone. But no one had the power to enforce the ratings. Before 1918 – when the British film industry revived from its shaky, underfunded pre-war beginnings – most movies were imported from America and generally considered silly and banal. Educational films – such as the record of explorations or glimpses of animal behaviour – had more merit, as did films showing royal pageantry. Nevertheless, audiences flocked to see American comedies and westerns, and an increasing number of venues applied for licences to convert themselves into picture palaces, not surprisingly sparking debate. Those opposed to the proliferation of cinemas, the historian Audrey Field writes, reflected the 'deep-rooted puritan conviction that one ought not to be pleased with that which is intended to give pleasure'.[15]

'What are the "movies" making of our children?' asked the secretary of the Pennsylvania Board of Motion Picture Censors in an earnestly hand-wringing magazine article. Their influence, he lamented, 'rivals that of all the stages, pulpits, lecture platforms, newspapers, and books hitherto known in the world', and they have 'widened the experiences, quickened the imagination, and satisfied the craving for romance of multitudes who are deprived of the education that comes from reading, travel, and human association'.[16] Prominent among those multitudes were aspiring young women.

Stars

Audiences created stars: actors and actresses they admired, even loved; men and women who represented the person viewers wanted to become, or the person, deep inside themselves, they believed they were. Stars were talented, real people, but they were also figments of quickened, romantic imagination. Profiles, interviews and publicity articles conflated screen characters with the actors' personalities and daily lives. On screen and in print, they appeared luminous, riveting and irresistible. In 1914 at the Grand Ball of the International Moving Picture Association in Chicago, more than 10,000 fans thronged at the event's entrance to glimpse movie stars. Stage actors had their fans, too, a front-page newspaper article noted, but they elicited no more than a refined gasp, while 'a celluloid favorite can start a riot'.[17] At the same time that moviegoing was a communal, social experience where friends gathered and new friends were made, and where courtships played out in the dark, it was a private experience, as well, that fuelled individual dreams. For young women, those dreams were about freedom and independence, with a slight halo of glamour, and the hope of love.

In cinema's early years, some companies did not allow actors' names to appear in cast lists or advertisements, so that they could be placed in both starring and bit roles. But in 1909 the Kalem Stock Company provided actors' photographs for display in theatre

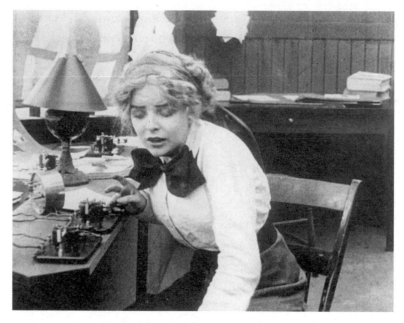

Blanche Sweet in *The Lonedale Operator* (1911).

lobbies, and by 1910 many other movie producers followed. To meet the huge demand for actors' photographs, one company offered postcards of stars' images, priced at 5 cents – as much as the cost of theatre admission. Trade magazines, such as *Moving Picture World*, *Billboard*, *Variety* and, in the UK, *Pictures and the Picturegoer*, began publishing interviews and gossip articles. Newspapers added film reporters: in the *Chicago Daily Tribune*, 'Mae Tinee' wrote 'Answers to Movie Fans' – readers who sent questions in droves – and Kitty Kelly offered 'Flickerings from Film Land'; Grace Kingsley covered the movie world for the *Los Angeles Times*, and the *San Francisco Chronicle* ran 'Gossip of Plays and Players'. The early 1900s saw the start of fan magazines, too, each issue awaited hungrily, especially by young women. The issues portrayed actresses as strong, lovable,

Blanche Sweet, who played the role of feisty ingénue.

sympathetic personalities, devoted to their craft, and each issue chronicled and idealized their lives, loves and aspirations.

Young women moviegoers discovered that many actresses they admired were the same age as they were, heightening their feeling of identification and intimacy. In 1911 the fifteen-year-old Blanche Sweet, for example, starred in a D. W. Griffith thriller, *The Lonedale Operator*, playing a plucky telegraph operator who outwits robbers trying to break into a railway station. Sweet, dubbed 'The Biograph Blonde' by the company she worked for early in her career, became identified with 'light ingénue roles'.[18] But those ingénues were fearless, forthright working girls, not swooning heroines. Like her contemporary Mary Pickford, who was seventeen when she moved from stage to screen, Sweet projected an image of boyish femininity.

Pickford's slender figure led to her being cast as adolescents and child-like women in the hundreds of films she made from her teens through her twenties, even after her widely publicized marriage. Although attractive to men, she seemed sexually innocent, flirtatious but not aggressive. Pickford was a phenomenon, a star so adored by audiences that she pumped her salary up to a startling $175 a week, many times higher than most of her colleagues. 'The little Lady is endearingly referred to as "Little Mary",' *The Billboard* reported in 1910, 'and she is on intimate terms with every person who patronizes the moving picture theatre.'[19]

As popular as Pickford, but since forgotten, Mary Fuller, the star of the twelve-episode serial *What Happened to Mary*, began her acting career at nineteen, playing the typical ingénue for many years after. A profile published when the series began portrayed Fuller as attractive, vivacious, girlish and daring. When movie roles required her to run over icy boulders carrying a child, jump from one speeding car to another, race in a motor boat, be thrown from horses or suffer shipwrecks and stabbings, she performed fearlessly. Courageous as she was, the reporter noted, Fuller was 'by no means a "mannish" woman, as some might suppose from a recital of her strenuous outdoor exploits', but instead 'charming of manner, pretty of face, and graceful of figure' – as strong and lovable as the characters she played.[20] To her audience, she felt like a friend.

For some young women, the intimacy they felt with stars translated into a yearning to be part of the film world, a possibility that film magazines and reporters encouraged by publicizing actresses who had made the leap from their ordinary, everyday lives to the glamorous milieu of movies. 'How Famous Film Stars Have Been Discovered' was the title of a column by Grace Kingsley that revealed the unusual trajectory of many stars – Mary Pickford, Blanche

LITTLE
MARY PICKFORD

Mary Pickford was a teenager when she began her movie career.

Sweet and the famous Gish sisters, to name a few – who had started out as film extras. 'Some of the most widely unknown people in the world have turned into great moving picture actors,' director D. W. Griffith attested.[21]

Gertrude Price, in her syndicated column about movie stars, pointed out another direction for involvement with film: 'The mental market place of the nation has been thrown open to women with wares to sell. Her originality and her perseverance and her brains are coming to be recognized on the same plane as man's.' The movie world, Price said, 'is bubbling over with novel opportunities for pretty girls, active girls, persevering girls, blonde girls, brunette girls, short girls and tall girls, athletic girls and studious girls'.[22] This world beckoned with enticing possibilities, and while their parents fretted, adolescents dreamed.

Animal dances

In 1914 the Chicago police major Metellus Funkhouser took charge of ensuring morals in a city notorious for vice. Supported by many women's groups, he vetted such film titles as 'The Scarlet Letter' and 'The Merchant of Venice', and banned movies featuring crime, brothels, the degradation of women, violence and one showing the controversial injection of morphine and scopolamine to induce 'twilight sleep', purported to relieve the pain of childbirth. 'The doctors tell me a promiscuous display of the pictures might encourage race suicide,' he told an audience. And besides, he added, 'I think in any event child birth is too sacred to be shown in moving pictures.'[23] He was just as vigorously opposed to a movie featuring the tango and the so-called 'animal dances' that were sweeping the country: the bunny hug, grizzly bear and turkey trot. Besides

dancers' moves that he considered salacious, he objected to seduc-
tively wild representations of dance halls in movies, which he was
certain – and he was right – would lure young movie viewers.[24]

Deeming dance a threat was nothing new. Many in eighteenth-
century society had roundly condemned the waltz after it was
introduced to Britain from Germany: they were shocked to see
partners pressing their bodies so closely to each other, shocked to
watch them swirling, with apparent abandon, around the dance
floor. One father 'whisked his daughter home from a party lest "she
be made a whirligig"'. In the early nineteenth century, Byron, no
slave to convention, denounced it; some derided it as 'hugging set
to music'.[25] By the 1900s, when the waltz had become a beloved
staple in anyone's ballroom – staid and even, truth be told, boring
– upright citizens found new dances to incite alarm, and new
youthful activities to condemn.

It started on San Francisco's Barbary Coast with the turkey trot,
danced to ragtime music, which so enchanted the ballerina Anna
Pavlova that she announced she would teach the steps to her students in her native Russia. As the turkey trot swept eastwards and
crossed the Atlantic, it was followed soon by the bunny hug and
the grizzly bear, a trio of popular dances that emulated the movements of animals, with the addition of elbows protruding, bottoms
jutting and arms draped languidly over each partner's shoulders as
they clasped each other closely, gyrated, flounced, twisted, contor-
ted and dipped. The tango came in for special notice: called the
'Argentine Largo' in Paris, where it was 'particularly fascinating',
the French believed it had come 'by way of South America from the
negro communities of the United States'.[26] If French society was
charmed, some white Americans were repelled, and they conjured
up their own genealogies, insisting that depictions of such dances

could be found on Grecian urns or Egyptian tablets, anywhere but from African Americans.

Whatever their origin, there was something defiantly erotic about the new dances, and of course, they needed to be stopped. In some cities, police departments prohibited the dances, slapping steep fines and even prison sentences on violators who danced closer than 9 inches from their partner. One city official demanded 'daylight waltzes': that is, a slice of light visible between a young man and woman, no matter what the dance.[27]

Clergymen, educators and reformers warned parents against allowing their daughters to go to dance halls, but those daughters wanted to dance, and when their parents forbade them to go to dances held in the evening, they danced in the afternoon. Restaurants, seeing a money-making opportunity, used the slack hours from four to six to open rooms for 'tea dancing', much to the dismay of some local officials. As New York's mayor discovered, high-school girls would tell their parents they were going to a club meeting, but instead meet their friends at a tea dance.[28] Crowded with 'girls and men', tea dances were more likely to serve gin fizzes and cocktails than tea, and observers were scandalized to see many girls smoking.[29]

Dancing, F. Scott Fitzgerald advised his fourteen-year-old sister in 1915, 'counts as nothing else does' if she wanted to be popular.[30] Growing up in a religious family in a Southern university town, one girl recalled feeling frustrated by her parents' disapproval of dancing. 'I cared for dancing intensely, having rhythm and poetry and romance in my very marrow,' she said. Because she was never invited to dances, she had no chance to meet boys, and she listened with envy as other girls her age 'talked about their beaux and dances and fraternity pins, about this college boy and that, and I felt an

Dancers trying out the latest steps, by noted illustrator John Held Jr, 1915.

aching loneliness that could not have been worse if I had been actually branded and cast out for human society'. But her mother never thought that she might want to meet some boys and 'have a chance for a social life that I was secretly dying for', a social life that centred around dances.[31]

Even parents who approved of dancing as pleasure and exercise tried to keep their daughters out of dance halls to protect them from abduction. The fear of white slavery was revived with rumours of men adulterating women's drinks or lurking outside of clubs and injecting young women with opiate-laced syringes. Even so sophisticated a reformer as Rheta Childe Dorr believed that 'White Slavers' lurked around dancing academies and dance halls:

'The dance hall . . . practically unregulated, has become a veritable forcing house of vice and crime in every city in the United States,' she wrote. 'It is a straight chute down which, every year, thousands of girls descend to the way of the prodigal.'[32] Young women were warned to look out for handsome young men who offered themselves as dance partners: they could be one of the 'tango pirates' or 'tango pickpockets' who were really after a woman's money – or worse, her virtue.[33] In New York and Chicago, debate over public dance halls was reported as front-page news, but the dance craze was hardly limited to big cities. 'The whole country is dance mad,' announced one public school dance teacher.[34]

In a fictionalized diary chronicling 'The Day-to-day Story of a Modern Girl', published in the *Ladies Home Journal*, the diarist disclosed that she knew girls who lied to their mothers and said they were going shopping several afternoons a week, but really arranged to meet men who took them to tea dances. She herself loved to dance, and at one club met 'the most independent girl I ever knew', who had studied art in Paris, flouted convention and 'gets herself talked about' – just the kind of young woman parents warned their daughters against. The diarist, though, cared nothing about gossip or threats to her reputation. She cared only that she was 'young and pretty and can dance like a breeze'.[35] Men interested her more as dance partners than life partners. 'I don't want to settle down – not ever. I won't!' she exclaims. But if she happens to wind up settling down 'in spite of myself, I'm going to crowd as much as I can into my youth'.[36]

The women who assembled in the ballroom of New York's renowned Delmonico's restaurant in 1912 for the annual meeting of the Committee on Amusements and Vacation Resources of Working Girls knew that the diarist's feelings were widely shared. The 'expensively clad' attendees, who included Mrs August Belmont, other society women and many settlement workers, took seats on gilt chairs five rows deep, around a waxed dance floor, with an overflow of latecomers ranged against the walls. They had come to see demonstration dancers do the two-step, rag their shoulders in the grizzly bear and show off their version of the chicken hop. At the end of the performance, when the applause and laughter had died down, the Rev. Dr Percy Stickney Grant took pains to 'minimize the deleterious effects of the dances witnessed' by advising the committee to ban alcohol from dance halls.[37] It was clear that no one would succeed in banning the buoyant dances, nor stop the proliferation of dance halls. By 1910 New York had upwards of five hundred. As the dance historian Mark Knowles discovered, 'in the lower East Side alone [a densely populated neighbourhood of immigrants] a dance hall could be found every two and a half blocks.'[38]

'The forbidding of the modern dances in public centers is dangerous,' Elisabeth Marbury wrote: 'It sets that alluring sign "Forbidden Fruit" upon what otherwise would arouse no prurient curiosity.'[39] She herself came into conflict with reformers who tried to shut down the popular Strand Roof in Manhattan, of which she was a sponsor, along with her friend Anne Morgan, who saw in dance halls an outlet for her newly claimed independence. Morgan lashed out against accusations that the Strand was immoral. Besides enlisting socially prominent women, such as Mrs William K. Vanderbilt, as chaperones, the Strand employed its own officer and detectives. 'They were constantly on the watch for disorderly persons,' Morgan said, 'and when they saw any one they recognized as a notorious character, or if they saw any young girl dance improperly, they interfered.'[40]

Tea dances became a popular afternoon pastime in London, where one dance teacher praised the 'cheery little "Thé Dansant" clubs, which have sprung up all over the West End'; one sat

> at a tiny table – one of the many which surround the dancing floor – set forth with the prettiest of gold and white china; to enjoy a most elaborate and delicious tea, served within a moment of one's arrival, while listening to an excellent string band playing delicious, haunting Tango airs, with an occasional waltz . . . or a lively rag-time melody . . . While chatting with friends, or joining in the dance, an hour or two slips by like magic, and it is time to go; but nevermind, the club meets twice a week, at least, and many of them every day.[41]

Sometimes these clubs were held at hotels, for members only:

> Well-known people are seen on every side. The dancing enthusiasts come early, and spend the whole afternoon; others drop in for half an hour; while many of the members bring parties of young people, who seem much to enjoy the novelty of dancing the afternoon, and seldom leave until after the last bar of music has been played.[42]

In New York, invitation-only teas were held by socialites Mrs William K. Vanderbilt Jr and Mrs William Astor Chanler, and a dinner dance was given by Mrs Stuyvesant Fish, where Vernon and Irene Castle gave an exhibition of the Innovation Waltz, 'a style of dancing the waltz in which the partners do not touch each other at all, even to hold hands'.[43] Stars shone on dance floors, just as they did on movie screens, and in the early 1900s the Castles – sleek, elegant Vernon and slender, alluring Irene – shone brightest. It was Irene whom F. Scott Fitzgerald called the model for the flapper, the woman, he claimed, who enticed nice girls and not-nice girls to mingle.

The fetching Mrs Castle

Elisabeth Marbury became the agent for the Castles after she saw them performing in Paris, where they danced at a renowned supper club, the Café de Paris. At one performance, Grand Duke Dmitri threw a hundred-franc note on a plate and passed it around the tables, collecting from the appreciative audience more than five hundred francs for Irene.[44] 'I had sensed the approach of the dancing madness,' Marbury said after watching the Castles.[45] The couple left Paris for Chicago, where they danced in clubs, but Marbury persuaded them to come to New York, where, in 1912, nineteen-year-old Irene and her 25-year-old husband Vernon astonished patrons with their performances at the Café de l'Opera in Times Square. Each evening, they would rise from their table at ringside, sweep onto the dance floor and dance – the foxtrot, waltz, tango – as no one had danced before.[46] Marbury convinced them to give private lessons and establish Castle House, their own venue, where they would perform at daily teas to music provided by the noted African American jazz and ragtime conductor James Reese Europe and his Society Orchestra. 'The success of the undertaking was pronounced from the very outset,' Marbury recalled: 'The place was jammed and the floor space inadequate.'[47] Vernon choreographed their steps, but Irene mesmerized the audience. As Marbury described her, Irene 'was extraordinary. Her body was lithe and graceful, her swanlike neck suggested the highest distinction, her features and coloring were beautiful.' Although many other dancing couples copied them, Marbury said, 'the Castles were never equaled, let alone excelled, neither have they ever been replaced.'[48] The arts critic Gilbert Seldes remarked on Irene's ethereal lightness: 'There was something unimpassioned, cool not cold, in her abandon,' he wrote: 'it was certainly the least sensual dancing in the world; the whole appeal was visual.'[49]

Castle House was followed by Castles in the Air, a roof garden, Castles on the Sea at Long Beach, New York, and performances on stage and film. Soon after the couple came from Paris, the impresario Charles Dillingham booked them for *The Lady of the Slipper*, to join a seasoned cast. To the vaudeville performer Elsie Janis, they seemed shy: 'They looked like two adolescent palm trees in Paris clothes.' And it turned out that 'their type of ultramodern dancing did not fit into the glorified pantomime atmosphere of our show.' Nevertheless, soon after, in 1913, they opened in *The Sunshine Girl*, a hit that played for months.[50] When Irene came to take her bows in the Broadway musical *Watch Your Step* in 1914, Marbury wrote, 'she was such a symphony of form and color that the audience fairly gasped in admiration. I have never seen a greater triumph born of a personality which was externally faultless.'[51] In 1915 the Castles starred in a musical, *The Whirl of Life*, and in 1916 Irene was voted the most popular movie star in America. Fans pushed and shoved for a chance to bid for a souvenir photograph of her, bidding that proceeded furiously and garnered high prices. 'The Fetching Mrs Castle' sat for an interview in 1916, the year that Vernon went off to war and she starred in a new movie, *Patria*, in which she played a dual role. 'I am perfectly mad about the work,' she gushed. 'I adore it, and I do not allow any one to double for me, all the diving, swimming, riding, etc., is done by me; all of the hair-breadth escapes

Irene and Vernon Castle, 1913.

are mine.' Irene 'fairly radiates charm', her interviewer wrote; 'she is elusive and fascinating; she is beautiful and she is chic, and every one knows if Mrs Castle should appear on Broadway wearing a barrel and suspenders that by the end of the week barrels would be the only fashionable raiment.'[52] Women who wanted to copy her did not have to resort to barrels: shoes, hats and other articles of clothing were marketed in her name.

As an adolescent, the petite, slim Irene had been beautiful, doted upon and a rebel. When she was fifteen, her parents sent her to National Park Seminary, a finishing school in Maryland, in order to separate her from a boy she loved. One day, before practising for the school's swimming team, she decided to cut her hair so it would dry quickly between classes. 'To my surprise,' she recalled,

> the rest of the girls began to follow suit. One by one, they snipped their locks and sent home snapshots of themselves grinning coyly beneath their new hairdos. The effect was thunderous. Parent showered the principal and the board members with irate letters. There was evidently going to be a great storm.

She escaped by hopping on a streetcar to Washington, DC, and then a train to New York where her Aunt Molly lived – 'She was an ardent feminist,' Irene noted, 'and the first woman surgeon to obtain a license to operate in the state of New York.'[53]

Irene's influence on her high-school classmates played out on a much larger scale in 1914, when, now a much-photographed celebrity, she made the impetuous decision once again to cut her hair into a short bob, adorned with a jewelled headband. 'Evidently women were just waiting for someone to do it first and give them enough nerve to face their outraged husbands.' The first week after her photograph appeared,

> there were two hundred and fifty Castle bobs; the next week twenty-five hundred. Stores began to feature the 'Castle Band to hold your hair in place.' Men's barbershops began to hang out signs reading 'Castle Clips here' and cartoonists pictured men dressing like women so they could stand a chance of getting a haircut in a barbershop filled with women.[54]

Her drapey, body-skimming dresses also started a trend. 'In those years before the First World War, there was no set style and no single fashion dictator to say what a woman should wear and what a woman should not wear,' she recalled.

> The clothes I wore were practical for me and that is the reason I wore them . . . I found that a frock with unclut-tered lines and flowing sleeves was more comfortable for everyday wear. And soon I was surprised to find myself with a following. I wore a Dutch bonnet in the early days of my dancing, which [a friend] brought me from Rotterdam, and other people began to wear Dutch bonnets.[55]

When she wore jodhpurs for riding, women followed that style, too, a far cry from the bloomers that an earlier generation of women boldly took up. 'If any one person is responsible for the appearance of the modern young lady of fashion whom we admire so much today,' the photographer Cecil Beaton observed,

Irene Castle, 1915.

it is certainly Mrs Vernon Castle, who was the first to cut her hair into the curly locks of a bob, who loosened hobble skirts with her voluminous chiffons and long flowing sleeves, and who, with her boyish figure, tight waist, sloping torso and arrow-like legs, discovered a new grace and fluid elegance so fresh and attractive that in comparison classic beauties were considered stolid and lifeless.

'And all this,' Irene responded, 'because I tried to be comfortable.'[56] Yet as much as she was admired, as much as she became a fashion icon, Irene still had to defend new ways of dancing from vociferous detractors.

Exhilaration

Planning for his inauguration in January 1913, Woodrow Wilson decided to ban the Inaugural Ball. First defending his decision as a cost-saving measure, he finally admitted that he was afraid 'there would be indulgence in the "turkey trot", the "bunny hug", and other ragtime dances, and thus provoke what might amount to a National Scandal'.[57] His condemnation set off 'a mighty fuss' that played out in the nation's newspapers. 'With only the waltz, the two-step, the minuet and the like . . . the dancers will go to sleep and fall on the floor, the wall flowers will wilt and the stags will stagnate,' complained the *Atlanta Constitution*. In the end, sister balls, allowing the turkey trot and all other ragtime dances, saved the dour inaugural season. And just weeks later, when President Taft left the White House for the last time, Mrs Taft danced the turkey trot with her husband looking on approvingly.[58]

'The rhythm of present day life is exhilarating,' one defender of the turkey trot wrote: 'the rhythm of the one-step is lively and inspiriting', and the only objection anyone could reasonably have against it is 'the close proximity of person which has occasioned the rather cheap witticism that the partner is "more danced against than dancing"'. New dances should not be prohibited, but instead taught correctly.[59] That was a mission the Castles were eager to undertake.

The new dances were condemned, Irene wrote, 'as not only unsightly, but downright immoral'. Even when she was in the hospital for an appendectomy, her doctors had opinions about dancing. 'Half of them tried to prove that dancing had damaged my appendix and caused the attack. The rest of them stoutly defended both my appendix and my dancing. Dancing was good clean exercise, they said, and definitely therapeutic.'[60] That defence was one of the Castles' selling points for lessons at Castle House and their book *Modern Dancing* (1914), which laid out the rationale and principles of their style. 'Our aim', Irene wrote, 'is to uplift dancing, purify it' and show 'that dancing is not only a rejuvenator of good health and spirits, but a means of preserving youth, prolonging life, and acquiring grace, elegance, and beauty'.[61] Irene's insistence that dancing promoted health was calculated to contradict medical objections to animal dances and the tango, which included physical exhaustion; the newly identified 'turkey leg', an inflammation of thigh muscles; insomnia from too much stimulation; and 'dancer's heart', which especially afflicted older men who danced with young women.[62] Elisabeth Marbury elaborated on Irene's claims: when the Castles taught the one-step, she wrote, they eliminated 'all hoppings, all contortions of the body, all flouncing of the elbows, all twisting of the arms, and, above everything else, all fantastic dips'. Their one-step was elegant and refined, and so was their tango, in which there was 'no strenuous clasping of partners, no hideous gyrations of the limbs, no abnormal twistings, no vicious angles' and no 'salacious suggestions'.[63] Although critics like Gilbert Seldes remarked on the Castles' lack of sensuality, Irene demurred: he left out, she said, 'the great sense of bubbling joy we shared together when we danced'.[64] Joy pervaded dance halls, and bubbled into the experiences of dancing girls.

6 A Culture of Their Own

‘Oh, it's good to be out in the world!’
Juliet Wilbor Tompkins, ‘Shelter’ (1916)

In the 1910s the troubling adolescent became the charming, unsettling, modern girl, as this bit of doggerel published in the *Washington Post*, titled ‘The Modern Girl’, reveals:

We knock and criticise her,
We scold, apostrophize her,
We wish that she were wiser,
More capable and kind.
Her path we're always stalking
To criticise her talking,
Her clothes, her ways of walking,
Her manners and her mind.
We say, ‘Oh, highty-tighty!’
She's frivolous and flighty,
And all her ways are mighty!
Undignified to see;

She dances and she chatters,
Our golden rule she shatters,
And laughs at serious matters
With unabated glee!
We chide and we correct her,
We shadow and detect her,
We study and dissect her,
With all her smiles and tears,
And find, on looking o'er her
(And learning to adore her),
She's just like girls before her,
For twenty thousand years![1]

But she was not behaving like girls before her: everyone knew that. She was changing, quite boldly, and she was impatient with detection and dissection.

Beatrice Van Norden, the sophisticated ingénue in Ruth Mitchell's comedy *A Modern Girl*, which opened on Broadway in 1913, was stubborn, impetuous and, one critic noted, 'no respecter of traditions'.[2] 'The modern girl smokes cigarettes,' observed another reviewer: 'She tangoes in and out of season. She wears superslit skirts. She reads Bernard Shaw. And, when she happens to feel like it, she makes an unchaperoned evening call at the apartment of a good-looking bachelor' – a bold transgression that propels the plot. To many of the play's viewers she seemed a fair rendering of 'a certain type of New York flapper, with her half-portion clothes and ideas to match'. Defiant, intent on having fun, this flapper – onstage, in movies, plays and novels in the years before the war – was 'the girl who almost did'.[3]

The long-legged pre-pubescent flapper of the turn of the century had evolved: one model was the independent, outdoorsy girl

– the grown-up tomboy – who golfed, rowed, hiked, cycled, went on sporting holidays and exuded a modest competence in everything she did. A *San Francisco Chronicle* article of 1913 praised her spunkiness: 'She is generally young, athletic, alert, and business-like,' brightly optimistic and friendly.[4] But another model, more controversial to be sure, was the girl who flouts convention: she is sexy, flirtatious, 'very pretty, very charming, very foolhardy', said Mitchell's collaborator Marion Fairfax, and a much more appealing ideal of girlhood than the 'tightly closed rosebud, the blank white page, the colorless, ingenuous, demure maiden' who needs to be watched over and protected. But as much as Fairfax admired her, she worried over her. The modern girl, she added, 'is walking along the edge of a precipice, and it's only luck that keeps her from tumbling over oftener than she does'. In order to take care of herself, the modern girl needed to have 'complete knowledge. She must know the possible results of late hours, cocktails, cigarettes, and unconventional calls on gentlemen.' 'A romantic half knowledge', Fairfax cautioned, is 'as bad as ignorance'.[5] Many girls growing up in the 1910s knew little about the consequences of sex and desire, and certainly some girls, if not completely ignorant, were not as worldly as Fairfax wished.

The screenwriter, novelist and memoirist Anita Loos was a modern girl who helped to shape the flapper's image in the 1910s with her movie scripts and in the 1920s with her saucy gold-digger Lorelei Lee, whose adventures Loos chronicled in her novel *Gentlemen Prefer Blondes*. Loos, whose adolescence began with the new century, gleaned romantic half-knowledge not from movies or racy books, but from the wife of a sea captain. As they sat overlooking the bay in San Francisco, the captain's wife, Loos remembered, whose 'great interest in life was sex', shared 'intimacies that my poor mother was too embarrassed ever to mention; but her slant on the subject was so extremely poetic that she never quite got down to cases'. The woman's revelations, though, left Loos

> with visions of mysterious bliss which might also be dangerous; for she warned me that a girl could love not wisely but too well, in which case a child might be born disgracefully out of wedlock. Her stories made such a powerful impression on me that from time to time feelings of excitement and anticipation mingled with downright fear used to come over me in waves.[6]

With her mother too embarrassed to answer her daughter's questions, Loos was left to work out for herself how far to yield to the many temptations in her path.

At the same time as *A Modern Girl* toured city theatres, another play, the British dramatist Cosmo Hamilton's *The Blindness of Virtue*, also took up the theme of the modern girl, underscoring her potential vulnerability. When a local girl returns home ruined, the town's vicar worries about his own seventeen-year-old daughter, Effie. 'Are you going to tell Effie things she should know,' he asks his wife, 'or are you going to let the child be lost in her ignorance?'[7] His wife reluctantly agrees to have the difficult talk, but before she musters the courage to do so, Effie innocently visits the family's young boarder's room one night, dressed in her nightgown, and is discovered by her father – precipitating a violent scene of accusation and remorse. Although the play ends happily, with the marriage of Effie and the startled young man, Effie's ignorance might well have resulted in dreadful consequences. The play's message, received as timely and urgent by some viewers, met with a sigh from others. 'I feel as though I'd been to Sunday-school and teacher had just let us out,' a female audience member remarked after the play ended.[8]

Effie's complete ignorance about what might happen between a young man and a young woman in a bedroom at night seemed, to that viewer at least, anachronistic, harking back to the advice disseminated in nineteenth-century advice manuals such as *Tokology* or *The Science of a New Life*. Sources of 'romantic half knowledge' were so abundant that the essayist Agnes Repplier, a long-time contributor to the *Atlantic Monthly*, protested that young women were given far too much graphic information about sex. Explicit descriptions of brothels, novels about degeneracy and nymphomania, and articles about venereal diseases were rampant, and schools taught sex education – hygiene, they called it – in gender-segregated classes. All these, Repplier said, 'are offered for the defense of youth and the purifying of civilized society'. But she believed the opposite was happening, and rued society's 'lamentable lack of reserve'.[9]

Repplier's observations were borne out by a survey conducted among two hundred English girls aged fifteen to eighteen, inquiring about their reading habits. These girls, it turned out, were steeped in popular fiction. Because girls went freely to public libraries, parents had lost influence over their daughters' choice of reading material. Dickens, Scott and Mrs Gaskell were, these girls said, boring. Much more exciting were contemporary romances and adventure stories, such as Anthony Hope's *The Prisoner of Zenda*, and pot-boilers – mysteries, love stories, suspense thrillers – that they bought with their spending money. Besides novels, most girls read several magazines each month, such as *The Strand*, which featured Arthur Conan Doyle's Sherlock Holmes stories and fiction by Grant Allen and H. G. Wells.[10] A reader in 1914 could find, besides short stories, articles that included 'Heroines of the Film' (a regular feature), 'Tips for the Tango' imparted by the dancer Phyllis Dare and a colloquium gathered by the eugenicist Dr C. W. Saleeby on 'Do Love Marriages Turn Out Best?'

'The age she lives in is one of knowledge,' the journalist H. L. Mencken wrote in a light-hearted portrait of 'The Flapper' of 1915, which appeared in *The Smart Set*, one of the modern girl's favourite magazines. 'She herself is educated. She is privy to dark secrets. The world bears to her no aspect of mystery.' She was at home 'in matinée lobbies and railroad stations', where she was alert to such dangers as white slave traders or gigolos, but she was not about to be victimized by them, or by anyone. She was titillated by the idea of love, but refused to cede power to men. 'She is opposed to the double standard of morality,' Mencken reported, 'and favors a law prohibiting it.' The flapper, Mencken observed with delight, 'has forgotten how to simper; she seldom blushes; it is impossible to shock her'. Mencken found her adorable, 'charming', with 'something trim and trig and confident about her. She is easy in her manners. She bears herself with dignity in all societies. She is graceful, rosy, healthy, appetizing . . . There is music in her laugh. She is youth, she is hope, she is romance – she is wisdom!'[11] Of course, she was youth: she was an adolescent.

Mencken's piece reflected widespread use of the word 'flapper' to apply to modern girls, a word that had become much transformed from its origins in nineteenth-century Britain, when it was tainted with illicit sexuality. The American flapper, according to Mencken, was part of a species: in France she was called *l'Ingénue*, in England simply the flapper, and in German *der Backfisch*. Her behaviour was the same worldwide. In London, reported *The Times*, no modern girl would think to go to a dance without a man, 'often with more than one man' so she never would lack a partner. 'The youth of the day', the report continued, 'live in an atmosphere of independence.'[12] In Germany, handsome 33-year-old Crown Prince Friedrich Wilhelm was besieged by *Backfisch* who wanted to dance with him, play sports with him and get him to sign their birthday books. 'And when Wilhelm sees flappers – especially if they are red-haired and thin – he gushes and wants to kiss their hands,' reported an American girl visiting Germany. According to the girl's article in the *Boston Daily Globe*, he played tennis with flapper Friedchen, aged sixteen, and rowed with flapper Grete, aged fifteen. His wife looked on with apparent equanimity; the prince, buoyed by his fans, exuded an attitude of 'effervescent youth'.[13]

Sex o'clock

In 1913 'Sex O'Clock in America', an article in the magazine *Current Opinion*, gave voice to anxieties – such as Repplier's – about the sexualized culture in which Mencken's appetizing flapper was growing up. The article quoted St Louis newspaper editor William Marion Reedy, who coined the racy phrase 'sex o'clock', noting with disdain the prevalence of sexual topics in all media, plays and books, and in bawdy cabaret shows frequented by rich patrons looking for an erotic thrill. Although Reedy insisted that women do not have the same sexual desires as men, he reprised Hall's assessment of a decade earlier, cautioning that adolescent girls deceptively hide their erotic feelings.

> Society is apt to regard the fourteen-year-old adolescent
> as a little dreamy school-girl who ties pretty ribbons in
> her hair, and keeps her dresses well confined to knee

length, forgetting all the externals of the child mask the seething turbulent ocean beneath.

'In the child', Reedy asserted, 'dwells a fully awakened woman', who, in his view, was coming of age in a perverse American culture.[14]

Like Fairfax, Reedy argued that adolescent girls needed to be made aware of the perils of giving in to their seething turbulence. A play like *The Blindness of Virtue*, he may well have thought, presented a much-needed cautionary tale. Another flag of caution, which Reedy endorsed, was raised by the novel *Hagar Revelly* by Daniel Carson Goodman, a physician turned novelist and screenwriter. Hagar was a working girl seduced and betrayed by her employer, a recurring plot in fiction of the time. But in this case, Goodman's novel became a cause célèbre when its publisher, Michael Kennerly, was brought up on obscenity charges under strident oversight of a federal law that prohibited sending sexually explicit material through the u.s. mail. The purpose of the book, Kennerly said in his defence, 'was to portray the evil influences to which girl workers were subjected, the reward of virtue, and the penalty usually paid by those women who attempt to defy the laws of nature and of society'.[15] Debate played out in newspapers and the courts, Kennerly was acquitted and the novel gained more attention than Comstock ever intended.

Sex, after all, sold. And one of the most notorious novels of the time was Elinor Glyn's *Three Weeks*. British reviewers denounced it as lurid when it was published in 1907; Americans made it a bestseller. The plot centres on the seduction of a handsome 23-year-old man by a mysterious, cosmopolitan Russian woman. Their affair, which lasts three weeks, begins with an exotic flourish, on a couch covered by a tiger skin and piled with sensuous velvet pillows.

'A Live Wire', 1914, illustration from *Puck*.

Although the man is no innocent, his lover has much to teach him, including how to kiss. After the lovers part, the woman becomes pregnant and is killed by her powerful husband. But despite this retribution, the novel seemed to British readers, and some Americans, contemptible. 'England has condemned the book without reserve,' wrote the *Chicago Daily Tribune* reviewer Jeannette Gilder, 'and England is right. It has absolutely no purpose except to show how deep a hold a siren of 35 may get upon a boy of 23.'[16] More than that: the novel showed a woman's aggression, a man's submission and the thrill of an affair.

When Glyn visited the U.S. soon after the book was published, she was inundated with attention. One newspaper called her 'easily the most talked-about woman in America', a 'ravishing beauty' who discoursed on the 'ultra fine points' of a love affair. Red-haired, green-eyed and dressed sumptuously in costumes designed by her sister, Lady Duff Gordon, who went by the professional name of Lucile, Glyn cut a glamorous figure. Married and, rumour had it, experienced in infidelity, Glyn was outspoken not only about the ultra-fine points of love, but on American culture. In contrast with England, America seemed to her 'the perfect kingdom of woman, and with a few exceptions, men are dominated by women more completely there, I am convinced, than in any other country in the world'. In colleges, according to Glyn, female students directed courtship, and after they married, demanded 'more and yet more comforts, luxuries and gifts', pressuring their husbands to work harder and harder. Women took charge of social life for their families. In the home, Glyn said, 'Mother-love throttles the individuality of the little boys' and by example, the little girls grow up to be 'tyrannous' adolescents, demanding

Elinor Glyn, a British novelist who celebrated women's sexual freedom.

> cars, furs, dresses, European trips, marriage settlements, and, finally, in all probability, heavy legal expenses in connection with one or more divorces, and the renewed burden of rearing and educating granddaughters who will grow up to repeat the process *ad infinitum!*[17]

If Glyn looked at this situation with derision and, truth be told, a bit of envy, it did play out in theatres where plots often featured women triumphing over the foibles of men; and in movies, where, beginning in 1910, the female vampire incited a rage.

Theda Bara was the most famous of those, so identified with the role that she earned the epithet 'The Vamp', a persona that – unfortunately for her – defined her as an actress. In 1915 in *A Fool There Was* she played a seductress who ruins the life of a married lawyer when his obsession with her results in the loss of his money, position and family. In *The Devil's Daughter*, after a lover abandons her, she sets out for revenge against all men. Louise Glaum, another actress branded as a vamp, starred in *Honor Thy Name* (1916) as a cabaret dancer who snares a wealthy college man, enraging his father, who conspires to get rid of her. The vamp, like the more cheerful gold-digger of movie comedies, was a predatory female: she represented woman's unleashed sexuality and rage.

Working girls

If the aggressive, seductive vamp fulfilled some girls' fantasies, a much more popular plot of American dime novels and movies involved the spunky working girl navigating her future, which meant facing the challenges of finding and keeping a job, and – sooner rather than later – finding a husband. In 1910 the number of girls in the U.S.

Louise Glaum, *c.* 1915.

workforce increased by more than two million compared with the number employed in 1900; in the UK, women comprised about 30 per cent of the workforce, slowly moving from domestic service to the business world. Besides jobs that had always been associated with women's work – teaching, nursing and domestic employment – young women increasingly worked in sales and in offices as clerks, copyists, stenographers, typists, bookkeepers, accountants, and telegraph and telephone operators. In many of these jobs they were hired by, and supervised by, men, who evaluated them on the basis of their skills and, most assuredly, looks, complicating girls' work experiences.

In 1916 Norma Talmadge starred in *The Social Secretary*, with a script by Anita Loos, playing a working girl who tries to get and keep a secretarial job. But she finds she is too pretty: her male bosses repeatedly proposition her, and female employers think she will steal their boyfriends or husbands. Finally, desperate, she disguises herself in glasses, a severe hairdo and plain clothing to land a job. The complications that follow end with marriage, of course. In movies, and in many romance novels, working girls envisioned their future as living happily ever after as a wife.

Loos herself was a working girl. Although under five feet tall, weighing 92 lb and with hair bobbed like Irene Castle's, looking and dressing like an adolescent – in demure sailor suits or outfits she bought in the children's department – she aspired to become a screenwriter. By the time she was 23 she had earned praise for her creative intertitles for silent films and she had submitted 105 scripts, many to the already famous director D. W. Griffith. Her romantic tales and snappy comedies made top stars of such actors as Norma Talmadge and Douglas Fairbanks.

She was determined to succeed in a field dominated by men, but at the same time Loos hoped that she would marry. Like many of her contemporaries, she found that because of her work some dates saw her as 'some sort of monster; I no longer seemed to be a girl.' So she decided to keep her working life secret, separate from her social life. For Loos, the 'sex revolution' had less to do with visiting a gentleman's rooms unchaperoned or wearing slit skirts than with 'the transfer of female emotions from the boudoir to the marts of trade', and a woman's consequent feeling that something was the matter with her if she felt more joy from work than from marriage. For some working girls, those marts of trade, rather than a man's attentions, were a source of self-esteem, 'so valuable and sweet that they even seem romantic'.[18]

As counterweight to the marriage plot, readers found stories – such as Juliet Wilbor Tompkins's 'Shelter', published in the magazine *Good Housekeeping* – that validated the idea that women could feel as satisfied by work as by marriage. In this story, Dorothy Eades, who grew up feeling cloistered, infantilized and bored in a world of 'pink teas, yellow teas, engagement teas', gets a job after her family is ruined when a fire destroys the town of Chiltern. When she sells her own car to finance her family's move to a nearby city, she thinks she has found her niche in car sales. Her suitor, George, is aghast that she feels she needs to work, but she retorts vehemently that she wants to escape from the 'dull hole' in which she felt she was 'a prisoner, condemned to hard idleness for life'. 'This may not be the ideal job,' she tells George, 'but it feels good!'[19] George says he wants to take care of her, but that is precisely what she does not want. 'I've been taken care of and taken care of till I'm half smothered!' she cries. 'I've just got out of my box, and you'd put me back in it, and feed me through a hole, and let a few chosen people come near enough to speak. No, George! No! I want to take care of myself!'[20] Taking care of herself meant more than financial independence: it meant freedom to choose what she did with her life, to find new interests and to make her own decisions. 'Oh,' she exclaims, 'it's good to be out in the world!'[21]

Dorothy's exuberant celebration of the working life seemed far-fetched to many girls who devoured the fiction of Laura Jean Libbey, one of the most prolific authors of dime novels. Libbey fed her readers' desires for liberation from work through marriage by offering romances that featured working-girl heroines who faced obstacles – orphanhood, being fired, pursuit by villainous, predatory men – that they overcame by a combination of virtue and luck. They were rewarded by love. A few sample titles reflect the formulaic plots that drove more than sixty books: *Leonie Locke; or, The Romance of a Beautiful New York Working-girl*, was one; *Pretty Madcap Dorothy; or, How She Won a Lover*, was another.

In 1910, 38-year-old Libbey, having become a household name with her romances, decided to make an entry into vaudeville, with a ten-minute 'Love Monologue' that she delivered bedecked alluringly in a chiffon gown. She also began contributing an advice column to the *Chicago Daily Tribune*, counselling her readers to guard their innocence as a rose protects itself with thorns. Her popularity soared in the next few years, leading to a daily column, 'Laura Jean Libbey Talks Heart Topics', in the *Los Angeles Times*. Day after day, the creator of romantic plots criticized the 'silly age in girlhood' – from fourteen to twenty – that comprised her eager readers. A girl of that age, Libbey wrote, 'thinks that all she has to do is frame up an ideal lover, hang his picture in her mind, carrying the duplicate of it in her heart, and watch out for the first fellow to come along who bears any kind of a resemblance to it'.[22] This romantic fantasy – fed by her own novels – might well lead a girl to inappropriate behaviour, which Libbey repeatedly advised against in all of her columns. Her warnings and bromides ('Everyone knows that the diet of honey soon cloys,' she wrote, insisting that girls save their kisses for marriage[23]) served as a barometer of the same anxieties about girls' sexuality that Reedy voiced. Flirting, kissing, meeting secretly, picking up men in dance halls, embracing in dark movie theatres: all these behaviours would send a girl on a downward spiral. 'No matter how much a man may admire a girl or how near he is to proposing marriage to her,' Libbey warned, 'if she accords him the kiss to which he may plead for – from that moment he ceases to think of her as the girl whom he would have for his wife!'[24] Some young women, Libbey lamented, 'regard all too lightly the conventionalities and by doing so invite much of the sorrow which comes to them. Nature intended all that was sweet and tender to be well guarded.'[25] The men a girl met in public venues were always suspect: they might be married, with a wife and children away; or they might be the kind of man who expects sexual favours in exchange for a movie ticket. 'Not in one case out of a thousand', she insisted, 'does a man ever marry a young woman whose acquaintance he has made without an introduction.'[26]

Besides her column, Libbey answered readers' questions: from girls of seventeen, for example, already married and too often giving in to their husband; girls engaged to men they did not trust; young working women wondering how friendly they should behave towards male colleagues; engaged girls whose parents disapproved of their fiancés; and girls, over and over, wondering how far to give in to the desires of the boys whom said they loved them. Hold back, Libbey said. Be sensible.

The sensible girl

The sensible girl kept her virginity until marriage. She did not quarrel with her parents; she stayed out of mischief; she accepted the idea that she was going to be a wife and mother, and she wanted to make herself as capable of fulfilling those roles as she could be. 'It is at last fashionable for women to be healthy, even athletic, also to be sensible,' announced *Good Housekeeping* in 1905. 'Neither man nor society is now attracted to the anemic, incompetent or silly.' The sensible girl's education might include Greek, but also 'a broader knowledge of the concrete – of the arts, sciences and social relations that make up human usefulness and happiness'.[27] The sensible girl was not necessarily plain, although the media made plain girls seem a surer bet as a wife and mother than their lovelier, often flightier, sisters.

In the u.s., as Elinor Glyn had observed, the sensible girl was overshadowed by the 'American Princess' – 'selfish, pert, self-centered' – whose brashness embarrassed her elders. In 1910 the *Ladies Home Journal* published an unsigned, detailed 'Open Letter to the American Girl Who Was Born Between January 1, 1892 and January 1, 1899'. The author, a woman, observed that this type of adolescent talked too loudly and too much, revealing ignorance cloaked in arrogance. At home, the author asserted, she was 'self-willed and heedless of others' comfort and pleasure', condescending to her parents, and focused only on her social life. The author blamed the development of this princess on several factors, such as overly indulgent mothers, who recalled their own 'self-denial and unsatisfied longing' when they were girls. 'She was forbidden pleasures which seemed to her perfectly innocent' and which she did not want to deny her daughter. Also to blame were bad models of behaviour by adult women who wanted to recapture the impetuous quality of youth. The letter urged girls to stop being self-indulgent and irresponsible: 'If only you could be stirred and thrilled by a knowledge of your power, you young girls who hold the future in the hollow of your hands!'[28]

In an effort to highlight just how sensible girls could be, the Mothers' Congress of Denver invited the city's high schools to send representatives to one of their meetings so that mothers could hear the girls' opinions at first hand. The girls were delighted to participate: they were eager to talk 'courageously and unhesitatingly' about 'the important three "D's" – dress, dancing and deportment', and to tell the mothers what was needed 'most urgently' for girls' welfare and happiness. What the girls wanted, the mothers learned to their surprise, was

> Better mothers.
> A dean of women for girls to consult.
> Dancing instructors in the high schools.
> More boys who knew the new dance steps.

A dean of women, the girls explained, would be someone who could counsel girls whose mothers were indifferent or 'not sensible'. The girls did not elaborate about what being 'not sensible' meant to them, but the term implies mothers who were too strict, old-fashioned or narrow-minded. The girls' suggestions seemed to the attending mothers to be quite reasonable – even their desire for a dancing instructor. 'It gets tiresome for us girls to dance alone,' the girls complained, 'and the boys seem to find the new steps intricate work, and for that reason stay away from dances. A dancing instructor could do a lot to promote a friendly feeling.'[29]

As Stanley Hall had observed, girls matured earlier than boys, who simply were not as interested in high-school dances as their female classmates. At public dance halls, girls found older partners, which was one reason their parents wanted to keep them away. In movies, the working girl was likely to marry her boss rather than a clerk her own age. One self-described flapper, aged eighteen, complained in a newspaper essay that boys were callow, awkward and sloppy; she wanted to be treated like an intelligent person, and a worldly, stylish older man seemed genuinely interested in what she was thinking.[30]

Girls' fantasies about marrying a sophisticated older man were fed by one of the most popular novels of the time, Jean Webster's *Daddy-Long-Legs*, which was published in 1912. Webster transformed it into a play in 1914, and Mary Pickford picked up the movie option, in which she starred in 1919. The plot involves Judy, a girl raised in a Dickensian orphanage who comes to the attention of a rich benefactor. He offers to pay her university tuition, provided that she writes to him each month and never seeks to know his identity. She thrives at a fictionalized Vassar College, where Webster was educated, and one day, seeing an elongated shadow of the man she thinks supports her, nicknames him Daddy-Long-Legs. Later, she meets a bachelor with whom she falls in love, who turns out to be that man. They, of course, marry.

The novel did more than fuel girls' romantic dreams: it inspired them to band together to help 'the loveless orphan asylum child, and raise funds for the rescuing of as many little Judies as possible'. Daddy-Long-Legs Leagues began at Webster's alma mater, where she had been a member of the College Settlement Association as an undergraduate, and the clubs spread wildly in high schools and colleges. In addition to raising money, members tried to foster adoptions. 'Bachelors seem to like little girls,' Webster observed, 'and old maids want boys.'[31]

Webster's membership in a university social service association reflected the club culture that helped to create a sense of community among girls and women. The American reformer and suffragist Rheta Childe Dorr extolled the influence of women's clubs in generating collective opinion and moving social reform. 'The immediate need of women's souls at the beginning of the club movement,' she wrote, 'was for education . . . and they formed their clubs with the sole object of self-culture,' but soon the members focused on service to the community.[32] Clubs were devoted to eradicating poverty, assimilating immigrants, educating workers, raising money for holidays for working girls, providing free medical care, chaperoning at dance halls and discussing salient social and political issues. Club members, Dorr said, 'look on life with the eyes of reasoning adults, where once they regarded it as trusting children. Women now form a new social group, separate, and to a degree homogeneous. Already they have evolved a group opinion and a group ideal.'[33] These women's groups found their counterpart in girls' clubs, such as Britain's Girl Guides and America's Girl Scouts. Girls formed clubs on their own, as well: book clubs, fan clubs, sports clubs, and tramping and camping clubs.

The club movement gave women and girls a sense of solidarity and, not least, of mass. Nowhere did that group ideal manifest itself as vibrantly as it did in the campaigns for votes.

7 Votes for Flappers

'Alone she kicks and bites her way
Through crowds of constables at bay;
Oh listen! All the world it seems
Re-echoes with the maiden's screams!'
'The Solitary Flapper', *The Observer*, 1909

In Britain and the U.S., the suffrage movement inflamed the spirits of girls and women, generating for many a sense of solidarity about shared values, potential and strength. But the movement also generated confusion and fear. Controversy over whether women should attain the vote became entangled in the ongoing debate about girls' education, capabilities and destiny. For high school and university girls who read about suffrage in thousands of newspaper and magazine articles, listened to speakers who visited their schools and communities, marched in parades and joined suffrage clubs, the prospect of political power was alluring. A woman with a vote was a woman with agency, a concept that anti-suffragists – men and women – found threatening. Suffrage campaigns in the UK and U.S. complicated girls' ideas about the risks and perils of women's power. A recurring theme in novels, stories, plays and even movies, suffrage was so much in the air that no girl growing up in the UK or the U.S. could avoid thinking about how it would, or should, affect her life.

'The Solitary Flapper', a poem published in the British *Observer* in 1909, caricatured the suffragette as a strident, militant, aggressive spinster, angrily wreaking havoc.

> Behold her, single in the street,
> > You solitary suffrage-lass
> Where 'coppers' with enormous feet
> > Decline to let her pass.
> Alone she kicks and bites her way
> Through crowds of constables at bay;
> Oh listen! All the world it seems
> Re-echoes with the maiden's screams!
>
> No peacock on a garden lawn,
> > No infant pig attacked by bees,
> No rooster at the break of dawn,
> > Can make such sounds as these;
> No jays can emulate the note
> That issues from her raucous throat;
> Such cries inebriates cannot raise,
> Immured in distant Holloways.
>
> Will no one tell me why she flings
> > (Like hooligans who used to throw
> Bad eggs, unhealthy cast-off things
> > And bottles long ago)

Fear of women's suffrage is evident in this cartoon from 1869.

Macadam gathered from the streets
At ev'ry Minister she meets?
Oh, is it just to cause him pain,
Or does she hope the vote to gain?

Whate'er her scheme, the spinster cried,
    As though her cries could have no ending;
I stood and watched her open-eyed,
    Her leather lungs distending.
I listened till I had my fill,
And, as she went on screaming still,
I termed her, in my heart, a bore,
And then – I thought of her no more.[1]

John Held's satirical cartoon 'The Only Way'
skewers women seeking the vote, 1912.

Calling her a flapper evoked, and intensified, all the negative associations of that term. This flapper was not a temptress, nor a flirtatious adolescent, but an unattractive, even repellent 'maiden'. As for being solitary, though, the poem was wrong: suffrage activists attested to feeling strong bonds with one another. Even when groups splintered because of opposing strategies, even when power struggles erupted, suffragists felt united by their commitment to a compelling cause.

The British suffrage campaign, which first emerged in the mid-nineteenth century, set an example for American efforts that gained momentum later. The Sheffield Female Political Association, organized in 1851, was followed in the next forty years by many other groups throughout Great Britain: organizations that saw bill after bill for women's suffrage introduced to lawmakers read and rejected

Emmeline Pankhurst, 1912.

over and over. The movement was re-energized in 1897, with the founding of the National Union of Women's Suffrage Societies (NUWSS). Its members, known as suffragists, hoped to win the vote through constitutional and, they insisted, ladylike behaviour: mainly by circulating petitions and holding informational meetings. In 1903 the charismatic, bold and indefatigable Emmeline Pankhurst, the 45-year-old widow of an activist lawyer, formed the Women's Social and Political Union (WSPU) intent on enacting a noisier and more visible strategy than its sister organization: boisterous public gatherings, marches, parades and a cadre of members who handed out its weekly 'Votes for Women', raising money and, they hoped, changing minds. Pankhurst's activists were dubbed, derisively, suffragettes – a term coined by a British newspaper in 1906 as a feminized, and therefore condescending, name for the outspoken WSPU members.

Although some members of Parliament assured suffragettes that their pleas would get a fair hearing, Pankhurst was convinced that all the government's proposals were, she said, 'intended for the future, a future so remote as to be imperceptible. We were beginning to understand this even in 1891.'[2] She became disillusioned with men who said they supported woman's suffrage, only to withdraw their support when it served their political careers, and her patience wore thin. The WSPU vowed to oppose any party in power because none of them – Liberal, Conservative or Labour – moved the suffrage cause forward.

The WSPU flared into public attention in the autumn of 1905, on the eve of Britain's General Election, when, during a Liberal meeting in Manchester, two WSPU members interrupted Sir Edward Grey as he was explaining his party's future plans. One of the disrupters was Emmeline's daughter Christabel, who, like her sister

Sylvia, had participated in the suffrage movement even as a girl. The other was Annie Kenney, who had been a mill worker since adolescence; she already had developed strong socialist leanings when she first heard Christabel speak at a suffrage gathering. The two women were the first of the suffragists to be arrested; given the choice of paying a fine or going to prison, they chose prison. The event proved decisive. At that moment, Emmeline recalled, the women's suffrage movement was languishing, with a paltry showing at meetings and general despondency. Her daughter and Annie Kenney changed that 'in a twinkling of an eye'. 'The two women,' Emmeline reported,

> put the fateful question, 'When are you going to give votes to women?' and refused to sit down until they had been answered. These two women were sent to gaol, and from that day to this the women's movement, both militant and constitutional, has never looked back.[3]

In 1906 three to four hundred women drawn from across London, from the poor East End to posh Mayfair, marched in the first suffrage parade, arriving at Parliament for its opening day. Deemed agitators, and derisively dubbed 'suffragettes', they dressed in white, with green sashes and violets pinned to their waists: the colours stood for purity, faith and courage. By the time they gathered for the parade, they knew that courage was the trait they needed most: they meant to interrupt and disrupt, and they were well aware of the consequences. Deemed agitators, suffragettes were dragged away by police and arrested. Between 1906 and 1914, when activists desisted their efforts because of the war, more than one thousand women were imprisoned, some held in solitary confinement, and many who went on hunger strikes were violently force fed.

The politician who incited their anger most was Herbert Asquith, who became Liberal Prime Minister in 1908 and who was unwavering, immovably opposed to giving women the vote. He claimed that the suffrage movement simply did not have enough support among the British population; Pankhurst intended to prove him wrong. On 21 June of that year, the WSPU convened an assembly in Hyde Park, but Pankhurst had no idea, when she sent out word, just how large it would be. She was astonished by the outcome: 'When I mounted my platform,' she recalled, '. . . and surveyed the mighty throngs that waited there and the endless crowds that were still pouring into the park from all directions, I was filled with amazement not unmixed with awe.' Women in white gowns and flower-trimmed hats 'gave the park the appearance of a vast garden in full bloom'. The next day, the London *Times* wrote that the estimate of 250,000 probably was doubled, if not trebled: 'Like the distances and the number of the stars, the facts were beyond the threshold of perception.'[4]

By 1911 Emmeline's daughter Christabel had taken a significant leadership position. Like Annie Kenney, many young suffrage workers testify to becoming awakened, and converted, by Christabel's oratory and example. 'It occurred to me', Emmeline said, 'that if the older suffrage workers could in some way join hands with the young, unwearied and resourceful suffragists, the movement might wake up to new life and new possibilities.'[5] Christabel and her mother infused the movement with what Emmeline Pethick-Lawrence, another prominent suffrage leader, saw as a fervour that went beyond politics. For the Pankhursts, she said, 'the cause of woman suffrage was a religion that demanded from them everything that they had to give.' Christabel, especially, seemed inspired 'not by pity but by a deep, secret shame – shame that any woman should tamely accept the position accorded to her as something less than an adult human being – a position half way between the child and the citizen'.[6]

By 1913 the suffragettes decided to wage guerrilla war, adopting militant tactics, including stone throwing, breaking windows (even those of royal residences), setting postboxes on fire and destroying property. They cut telephone wires, scorched golf courses with acids and smashed the glass of the orchid houses at Kew Gardens. The orchids died from the cold. They broke a showcase in the Jewel Room at the Tower of London and burned down a refreshment house in Regents Park.[7] They wrapped stones in brown paper, making it obvious that they had planned their attacks, not acted impetuously.

The media portrayed them as furies. 'Newspapers which had heretofore ignored the whole subject', Pankhurst said, 'now hinted that while they had formerly been in favour of women's suffrage, they could no longer countenance it.'[8] Men called them 'old cats mewing together because they can't get married'.[9] Some women withdrew support, as well, because they objected to breaking the law. The figure of the suffragette was vilified in essays, editorials and cartoons, condemned as 'an Outragette, a window-smasher, rioter, wrecker and incendiary', but Pankhurst blamed the government for turning law-abiding women into defiant rebels.[10] Condemnation, she said, only made them stronger. As one character put it in suffragist Elizabeth Robins's play *Votes for Women!*, ridicule may defeat a man, but it 'steels a woman. We've educated ourselves so that we welcome ridicule. We owe our sincerest thanks to the comic writers. The cartoonist is our unconscious friend. Who cartoons people who are of no importance?'[11]

'His Daughter!', satirical cartoon, 1915.

American readers attentively followed reports of British suffrage activists. During a visit to New York in 1913, speaking to large audiences, Pankhurst defended suffragettes' militancy. Men, she said, 'know perfectly well that there never was a thing worth having that was not worth fighting for'. Surely men would not sit quietly by if they had no constitutional rights, if they had to look pleasant and always obey, if they saw that their fate, and the fate of their children, was decided by women who claimed they knew 'what was good for you better than you knew yourselves'.[12] British suffragettes were outraged that their lives were governed by men; that they were denied the vote along with lunatics and criminals; that even if they met the same qualifications as male voters, they were discriminated against because of their sex. 'Our demand is a perfectly reasonable, constitutional and logical one,' Pankhurst asserted in a WSPU leaflet. 'It is simply that Taxation and Representation shall go together – that women who pay the taxes shall be represented in the legislation.'[13] But decades went by, and still their demand was not met.

Men opposed to giving women the vote, she concluded incredulously, must believe that women were a different species than they were:

> to men, women are not human beings like themselves.
> Some men think we are superhuman; they put us on
> pedestals; they revere us; they think we are too fine and
> too delicate to come down into the hurly-burly of life.
> Other men think us sub-human; they think we are
> a strange species unfortunately having to exist for
> the perpetuation of the race. They think we are fit
> for drudgery, but that in some strange way our minds

are not like theirs, our love for great things not like theirs,
and so we are a sort of sub-human species.[14]

Besides the time-worn arguments that women belong in the home, that having the vote would distract them from their family's needs and that they had no experience in making political decisions, there loomed over the government's deliberations the fact that women in the UK outnumbered men, by the astounding majority of one million.[15] Male legislators feared that they would vote in unison for such measures as temperance and the outlawing of prostitution. Christabel Pankhurst tried to set them straight. 'As a matter of fact,' she said, 'the only question likely to unite all women against all men is the present refusal of men to grant women the vote.'[16] This fear surfaced in the U.S., as well, where women also were in the majority. As one American anti-suffragist announced with alarm, 'When the majority of women and the minority of men vote together, there will be no such thing as personal liberty left in the United States.'[17]

Suffragette Sally and her friends

Among the many novels and stories published during the rise of suffrage campaigns, Gertrude Colmore's *Suffragette Sally*, published in 1911, offers a realistic portrayal of the British experience. The novel follows the growing militancy of three British women from different educational, economic and social backgrounds who join the cause: a young working girl, a middle-class woman and an aristocrat.

Sally Simmonds, employed as a general maid by the Bilkes family, is roused when she hears a talk by the elegant and eloquent Geraldine Hill. Treated condescendingly by Mr Bilkes, a blustering, leering businessman, Sally feels demeaned by her work, and she sees that the suffrage campaign offers her something she cannot find elsewhere: respect, understanding and a sense of community. Sally boldly decides to leave her job to devote herself to the movement, and she ends her relationship with her boyfriend, as well, because he cannot support her efforts, telling him to marry a more 'womanly woman'. For Sally, suffrage means far more than gaining a political voice: it means liberation from the oppression of domestic service and a revised image of her identity and her future.

Edith Carstairs represents the cautious, but open-minded, contingent of middle-class women whose sympathy for the movement was constrained by a fear that somehow voting would undermine one's femininity. But listening to an anti-suffrage speaker makes her rethink her position. When the speaker argues that 'the ryot in India and the negro in the Sudan' would 'be at the mercy of unsexed women' who intruded into politics, Edith wonders

> if the danger of introducing morality into politics
> was not exaggerated; for, if women, on entering a polling
> booth, became unsexed, out of that polling booth surely
> the dreaded attributes of the woman could not come
> forth to affect the negro in the Sudan and the ryot
> in India.[18]

Men exalted their mothers for their high and sacred moral standards, Edith reflects, but she begins to question if 'the really noble way of rewarding those mothers is to give them no say in the laws which affect their children'.[19] Wives and daughters were to keep out of politics, except when men needed them to campaign to get them elected to office. Despite the opposition of her brother and a suitor, Edith makes her own daring and independent decision to join the suffragettes.

Edith's trajectory echoed that of many middle-class suffrage workers who came to the movement with trepidation and concern. Evelyn Sharp, for example, left her home in Buckinghamshire in 1894, at the age of 25, to go to London in the hope of earning a living. The journey, she said, was the most adventurous of her life, not because it was so long – only about 72 kilometres (45 miles) – but because it marked a declaration of independence. Her family did not stand in her way, although, she said, 'they naturally disapproved', not being among those who held 'advanced ideas about the education and economic independence of women'. It was unusual for a middle-class girl such as she 'to have any other ambition in life than to sit at home and wait for a problematic husband'.[20] Like Henry James's Isabel Archer, the protagonist of *The Portrait of a Lady*, Sharp was destined to assume 'attitudes more or less gracefully passive', in anticipation of a man to fulfil her with a destiny.[21] Only with the encouragement of a teacher did she embark on this move, 'rather like running away', which her mother saw as 'nothing but original sin'.[22] But Sharp felt an indefinable force driving her from her home, and from a future that seemed bleak.

She first took a teaching job in London, and through her writing became involved with the 'Yellow Book' group of writers and artists – society that made her feel 'it was very heaven to be young' and 'on the crest of the wave that was sweeping away the Victorian tradition'.[23] It was an exciting time for Sharp, who discovered a world far different from her family's country life and from the conventions and moral strictures that she had been taught as a girl. She became a successful journalist and, like many educated women at the time, joined in reform efforts, working in girls' clubs, the

Anti-Sweating League to protest working conditions in sweatshops, and the Women's Industrial Council. Recognizing 'the political futility of the voteless reformer', she became a suffragist, a decision, she said, that changed her life.[24]

Women, she realized, were demanding more than the franchise: they saw the achievement of the vote as a step towards social and economic freedom. 'For the sake of a quiet life,' Sharp said,

> the majority of women had left their men-folk in ignorance
> of the extent to which they chafed under their disabilities;
> and I think some women welcomed the militant move-
> ment because it enabled them to express their discontent
> publicly without appearing to reproach any individual
> man in the home.[25]

Repeatedly imprisoned, pelted with mice and chestnuts when she took the platform to speak, Sharp remained committed to a cause that many of her contemporaries, on both sides of the Atlantic, saw as threatening the natural order of life.

Fictionalizing her experiences, Sharp wrote a story in which the narrator, collecting money for suffrage, has a typical encounter:

> 'Is not this a terrible condescension on your part?' asked
> one disapproving lady, putting up her lorgnette to read the
> inscription on the box. 'Oh, I quite believe in your cause,
> but why do this sort of thing? How much better to get
> round the men another way!'

The narrator explains she would consider wheedling and manipulation to be 'a condescension, and so would the right sort of man'.

The woman, she added, 'seemed to belong to a strange world . . . in which helplessness had a market value'.[26]

Mrs Brown, the protagonist of Katherine Roberts's semi-fictional *Pages from the Diary of a Militant Suffragette*, published in 1910, told a story similar to Sharp's. Brown believed that everyone should have the right to vote, but did not understand why women wanted to until she attended one of the many At Home meetings where newly released suffragettes talked about their prison experiences. Suddenly, she saw that the women looked upon the vote 'as a symbol of citizenship – in other words a latchkey, which will open a very big door'.[27] Realizing that she really had been a militant suffragist for her whole life, she dived fully into working for the cause, standing up to anti-suffragists who barked, 'Which would you rather have, a husband or a vote?'[28] Married, with two young sons, Brown was not threatened. 'This is not a sex war,' she retorted. 'It is the men and women of the future against the men and women of the past.'[29] Brown came to admire the camaraderie among the suffragettes, 'their mutual love for each other and for the leaders of the movement': the Pankhursts, Pethick-Lawrence and the notorious Lady Constance Lytton.

In Colmore's novel, Lady Constance was the model for the mesmerizing Geraldine Hill, a member of the aristocracy with ties to the government who represented the upper end of the social scale. Lady Constance joined the movement when she was in her late thirties, and, she said, had reached 'that place in the lane of life when the probable alternatives of the future are fairly visible'.[30] For the previous fourteen years, she had pined for a man who barely encouraged her affections; when it became clear that he never would marry her, she resigned herself to a life of engaging in mild good works and tending to her demanding mother, who treated her like a child. Subject to depression and assorted illnesses, some of which, her biographer concludes, were psychosomatic, she became energized by the suffragettes she met in the summer of 1908.

Like many upper-class British women at that time, Lady Constance knew little about the suffrage movement. 'My sympathies had been spontaneous with regard to the wrongs of animals, of children, of men and women who belonged to down-trodden races or classes of society,' she admitted, 'yet hitherto I had been blind to the sufferings peculiar to women.'[31] A meeting with the warm and charming Emmeline Pethick-Lawrence converted her. With Emmeline, she attended At Homes, where she listened raptly to the speakers and was thrilled by their courage; she studied the suffrage issue intently, read back numbers of *Votes for Women*, and became transfixed, as so many other women had, by the Pankhursts. Their example gave her the strength, at last, to stand up for herself against her mother's disapproval: 'Wild things are like me,' she proclaimed. 'I shall probably do them.'[32]

As she involved herself in the movement, it became clear to Lady Constance that she, and other well-connected women, were given preferential treatment when they were arrested: they received lighter sentences, were incarcerated in a hospital rather than the oppressive Holloway prison, and, once they engaged in hunger strikes as a protest, they were less likely to be forcibly fed. Uncomfortable and guilty, she decided to expose the inequality and to express solidarity with young women like Sally Simmonds. When next she participated in a demonstration, she took on the identity of a working woman, a seamstress, taking the name Jane Warton – Jane, for Joan of Arc, and Warton, a shortening of the name of a distant relative.[33] Dressed in plain, cheap clothing, with a bad haircut and unflattering eyeglasses, she was treated, as she had expected, with horrifying cruelty: when she refused food, doctors snaked a tube down her nose and throat, several times a day. After she was released, her exposure of torture generated public outcry, but only an equivocal victory: the Prisoners Temporary Discharge for Ill Health Act of 1913 allowed prisoners to go on a hunger strike until they were perilously weak. Discharged in order to recover, they were subject to rearrest in order to finish out their sentence. Because the government seemed to be toying with their lives the way a cat plays with a caught mouse, the Act was known popularly as the 'Cat and Mouse Act'. Not surprisingly, some of the mice disappeared after they were released, continuing their activism while in hiding.

Margaret Haig, founder of the progressive magazine *Time and Tide*, spoke for many of her contemporaries who came of age at the height of the suffrage movement: 'for me,' she said,

> and for many other young women like me, militant suffrage was the very salt of life. The knowledge of it had come like a draught of fresh air into our padded, stifled lives. It gave us release of energy, it gave us that sense of being of some use in the scheme of things, without which no human being can live at peace. It made us feel that we were part of life, not just outside watching it. It made us feel that we had a real purpose and use apart from having children . . . It gave us hope of freedom and power and opportunity. It gave us scope at last, and it gave us what normal healthy youth craves – adventure and excitement.[34]

Awakenings

When Emmeline Pankhurst first visited the U.S. in 1909, she was disappointed to find the suffrage movement 'in a curious state of quiescence', even though the first suffrage parade was held in New York in February 1908. Women were sympathetic to the idea of enfranchisement, but, like Mrs Brown in Katherine Roberts's novel, they did not quite understand why they would want to vote. But by the time she left, after meeting groups all over the country, Pankhurst felt encouraged: 'It was when talking with the younger women', she said,

> that I came to feel that under the surface of things in America, a strong suffrage movement was stirring. These young women, leaving their splendid colleges to begin life, were realising in a very intelligent fashion that they needed and would be obliged to secure for themselves a political status.[35]

When she returned the following year, the movement had come alive, in no small measure through the work and example of Alice Paul, who had worked with the WSPU in 1908 and 1909, when she was a student at the London School of Economics. At first doing nothing more than attending meetings, she was enjoined by the Pankhursts to take part in a deputation that, Paul knew, would end in her arrest. She did not hesitate to agree; and when she returned to the U.S., she brought with her the British suffragettes' burning spirit.

Paul, at 25, was described in a newspaper article as 'a slender, fragile appearing young woman with dark brown hair, calm gray eyes, and pale olive skin'. She did not look like a militant, at least not the way they were characterized in the British press. But when she spoke at the headquarters of the Equality League of Self-supporting Women in 1910, she told of her seven arrests, three imprisonments and experience of being forcibly fed through her nostrils twice a day for four weeks.[36]

The suffrage movement in the U.S. did not meet with the same violent resistance. It may be that Elinor Glyn was right when she noticed the difference between the way British and American men treated women: 'The traditional contempt for woman, as the weaker vessel, which the average Englishman has inherited as a second nature,' she claimed, 'was cancelled in America by genuine respect for the gallantry of the women who endured the hardships and shared the risks of pioneering days.'[37] This respect for the pioneer spirit might be why women first gained the vote in the west: Wyoming (since 1869), Colorado (1894), Utah and Idaho (1896).[38] The state of Washington granted the vote to women in 1910, and California in 1911. In some states, even before women had the vote, they attended city council meetings to witness what male representatives were doing. 'They don't say anything,' suffragist Rheta Childe Dorr reported.

> They don't have to say anything . . . More than once the
> deep-laid plans of the most powerful politicians in Salt
> Lake City have been completely frustrated by a silent warning from the women. The city council has not dared to pass
> grafting measures with a roomful of women looking on.

Women's presence is powerful.[39] Although suffrage bills in New Hampshire, Rhode Island, South Dakota and Michigan, among other states, were voted down, the movement was gaining popular support.

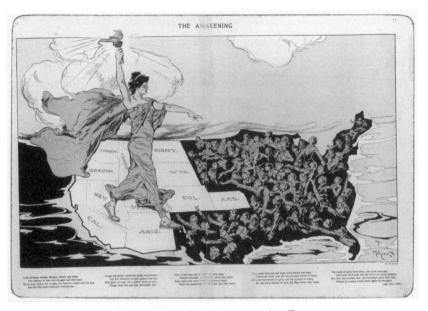

'The Awakening', showing women's suffrage
spreading across the u.s., 1915.

Dorr saw that women 'have learned that they cannot have everything they want merely by asking for it. Also they have learned
. . . that the old theory of women being represented at the polls by
their husbands is very largely a delusion.'[40] After Pankhurst's first
two visits, Dorr said,

> American suffragists everywhere began to view their cause
> in the light of a political movement. They began to adopt
> political methods. Instead of private meetings where suf-
> frage was discussed before a select audience of the already
> convinced, the women began to mount soap boxes on
> street corners and to talk suffrage to the man in the street.[41]

But they were not ready to mount a guerrilla war.

When Pankhurst made her third, and last, visit to the u.s. in 1913, her reputation as a militant caused consternation even among some suffrage supporters, who feared that she would incite guerilla tactics in the u.s. After being detained at Ellis Island when she first arrived, she was released only with the stipulation that she would leave the country as soon as her lectures were over. As she assured her audience at her first talk in New York's massive Madison Square Garden,

> It has not yet been necessary in the United States for women to be militant in the sense that we are, and perhaps one of the reasons why it is not necessary and why it may never be necessary is that we are doing the militant work for you. And we are glad to do that work. We are proud to do that work.

What she wanted from Americans was not imitation, but moral support: 'All that we ask of you is to back us up,' she pleaded.

> We ask you to show that although, perhaps, you may not mean to fight as we do, yet you understand the meaning of our fight; that you realise we are women fighting for a great idea; that we wish the betterment of the human race, and that we believe this betterment is coming through the emancipation and uplifting of women.[42]

Among Pankhurst's escorts during her trip was Rheta Childe Dorr, a journalist whose position about suffrage was made clear in her 1910 book *What Eight Million Women Want*. Dorr had been a suffrage supporter since the age of twelve, when, disobeying her

Official programme of the Woman Suffrage Procession, 1913.

father, she went to hear Elizabeth Cady Stanton and Susan B. Anthony speak; handing over a silver dollar, she became a member of the National Woman Suffrage Association (NWSA), and her feminist ideals intensified year by year. 'It was a family joke', she recalled in her autobiography, 'that from infancy it was easy to irritate me by a most casual allusion to the tradition of male superiority.'[43] A tomboy who resented that her freedom was curtailed as soon as she reached puberty, the young Rheta taxed her parents' patience. Hoping to give her some direction, her father enrolled her at Nebraska State University; mostly, she was bored, but in her second year an English teacher gave her a copy of Ibsen's *A Doll's House*, which, she said, 'cleared most the fog out of my mind'. Suddenly, she saw 'all women's mental, moral and economic parasitism'. Deciding that she no longer wanted to be economically

Suffragettes with flag, *c.* 1910–15. The photo shows Jessie Stubbs and 'General' Rosalie Jones, who led the woman suffrage hikes to Albany, NY, and Washington, DC.

dependent on her father, she dropped out of school to earn her own living.

Her family was scandalized: a working girl reflected badly on the man of the house, implying that he could not support his wife and children. But Rheta prevailed and found a job at the post office, where she had a front-row seat to human drama, including the clandestine affairs – facilitated by the post – engaged in by restless housewives. She quit after two years, acting on a friend's suggestion that she join her in New York to study art. After a time at the Art Students League, she discovered, however, that she had more talent for writing – verse, fiction and reporting – than drawing or painting, and she was delighted when she was paid for her work. Never short of admirers, she found herself attracted to John Pixley Dorr: forty, handsome, well read and, she thought then, urbane. They married and moved to Seattle, where John Dorr was a businessman.

Their first years of marriage were happy, but soon Rheta noticed that her husband had rather old-fashioned taste in literature and, sadly for her, old-fashioned ideas about women. 'The man who really broke up our home', she admitted, 'was Herbert Spencer', whose insistence on women's mental inferiority incensed her. Unfortunately, John agreed with Spencer. 'To him I appeared a foolish iconoclast. To me he appeared an intellectual dodo.'[44] She felt trapped in her own doll's house, and in 1898, with $500 and her two-year-old son, she went back to New York.

Having continued to publish in Seattle, she hoped to find an editorial or writing position, but soon learned that those positions were given to men. After several economically precarious years as a freelance writer, she finally landed a newspaper assignment on the women's pages of the *New York Evening Post*, where she wrote about fashion and home decoration, but also philanthropy and women's clubs. Meeting women active in social reform led her to resign from the *Post* to dive into causes she considered more serious and socially critical, working against the exploitation of women workers and serving as chairman of the Committee on Industrial Conditions of Women and Children. Magazine assignments paid for travels to Norway, Russia and England, where she met Christabel Pankhurst. Ignorant of the battle for suffrage in the UK, she returned home transformed, she said, 'from a complete individualist to a socialized human being'.[45] By 1912 she was active in the American suffrage movement, which had awakened from the doldrums of its earlier years. She was an apt choice, then, to write an article about Emmeline Pankhurst, commissioned by the editor of *Good Housekeeping*. The magazine sent her to Paris to interview Pankhurst, and they worked together on the voyage to New York for Pankhurst's third visit, and then, after her lecture tour, back in England. The result was both the article and Pankhurst's autobiography, for which Dorr was the ghostwriter.

Votes and kisses

When Pankhurst visited American universities, she found students energized around the issue of suffrage at major institutions – Cornell, Northwestern and New York University, to name a few – and prominent women's schools. The colleges of Barnard, Wellesley, Smith, Radcliffe, Vassar and Bryn Mawr each had a suffrage club, and in 1910 Mrs Clarence MacKay, president of the Equal Franchise Society, organized women students to mount a radical, innovative campaign. 'Each of the college suffragists', reported the *Los Angeles Times*, 'will bind herself to forswear the marriage vow until she has won over to the women's suffrage cause 500 bona fide men voters.' MacKay was confident that men would jump at the chance to endorse their girlfriends' cause. 'When the girl member will have signed up 500 real live men,' MacKay said, 'she will get a "clear bill" permitting the wedding bells to ring.' Some of the real-live men, girls were advised, could be politicians – a u.s. senator was worth two hundred points; a congressman one hundred; and a state senator fifty – without the promise of wedding bells.[46] 'No Vote, No Husband,' declared 250 girls in Spokane, Washington.[47]

'There is not a man in America whose vote cannot be bought for a kiss,' one suffragist claimed, urging the suffrage party to send 'some pretty people' to make personal contact with senators and assemblymen.[48] At Wellesley, though, suffrage activists among students and faculty objected that kisses 'have no place in politics or in obtaining women's rights and that the bestowal of such favors publicly and promiscuously would bring the cause into disrepute or ridicule'.[49] That was the experience of a young delegate of the East Side Woman's Suffrage League when she entreated New York assemblyman James Oliver to support a suffrage bill. He refused, saying he did not want to be bothered, but he offered some advice: 'What you want to do is go to some young Assemblyman and give him a hug and a kiss, and then you will get it,' he said. 'That's the way the girls on the street get what they want.'[50] The delegate, one Miss Mercy, went away disgusted.

Much of the media depicted young American suffragists far differently from the way they were characterized in the UK: as 'stunning', smart and saucy. 'We must attract and allure men,' became one group's campaign slogan. 'The dowdy suffragette is a thing of the past, a memory of the dark ages before society lent its prestige and influence to the cause,' a suffragette remarked, displaying a skirt that she was altering into a trendy style.[51]

As the suffrage movement gained strength, so did the opposition, anti-suffragists who regretted young women's activism for reform in general and suffrage in particular. Even so stalwart a feminist as Dorr confessed that the 'modern girl' puzzled her. 'The bobbed-haired young female who will be the woman voter of tomorrow', she said, 'often appears to me to lack certain desirable qualities.' 'She does not read much,' she lamented, and has not be influenced by 'master-minds of the past'. Although she rejoiced 'in the wider freedom claimed by young girls', she felt uneasy by the direction they seemed to be going, and their blithe disregard of their predecessors.[52] Dorr's misgivings were strongly underscored by anti-suffragists, whose views were articulated well by the popular novelist Margaret Deland.

Deland was nearly sixty when she published *The Rising Tide* in 1916. Ten years earlier, *The Awakening of Helena Richie* had shocked some readers, dealing as it did with a woman who leaves her drunkard husband and goes off with another man, whom she tries to pass off as her brother. When her real relationship with her lover comes to light, an orphaned boy she has been raising is taken from her, and, horrified and chastened, she realizes that she loves the child much more than her lover. Helena's predicament resonated with readers: a woman rebels against her husband's maltreatment, seeks happiness, but finally must face the consequences of her actions. Motherhood, the novel argued, is woman's greatest gift and satisfaction. The novel's first edition sold out in two weeks, it was made into a play that won acclaim on Broadway, and in 1916 it was made into a silent film.

In *The Rising Tide*, Deland once again found a timely theme: the fate of intelligent, educated, energetic young women who wanted, Deland wrote in an article in the *Ladies Home Journal*, 'to make the world over'.[53] Frederica Payton, 25 years old, is a defiant New Woman who believes 'the ballot is the key' to free women from oppression.[54] Slender (she walks her dog for miles to keep thin), wearing short skirts and silk stockings, and smoking cigarettes, Freddy (as she is called) is the image of a flapper. She outrages her mother, aunt and grandmother by speaking her mind about sex, men, birth control and marriage, making such declarations as, 'I don't want a man; I want an occupation,' and 'The child is the jailer that has kept women in prison.'[55] Although she will someday inherit family money, without a remunerative occupation Freddy lives at home, where she feels alienated from her fussy, widowed mother, who spouts values that Freddy vehemently rejects. She calls her mother a parasite because she has lived off her husband's considerable wealth, and she condemns her for never standing up for herself when he erupts in a violent temper or when he drinks to excess and betrays her with other women. Freddy believes that her adult brother's mental affliction, which appears to be brain damage or severe autism, was caused by a venereal disease transmitted by her father. Men should not be allowed to marry, Freddy announces, 'unless they have a health certificate'.[56] Mrs Payton, who spends her time doing jigsaw puzzles, is shocked by Freddy's attitudes and behaviour. 'Mother's mind stopped growing when her first baby was born,' Freddy remarks.[57]

The novel's narrator, noting Freddy's 'shallow generalizations' about women's suffrage and various social injustices, echoes Deland's views about Freddy and her comrades, women who think they can 'produce spirituality by legislation', without accounting for human nature; 'there seems to me a certain arrogance in our bustling, feminine haste to make the world over . . . as if we thought ourselves so important that nothing could go right without us.'[58] Still, Deland allows Freddy to become increasingly sympathetic as she confronts her own desires and faces realities that she cannot control.

Among her desires is finding a way to earn her own living. She rejects working with the poor, as many women of her class did, and feels no calling to be a nurse. Instead, she comes up with the idea of finding apartments for single women, earning a small commission for her efforts. The family's financial adviser, Arthur Weston, the executor of Payton's estate, cautions Freddy that she will never make enough to support herself, but she is undaunted. Among her first clients are two spinster sisters, who are sometimes amused, sometimes shocked, by Freddy.

As in most novels about New Women, the feisty protagonist is portrayed beside a more womanly woman: sweeter, quieter, softer and endearing to men. In this case, Freddy's cousin Laura becomes the love interest of Howard Maitland, a hearty, rich young man fascinated by conchology: the collecting of shells. He is enthralled by Freddy – he can talk to her 'just as I can to a man', he tells her – but is taken aback when Freddy boldly proposes marriage.[59] Men don't marry pals, this novel teaches. Freddy, deeply embarrassed by her misreading of Howard's attentions, asks him not to tell Laura. 'You can talk all you want to about "new women" . . . I guess human nature doesn't change much,' Howard decides, reflecting on Freddy's emotional request.

Howard, it turns out, is in love with Laura – they marry and soon are expecting a baby, while Freddy nurses her emotional wounds, growing thinner, older and apparently wiser. 'The welfare of the child demands a permanent relation between the father and the mother,' she comes to realize – just as Helena Richie did. New Women need to nurture their beauty and dignity, because these qualities, Freddy sees, lure men.[60]

Freddy's yearning for love does not conflict with her adamant support of suffrage. She derides women 'antis' as having 'no brains', and the novel reveals views held by many anti-suffrage men: 'Our grandfathers made a mess of it, by dealing out universal male suffrage,' one man emotes, 'and our fathers made a worse mess in giving it to the male negro . . . .'.[61]

Deland was sympathetic to this view: she was opposed to suffrage for unqualified (that is, poor, uneducated) women, just as much as for unqualified men. Prominent educational activist Annie Nathan Meyer, whose efforts resulted in the founding of Columbia University's women's college, Barnard, took the same position in a letter to the editor of the *New Republic*. The vote, she said, is 'a necessary expression of class interests, but . . . sex is not a class'. Meyer believed that men of one class well represented the women of their own class more accurately than women of different classes could represent one another.[62] Giving the vote to women, both Deland and Meyer contended, would just compound social problems. Even Howard Maitland, who never contradicts Freddy's pronouncements, becomes an 'anti' when Freddy and Laura are arrested after a pro-suffrage event. Freddy finds love – Arthur Weston, twenty years older than she, confesses his adoration – but only after she is hurt and chastened.

'Shallowness' was Deland's term of approbation for women who thought having the vote would solve endemic social problems, and it is a term repeated many times in 'The Change in the Feminine Ideal', an article she published in the *Atlantic Monthly* in 1910. Although she acknowledged 'that the condition of women is full of hope', she also perceived in the behaviour of young women like Freddy a threat to family stability.[63] The girl, she says, 'apes the independence of the boys and often emphasizes it with an affected and ludicrous swagger (which the boys, at any rate, see through, and do not really like)'.[64] In school, girls discover that their horizons are greatly expanded from what their mothers experienced. Teachers tell them to 'make the most of your own life', to fulfil their own desires and to contribute to the community. But the family, Deland worried, was becoming secondary.[65] 'The individualist', she wrote, 'believes that happiness is the purpose of marriage – whereas happiness is only an incident of marriage'; the individualist seeks happiness, without considering that marriage 'is civilization's method of remaining civilized'.[66]

When women rule

It is no surprise that an issue as incendiary as suffrage made its way into movies. In some, women were shown dressed in male attire to emphasize their loss of femininity and their usurping of male roles in society. Often, suffrage was satirized in comedies: *When Women Vote* (1907), *When Women Win* (1909), *Oh! You Suffragette* (1911), *When Helen Was Elected* (1912) and the ominously titled *When Women Rule* (1912). In that movie, says the film historian Shelley Stamp, 'equal enfranchisement is figured as a feminine invasion of public space,' a scenario that made its way into cartoons, as well: in one, mannish women smoke cigars and sidle up to the bar in a pub; in another, an earnest young woman with a large broom sweeps corrupt politicians out of office. Men had much to worry about.

Sometimes, a movie took a humorous view, as in *When Women Win*, which showed 'the flowery touches' women would bestow once they had the vote: 'fastidious, white-gloved ladies clean city streets, business meetings become chatty tea parties, and Friday is declared bargain day at the market.' In other movies, romance interferes with women's expanded public roles.[67]

Suffragists themselves saw the potential of movies to serve their own ends. Between 1912 and 1914 the National American Woman Suffrage Association (NAWSA) released four movies that argued their case, screening them all over the country, at movie houses and public meeting halls. In *Votes for Women*, Jane Addams and NAWSA's president Dr Anna Howard Shaw were cast, giving viewers a chance to see the women they had previously only read about. During her 1913 visit, Emmeline Pankhurst was filmed giving an introduction for the silent movie *What Eight Million Women Want*. The movie introduced Pankhurst to a large population who had no chance of seeing her in person, and her appearance – gracious, delicate, elegant – gave the lie to the rumours about her that had come from the British press.

No woman begins as an agitator, says the main character in Elizabeth Robins's play *Votes for Women!*: 'Every woman's in a state of natural subjection – no, I'd rather say allegiance to her idea of romance and her hope of motherhood. They're embodied for her in man. They're the strongest things in life – till man kills them.'[68] Women, she says, need to work together to make life fairer: 'We have all (rich and poor, happy and unhappy) worked so long and so exclusively for men, we hardly know how to work for one another.'[69]

The question of suffrage – pervasive, noisy, unavoidable – shaped girls' notions about their independence, authority and power. In a cartoon published in 1915, a small girl leans defiantly towards a bewildered little boy, insisting:

> For the work of a day,
> For the taxes we pay,
> For the Laws we obey,
> We want something to say.

'Votes for Women', cartoon, *c.* 1913.

Only after the war did married or property-owning women over thirty succeed in getting the vote in Britain, with the passage of the Representation of the People Bill in February 1918. It would be ten years more until women over 21 – more than five million of them – were able to vote, with the passage of an expanded law. American women won full enfranchisement in 1919. For many decades before, women's grit and ambition had infused the world in which girls grew up, and infused, as well, their hopes and dreams about the future.

8 The Age of the Girl

꒰

'Every tendency of today seems to favor
the predominance of youth.'
Chicago Daily Tribune, 1912

Girls were sexually alluring: that was no news, but by the 1910s
the past several decades of investigation and debate about adolescent sexuality had effected changes in the way girls and women
looked, dressed and behaved. Men loved girls: that was no news,
either; and women who wanted husbands grasped at youth to make
them competitive in the marriage market. Even before the war that
drastically diminished the male population in the UK and America,
there were over a million more women than men in each country.
To be a 'surplus woman' was a sad fate. Although girls strived for
education, independence and the vote, still they realized, as their
mothers and grandmothers had realized, that marriage would give
them status and stability, not to mention companionship, children
and, possibly, love.

In *The Getting of Wisdom*, published in 1910, the novelist Ethel
Florence Lindesay Richardson, writing as Henry Handel Richardson,

told the story of Laura Rowbotham, who takes classes in physiology at her boarding school, where the girls 'were required to commit to memory every bone and artery in the body, yet all that related to a woman's special organs and chief natural function was studiously ignored'. Not surprisingly, Laura reports, 'the fancies woven by quite big girls, for instance, round the physical feat of bringing a child into the world, would have supplied material for a volume of fairy-tales.' And equally distressing,

> out of it all rose the vague, crude picture of woman as
> the prey of man. Man was animal, a composite of lust
> and cruelty, with no aim but that of taking his pleasure:
> something monstrous, yet to be adored; annihilating,
> yet to be sought after; something to flee and, at the
> same time, to entice, with every art at one's disposal.[1]

What does not change for girls, Laura realizes, is the unalterable goal of marriage, 'the great consummation', which occurs 'without fail directly the college-doors closed behind them'.[2]

Laura rebels against that prescribed plot. When one of her teachers characterizes a woman's brain as 'vague, slippery, inexact, interested only in the personal aspect of a thing', Laura takes the taunt as a dare. It was, she thought, as if 'an invisible hand had opened the door to an inner chamber, and light broke on her'. Humiliated, she decides that 'she did not want to have a woman's brain, thank you', and she would not become a girl with a tiny waist who flirted with boys and aimed only for 'the great consummation' of marriage.[3] Still, even if ambitious girls like Laura wanted to use their brains and talents, marriage stood as an undeniable goal. The modern girl faced the struggle of negotiating independence and ending up as a wife.

Marriage meant a girl was desired. 'If through lack of beauty or fortune, or both, she failed to marry,' noted an article in *Appleton's Magazine* in 1908, 'she became that most pathetic of all human creatures, a gentle and purposeless "old maid" dependent.' Even girls who went to university and were brought up to be independent had marriage in view from childhood, and it was a goal for which they knew they had to compete. Beauty, of course, was an asset, and in the 1910s beauty was synonymous with youth. The key to perpetual youth, the *Appleton's* writer concluded, 'lies in arresting adolescence'.[4] That conclusion increasingly made sense to women: arresting adolescence became an obsession.

In George Egerton's short story 'A Nocturne', a man finds a woman near fainting in the street late at night and takes her to his apartment, where he gives her tea and a place to rest and regain a bit of strength. When he learns that she is looking desperately for a job, he gives her a reference to an 'editress'. Although he seems to be a thoughtful and educated man, when he guesses that the woman is about thirty, he considers her unattractive: 'there is nothing like milk-fresh youth,' he thinks. 'The plainest fresh-skinned wench with the dew of life in her eyes is worth ten of any beauty of thirty-five.'[5]

No woman wanted to be seen as mature; every woman, if newspapers and magazines are to be believed, wanted to be a girl. Youthfulness, reported J.O.B. Bland in the *Chicago Daily Tribune*, 'is something more than skin deep. It is the outward and visible sign of an inward and spiritual revolt against the withering hand of Time, a proof of mental and moral resistance to the insidious attacks of the Scythe Bearer.' An attitude of *carpe diem*, a penchant for wildness, swept into women's lives. And to be wild necessitated being young and cultivating 'the Peter Pan quality of mind, which . . . steadfastly refuses to grow old'.

Fashion encouraged women to scrutinize their shortcomings, 1913, cartoon.

Fashion designers shaped and responded to women's desires, 'making no distinction between the matron's gown and the frock of sweet 17, so that, seen from a short distance the sprightly grandmothers of to-day are not to be distinguished from "flappers"'.[6] The cartoonist and commentator Nell Brinkley declared that after 1910, unmarried women were living in the 'Day of the Girl'.[7] She should have included married women, as well. 'There are no longer any grandmothers to be found and even mothers are becoming rare,' observed theatrical agent Elisabeth Marbury. 'Women of all ages search for the Holy Grail of youthfulness in rejuvenating creams and beauty parlors.'[8] Advice columns in newspapers and magazines offered a plethora of helpful hints for achieving a glowing, dewy, youthful complexion. But a natural glow was not sufficient: artifice was necessary to enhance a woman's allure.

Between 1909 and 1929, according to the historian Kathy Lee Peiss, 'the number of American perfume and cosmetics manufacturers nearly doubled.'[9] Among them were Elizabeth Arden, Helena

'Costumes Parisiens', 1913.

Rubinstein, Max Factor, Madam C. J. Walker and Maybelline – all founded during this period of burgeoning opportunity, offering products more affordable than the expensive paints and potions from Paris. New firms and old promised the same results: a youthful, dewy glow. Madam Walker invented products to straighten the hair and lighten the skin of her African American clientele. Helena Rubinstein, with a shop in London's Mayfair, aimed to instil a 'cult of beauty' in the UK. The French favoured cover-ups with the heavy application of make-up, she said; the Americans preferred 'electrical and surgical remedies', but the Viennese, like herself, had invented special, youth-giving creams.[10] Rubinstein became a star among cosmeticians, with shops in Manhattan, Chicago and Paris. As popular as she was, though, using her vanishing, firming and moisturizing creams struck most girls as insufficient.

High-school girls dabbed on rouge and lipstick; they wore high heels, low-necked shirtwaists, short sleeves and sheer stockings. In Cincinnati, Ohio, one women's group started a dress reform movement, resolving to set an example for girls by choosing to wear simple, healthful and modest clothing.[11] At a meeting of the State Mothers' Congress in Colorado, a delegate complained about girls who 'wear their waists too low and their skirts too high. They go to school clad like nymphs in a Greek dance and they paint and powder like Comanches on the warpath.' But one mother defended herself for not denouncing her daughter's choice of clothes. 'If a girl expects to land a husband in New York,' she said, 'she has best to begin looking for him when she is still in school, and what chance has a little girl in a middy suit, with braided hair and a natural color, against girls dressed in silks' and wearing lipstick and rouge.[12] Girls, however liberated they aspired to be, dressed for men's admiration.

'Why not resort to artificial means to beautify one's self?' a girl asked rhetorically during a debate about cosmetics held by members of the Young Women's Elocution Class at Cooper Union in New York in 1913. If a girl 'has any ailment doesn't she consult a doctor? Isn't ugliness an ailment?' To the opposing view that nothing can be done to conceal 'defects', the majority of girls retorted that cosmetics 'cleverly applied' are a boon to women. 'It's human to look pretty, isn't it? . . . A homely woman has to resort to artificial aids to beauty in this day and age,' one girl asserted, 'if she desires to compete with her more fortunate sisters in certain contests that women have always had to fight for.'[13]

'Let me say here that fellows are not "scared off" by cosmetics,' wrote a *New York Times* reader. 'The girls who use them do so to attract attention, and, believe me, they succeed!' This writer was convinced that girls used make-up to lure men, with the object of marriage. All girls want a home of their own, this writer believed, even though the image of the 'despised old maid has become the admired spirited bachelor girl, who earns her own living and lives contentedly without fear of comment'.[14] Girls in the 1910s, raised by mothers who believed women's destiny was to be a wife, were not so sure that they wanted to become spirited bachelor girls.

The eternal doll

Ever-changing styles in cosmetics and fashions compelled girls to look in the mirror and assess themselves constantly. They made judgements about their facial features – nose, lips, brows, cheeks, chin; they decided if they were too thin or, more likely, too fat. All girls (single or married) were increasingly out in the world – at movies, dances, in shops and restaurants – and that world of other girls and, more assuredly, men was quick to evaluate them. To be out in the world meant to perform, like the movie stars they saw enlarged on the screen, and girls became astute at examining themselves as minutely as they examined the stars. Were their eyes too hooded, their pores too large, their hips too broad? Increasingly through the 1910s, girls finely honed their dissatisfaction with themselves, and they looked for ways to correct their defects.

In the early 1920s, F. Scott Fitzgerald captured girls' tireless scrutiny, of themselves and one another, in his ruefully satirical story 'Bernice Bobs Her Hair'. When Bernice visits her cousin Marjorie, a popular adolescent, she is ignored and shunned, much to her dismay. Bernice, the narrator observes, 'had been brought up on novels in which the female was beloved because of certain mysterious womanly qualities always mentioned but never displayed'.[15] But Marjorie is openly flirtatious, manipulative of her hapless boyfriend Warren and brazenly sexual. The womanly woman, she thinks, is hopelessly old-fashioned. When Bernice asks Marjorie for advice about how to become popular, Marjorie eagerly points out her cousin's deficits: she needs to brush her scraggly eyebrows, have her teeth straightened and cut her hair. She also needs to flirt, even with the boys that Marjorie calls 'sad birds'.[16] Bernice eagerly acts on Marjorie's advice, inviting one of the most popular boys to watch her get her hair bobbed, an outing that turns out to be a great lure for Marjorie's crowd.

Bernice is filled with trepidation about getting her hair cut, but she strides valiantly into a hotel barbershop and, surrounded by her excited witnesses, is shorn of her long, dark tresses. She hates the haircut, and so does Marjorie's mother, who is shocked by Bernice's rash decision. Even Marjorie agrees that it was a bad idea. Bernice gets a bit of revenge against her cousin – she cuts off Marjorie's blonde braids when the girl is asleep, and then flees for home – but she also learns an important lesson about the modern girl's life and 'the drama', as Fitzgerald's narrator puts it, 'of the shifting, semicruel world of adolescence'.[17]

It is no wonder that when the renowned French dress designer Paul Poiret visited the U.S. in 1913 he deemed American girls too conservative, afraid to try new fashions, afraid to stand out and, most of all, fearful of revealing their personality through dress. Poiret famously designed theatrical, sumptuous, body-skimming dresses. He used soft, clinging fabrics that emphasized a woman's shape, which ideally was slender and petite, like his wife, on whom he modelled his creations. Such women did not need corsets, he insisted, and he exhorted women to throw away those constricting undergarments. His elegant outfits were truly outstanding; however, girls in the 1910s made fashion choices not to stand out, but to conceal and to conform.

Many historians of this period cite Warren Susman's observation that nineteenth-century celebration of an individual's strength of character was transforming, in the first decade of the twentieth century, into a culture of personality. Developing one's unique personality was the subject of the many advice manuals that Susman investigated, and they revealed a curious paradox. 'In virtually the same breath,' he discovered, 'the reader is . . . urged to "express your individuality" and to "eliminate the little personal whims, habit, traits that make people dislike you".' Readers were instructed to try 'in every way to have a ready command of the niceties, the manners, the ways of speech, etc. which make people think "he's a mighty likable fellow"', or a very appealing girl. Susman found a 'singular emphasis not only on the need for self-confidence but also on the importance of not feeling "inferior"'.[18] Women were advised to enhance and, with the help of cosmetics and clothing, to create beauty and to learn mannerisms that would draw others to them. 'The social role demanded of all in the new culture of personality', Susman astutely saw, 'was that of a performer.'[19] Girls learned how to shape and develop their 'performing self' from movies, magazines and other girls. The culture of personality, for girls growing up in the 1910s, trapped them in prescribed models of behaviour and fashion.

Fashion dictated slimness. Clothing featured waists lowered to the hips or below, with a straightened line from the shoulders to the hem. The bosomy, hourglass shape of the 1890s Gibson girl gave way to what was called, derisively, the silhouette slouch – also called the slinker slouch and the debutante slouch: shoulders pushed forward, weight resting on hips and, to complete the look, hands thrust in pockets. 'No one could have dreamed a few months ago', reported the *New-York Tribune* in 1913, 'that the angular woman would become the model of fashion, or that the slouching woman would attract the envious glances of her sisters. But so it has some to pass, and the tight skirt is responsible.'[20]

The tight hobble skirt had been around for more than a few months, rising in popularity in 1910, and fading by the time the silhouette slouch became a source of comment. The hobble was so narrow that the wearer could not dance or take the long strides that marked the gait of the healthy, athletic girl. 'We are all as tired of the kind of gait produced by the hobble skirt as of a bad joke repeated in and out of season,' remarked a writer in the London *Times*.[21] Especially when worn with high heels, the hobble skirt hampered movement as much as layers of petticoats. But since it emphasized fashion's svelte line, women adopted it, at least for a while. As it happened, the fad was short-lived – Irene Castle, for one, was quick to reject it – and was followed by a style that was more practical but, it turned out, more shocking: the slit skirt.

'Last year we were hobbled,' wrote the *Los Angeles Times* columnist Alma Whitaker, a wry observer of society and its foibles:

> Skirts were not only all-enveloping, but they were almost sealed. Then some bright girl who tried to step from the road to the sidewalk on a rainy day in Los Angeles met with an accident at the seam – and behold, the slit skirt. The effect was quite artistic and certainly comfortable. Bien! Why mend it?

At first, Whitaker admitted, the skirt seemed 'a little sly'. But, she said,

> that slit lured us. There is a suggestion of the debonair,
> the insouciant, about an efficient slit skirt – a seductive
> swish, a captivating swagger, a feeling of free and untram-
> meled independence. It seemed so entirely to fit in with
> our modern mood, a sense of trying our wings and finding
> them gloriously capable.[22]

It was so logical: a skirt slit a mere 15 cm (6 in.) from the hem, but to some it seemed positively immoral. Four women were arrested in Louisville, Kentucky, for wearing their slit skirts; schools forbade them; priests condemned them, and so did assorted male pundits. Many girls were incredulous that the sight of their ankles proved so scandalous. 'The truth is, you see,' one British writer explained in a cable to the *Detroit Free Press*,

> we women have really accustomed ourselves to the fact
> that we possess lower extremities. Realizing at last that we
> have feet and ankles, we really are not ashamed of other
> people knowing it, particularly as it is so much easier
> to walk when they are unhampered with a superfluity
> of skirt.[23]

Some British women, however, worried that their feet were too large, especially compared with the smaller size of French women's feet and the narrowness of those of the Americans.

Whether or not girls chose the hobble or the slit skirt, all new fashions looked best on slim, flat-chested, 'boyish' bodies. Except for young adolescents, however, few had the required body type, and consequently height, weight, breasts and hips were the focus of ruthless scrutiny. As the fashion designer Georges Doeuillet observed in 1913, 'Today in the world of fashion, all women are young and they grow more so all the time. It is an age of elimination. Hips were the first to go. Then exit the waistline.' As far as hairstyles, women opted for 'the close boyish coiffure of the day' that gave the illusion of youthful ingenuousness. 'Years, either of discretion or indiscretion, are quite démodé', Doeuillet added, 'and must be forgotten by yourself and by others.'[24]

One social statistician, questioning 99 women, 'found that not one was the weight she wanted to be'. By far the majority believed themselves to be too fat, and these women were advised immediately to buy a bathroom scale and weigh themselves every night and morning. So-called self-weighing bathroom scales were easily available, costing around $8.50. Doggedly keeping track of their weight, women needed to keep the number in mind all day: while they took their daily exercise (walking and gymnastics) and ate spartan meals (breakfast of coffee and hot bread, a large lunch and a dinner of no more than fish and dessert).[25] A group calling itself the Slim Club advised that women's hips should correspond to the width of their shoulders: 'sloping hips are what you must aim at.' This could be achieved through exercise that included swaying, bending from side to side and playing hopscotch. Wearing heels, too, could make hips look slimmer.[26]

Fad diets proliferated as women struggled to be as thin as possible. 'Dieting', one physician observed, 'with some women means going without food to the very limit of existence.' They ate apart from their families because 'the idea of a regular meal has become repulsive to them'; instead, they sustained themselves on buttermilk, or toast and hot water, or fruit and crackers, or peanuts and lettuce.[27]

The Hollywood Eighteen Day Diet and the Medical Millennium Diet had daily food allowances as low as 585 calories. Lulu Hunt Peters's *Diet and Health: With Key to the Calories*, published in 1918, was a best-seller, bought by more than two million women. Peters, a physician, had been overweight herself and convinced her readers that calorie counting was the only way to control weight. It was difficult to sustain such restrictive diets, so girls looked for help: Silph Chewing Gum, Slends Fat Reducing Chewing Gum and Elfin Fat Reducing Gum Drops, containing a laxative, sugar and wintergreen, worked to suppress the appetite, as did smoking, which was advertised as the 'Modern Way to Diet!'[28] Since dieting depended on strict self-denial, slenderness came to signify a girl's inner strength. Excess weight, on the other hand, revealed laziness and sloth.

Women impatient for results from dieting or short on willpower bought elasticized undergarments, such as the Miracle Reducing Rubber Brassiere and the Bramley corsele (combination bra and corset) that compressed breasts and hips. Corsets became longer to produce a slender, hipless figure. 'Hips, indeed, are extremely bad form,' reported one newspaper in 1909. 'This is not . . . the season for the plump woman – unless she wears the proper corset,' extending from arms to knees.[29] As an alternative to corsets, manufacturers offered hip confiners and lightly boned brassieres. *Vogue* magazine carried an advertisement for P. N. Practical Front Corsets that promised to remould a woman's figure with its 'feather-light elastic vest'. 'To carry the look of youth your form must radiate the magnetism and virility of girlhood,' the ad proclaimed. 'The certain way to cultivate and hold the figure of a girl-woman is through natural and personalized corsetry.'[30] Where formerly women would choose undergarments at home, selecting from a few items sent by

Corset for the new fashions, 1912.

a shop, by 1914 buyers were advised to seek expert sales advice and try on items in the shop's dressing room.

In 1922, allegedly at the height of flapperdom, the fashion columnist Annette Donnelly announced confidently that the corseted figure was back. 'No new model, unless particularly favored by Providence, can well appear corsetless with the new, clinging, slinky frock, which calls for the illusion of grace and slenderness.'[31] Even Poiret, taking a closer look at his clientele, demanded that women

Fashion dictated a slim, straight line, as John Held portrayed
in this illustration of flappers at the beach, *Puck*, 1914.

return to corsets.[32] The *Chicago Daily Tribune* helpfully instituted a
daily column devoted to 'Corset Facts'.

In their desperation to look like adolescents, women who
yearned to liberate themselves from constricting undergarments,
whale bones, petticoats, long skirts and circumscribed lives found
new means of repression in diets, exercise and elastic. 'Most women
today must live by pleasing men in one way or another,' wrote the

feminist, spiritualist, philosopher and poet Henri Antoine Jules-Bois in his novel *The Eternal Doll* (1894).[33] Like August Villiers de L'Isle-Adam, who imagined the perfect woman as an automaton in his 1883 novel *Tomorrow's Eve*, Jules-Bois portrayed, with dismay, a doll-like woman, a marionette whose arms and legs moved 'with the rhythm of laughter – as though pulled by strings from beyond in the hand of some epileptic demon'.[34] She was the New Woman, redesigned.

Who wants to be beautiful?

That was the question that the columnist Barbara Craydon asked in the *San Francisco Chronicle* in 1920. 'Everybody has a chance,' she reported, 'now that science is making over mouths, chins, noses and even faces, changing brunettes to blondes and even imparting complexions that will never wear off.'[35] Lipstick, rouge, powder and vanishing creams had their limit in creating an illusion of youth. Now science offered paraffin to fill out hollows or wrinkles, but this material melted and migrated, making it less than desirable. More successfully, nerves in the forehead could be cut underneath the hairline, relaxing furrows. 'One cannot frown,' noted one report, 'but then frowning is considered unnecessary.' What was necessary was the opportunity to reinvent one's looks: 'Being bored with one's face is no longer the sad experience that it used to be.'[36]

Seeking to alleviate boredom and sadness, women went to surgeons with precise requests to rid them of double chins, jowls, nasolabial folds, drooping eyelids and other features they deemed repulsive. Actresses were eager clients, and reports of their procedures inspired other women to follow. From 1901, when the first facelift was performed, throughout the next several decades, cosmetic reconstruction offered a new way to capture the Holy Grail of youthfulness. Cosmetic surgeon Charles Willi assured patients, 'There is no pain, there is no danger, it is an instantaneous and painless rejuvenation.' Another, Charles Conrad Miller, insisted that 'signs of maturity in women must go', even at the risk of some scarring.[37] Besides facelifts, some women of means went so far as to opt for breast- or hip-reduction surgery to transform the figure of a woman into the figure of a pre-pubescent girl. As skirts migrated to the knee, calves came in for scrutiny, leading to calf-slimming surgery, which, if it failed, sometimes resulted in amputations.

Instead of submitting to a knife, women discovered that science offered another option: they could undergo a treatment in which X-rays were directed at the ovaries, allegedly reactivating them and revitalizing the endocrine system. The American novelist Gertrude Atherton had the treatment in 1922, when, at 65, she was despondent about her appearance and persistent feeling of listlessness. Even as a younger woman, she vowed to resist ageing. Her mother, she recalled, 'resented bitterly the passing of youth. She would have been reconciled to anything if she could have kept the first freshness of her beauty.'[38] Atherton, sharing those feelings, found that creams and make-up did not suffice: she put her ardent hopes in X-rays.

The treatment, administered to Atherton by the physician and endocrinologist Harry Benjamin, in his New York office, had been developed by Eugen Steinach, a Viennese physiologist whose early career was focused on men's complaints about impotence and the debilities of ageing. Vasectomies, Steinach believed, allowed cells of the testicles to release youth-giving secretions, resulting in increased vigour and strength. His patients testified that the result was miraculous, and Steinach turned to women, theorizing that exciting the ovaries with X-rays would act in a similar way.

A week after finishing the eight-session series of X-rays, Atherton felt 'the abrupt sensation of a black cloud lifting from my brain, hovering for a moment, rolling away. Torpor vanished. My brain seemed sparkling with light,' and she flung herself into work on a new novel. Five months later, she had written 110,000 words 'at a speed', she said, 'I had never commanded before'.[39] Filled with energy, Atherton imagined a world in which mature women could reactivate their youthfulness through ovarian treatments, and yet still retain their mature outlook, their sophistication and their depth. Surely that combination would triumph over shallow, silly flappers; surely these rejuvenated women would be irresistible to men. That utopian vision became the plot of her 1923 best-selling novel *Black Oxen*.

Her protagonist is Mary Ogden, a beautiful woman who had moved from America to Europe, where she married a Hungarian diplomat, Count Josef Zattiany. During the First World War she ran a hospital, an effort that exhausted her. After the war, the philandering Count died; a wealthy widow of nearly sixty, she felt that her life had no direction. Used to men's admiration when she was younger, she resented losing her power to seduce. Eager, like Atherton, to regain her energy and, she hoped, her beauty, she learned of the Steinach treatment. When she returned to New York as Mary Zattiany, she was a startlingly attractive woman who looked to be in her thirties.

Soon she meets Lee Clavering, a drama critic who is bored with his job and, even more, with life. At 34, he already feels threatened by younger writers who he thinks would eclipse him if he took a break from journalism. 'One was forgotten overnight,' he told himself, 'and fashions, especially since the war, changed so quickly and yet so subtly that he might be another year readjusting himself' if he left his position.

Or find himself supplanted by some man younger than
himself whose cursed audacity and dramatized youthfulness would have accustomed the facile public to some
new brand of pap flavored with red pepper. The world
was marching to the tune of youth, damn it . . .[40]

He was dissatisfied with young women, too, finding them facile
and shallow. And then he meets Mary: 'What interested him keenly
was her deliberate, quite conscious attempt to enslave the two men
beside her, and her complete success.'[41] The older men seem totally
captivated by her, and, moreover, to transform before his eyes into
men younger in spirit, merely by being in Mary's presence.

When he finally gets to talk to Mary, they agree, ruefully, that
the country 'has gone crazy over youth. The most astonishingly bad
books [here, a dig at writers like F. Scott Fitzgerald] create a great
furore because from end to end they glorify post-war youth at its
worst, and the stage is almost as bad.'[42] Clavering regrets that the
culture associates love with youth; Mary admits that young women
lack depth, but acknowledges that men cast off mature women in
favour of girls.

When Mary discloses her real identity – and the reason for her
youthful appearance – to women of her own age, a few are repulsed,
but more admit how desperately they have dreamed 'of becoming flappers overnight, and formidable rivals, with the subtlety
of experience behind the mask of seventeen'. They are unhappy,
though, 'to learn that they must submit to the claws and teeth of
Time until they had reached the last mile-post of their maturity'.[43]
The Steinach treatment could only be given after menopause, years
after many women register their own dissatisfaction with their face,
hair and sagging bodies.

In *Black Oxen*, the flapper is represented by Janet Oglethorpe, a character Atherton despises. Made up with powder and mascara, Janet still looks 'like a child – a greedy child playing with life', brash and calculating.[44] Janet admits to Clavering that flappers deliberately flaunt their sexuality in order to compete with girls whom men 'fairly raced after' because 'they could have a free and easy time'. 'Sensible' girls, 'waiting for men to call and wondering if they'd condescend to show up at the next dance . . . didn't have a chance', Janet complained. 'So, we made up our minds to compete in the only way possible. We leave off our corsets at dances so they can get a new thrill out of us, then sit out in an automobile and drink and have little petting parties of two.'[45]

Mary far eclipses Janet as a love interest for Clavering, who deems her an example of bad parenting. But he confesses to his friend Gora Dwight, a successful novelist, that he is afraid of Mary's 'force power . . . I prefer to be stronger than my wife.' But Gora firmly disabuses him of that idea: 'Don't flatter yourself,' she says, 'women are always stronger than their husbands . . . the average woman . . . has a moral force and strength of character and certain shrewd mental qualities, however unintellectual, that dominates a man every time.'[46] Although Mary tells Gora that it is 'woman's peculiar gift, you know, to convince the dominating male that he wants what she wants',[47] Gora cautions Clavering against marrying her: power 'had become the master passion of her life', Gora observes. 'Madame Zattiany has long since reached the age when power means more than love.'[48]

In the end, Gora proves correct. Mary is flattered by Clavering's interest and nearly agrees to marry him, but her aristocratic admirer Prince Moritz Hohenhauer convinces her that with her 'rare gifts' and 'renewed youth' she could become 'the most famous woman in Europe, and perhaps the most useful'.[49] She gives up the idea of taking a young American husband, and she returns to Europe to fulfil her destiny to change the world.

After the book was published, banned in some cities and selling wildly in others, Atherton was besieged by 'overwhelming correspondence' from women asking if the book was 'a fairy-tale or if it were really true they might hope to renew their youthful energies'.[50] She answered each letter, she said, and sent the women to Dr Benjamin or, if they lived abroad, to physicians in Berlin or London. To women who condemned the book as immoral, Atherton had one response: 'We live in an age of scientific marvels, and those who do not take advantage of them are fools and deserve the worst that malignant Nature can inflict upon them.'[51]

Florrie the flapper

In 1914 the American vaudeville performer Elsie Janis debuted in London a number she called 'the best song I have ever sung', titled 'Florrie was a Flapper', by Herman Finck and the lyricist Arthur Wimperis. She decided to wear men's clothes for the performance – buying a suit from a men's tailor – and to deliver the lyrics in a posh Oxford accent. With scenery 'more intimate than any boudoir', she was an overwhelming hit, earning, she said, her 'first personal London cheers'.[52]

Women taking men's roles was nothing new for theatre: Sarah Bernhardt and Maude Adams certainly were not alone in choosing, and winning acclaim for, those parts, and performing in drag was not new for vaudeville acts, either: among many others, there was the much-lauded Vesta Tilley, who had made her career dressed in men's clothes from the time she began performing as a child in the

Vesta Tilley, a famous cross-dresser.

1870s; later, Florence Tempest vied with Tilley as the greatest male impersonator. At a time when women were afraid of being called mannish, implying that they were lesbians, shrews or physically repulsive, and when men were afraid of being seen as weak and effeminate, a funny, flirtatious, cross-dressing performer underscored the sexy appeal of boyish women, yet also tweaked men's anxieties about their loss of stature, anxieties that had never been assuaged since the turn of the century. 'The Prince, the Hero, no longer exists,' F. Scott Fitzgerald admitted: 'I think women have come to believe that they have nothing of value to learn from men.'[53] Tilley, Tempest and Janis could pretend to be men making fun of the flapper women who seemed able to manipulate them, entrap them and threaten their sense of self-importance.

With her song about Florrie, Janis managed both to take a man's view of flappers and to underscore the flapper's overt androgyny: her desire not only to hone a boyish physique, but to adopt men's fashion styles. Despite a return to flared skirts and waistlines around 1914, women's fashions decidedly incorporated menswear: pockets, long Norfolk jackets and, soon after the war began, military fabrics (khaki), colours (tan) and styles (the trench coat). Women bobbed their hair, the better to wear a cloche hat, a beaver felt topper or a military cap. Even more masculine than the bob was the shingle, with the back cut close to the scalp and the nape as short as a man's haircut. Zelda Fitzgerald completely embodied that image, as her husband described her: 'Slim, pretty like a rather young boy . . . her hair as short as possible, slicked back'.[54]

Just as women were adopting – some thought usurping – men's fashions, it seemed to many observers that men were opting for styles that seemed feminine: baggy trousers, reminiscent of pantaloons, for example, that were cinched at the ankle. Some men were as concerned as women with slimness, wearing elasticized bands to hide any hint of waistline fat; they wore cologne and slicked back their hair. Edgar Leslie and James Monaco's 'Masculine Women! Feminine Men!' was performed with glee in nightclub revues and vaudeville acts, satirizing what many observers saw as unseemly gender confusion. At first glance, and often second glance, as well, it was hard to tell men from women.

Dressed in drag, Janis advertised the flapper's fluid sexuality, the paradox that although she lusted after men, she could be titillated by sex with women. Janis's Florrie was the seductive prototype of Loos's Lorelei Lee, collecting wealthy admirers who showered her with expensive jewellery. 'Clever', 'sweet', 'a fascinating kid' – she traded on her girlish looks. It was a bold decision to perform the piece dressed as a dapper young man. 'Florrie' was an exuberant reflection of the complicated flapper image as it was in 1914, and as it continued to be throughout the 1920s.[55]

9 The Flapper Paramount

ℰ

'It is really most amusing to play at being
wicked when there is a delightfully scandalized
audience to appreciate one's efforts.'
Alice F. Parker, Smith College student, 1922

When *This Side of Paradise* appeared in 1920, it quickly became
a publishing phenomenon. With twelve printings within the first
year, the novel made its 23-year-old author – the blond, handsome
Princeton graduate F. Scott Fitzgerald – into a celebrity, like a movie
star. Critics praised him, though, less for his writing style than his
revelatory perspective on his own generation, born at the turn of
the century (Fitzgerald was born in 1896), idealistic, romantic, brit-
tle and confused. Widely thought to be autobiographical, the novel
centres on Amory Blaine, a Princeton student with literary ambitions, questing for success, recognition and true love. There are
girls in the novel: girls who enjoy petting parties and who become
engaged 'every six months between sixteen and twenty-two'; girls
who stay out until three o'clock in the morning; and girls who
talk about 'every side of life with an air half of earnestness, half of

mockery'. As Amory notices, the girl who in the 1890s had been called a 'belle' or a 'flirt' had evolved into a 'baby vamp', willing to kiss a boy she hardly knew, just for amusement. She was a girl jaded enough to expect every boy to have a pick-up line, and savvy enough to have come up with a line of her own. Amory looks upon his generation's culture 'as one vast juvenile intrigue'.[1]

These girls reappeared in the magazine stories that Fitzgerald collected in his next book, *Flappers and Philosophers*: Ardita Farnam in 'The Offshore Pirate', already disheartened with 'the bleakness of living'; Sally Happer in 'The Ice Palace', who warns her suitor that a part of her 'makes me do wild things'; and Marjorie Harvey, Bernice's manipulative cousin in 'Bernice Bobs Her Hair'. Fitzgerald's girls – 'bright, quite selfish, emotional when aroused, fond of admiration' – were his contemporaries when he was growing up the 1910s.[2] They were wealthy and pampered and they had discovered, he said, 'the mobile privacy of that automobile given to young Bill at sixteen to make him "self-reliant"'. Petting, at parties and in cars, was one of these girls' 'more audacious' activities. But Fitzgerald admitted that the girls he knew were in a minority; for most others, 'a kiss meant that a proposal was expected.'[3]

If Fitzgerald's gilded, privileged flappers did not represent most girls' experiences, neither did another image of girlhood that emerged from Victor Margueritte's novel *La Garçonne* (The Bachelor Girl), published in Paris in July 1922. Decried by some readers as pornography, the book had sold more than a million copies in France by the end of the decade, was translated into fourteen languages and incited a scandal that quickly crossed the Atlantic. A movie based on the novel was summarily quashed, and Margueritte suffered the ignominy of being dropped from membership in the French Legion of Honour. Newspaper articles chronicling his troubles, though, served as free publicity, drawing readers eager to discover what all the fuss was about.

According to one American critic, the novel was 'as honest an effort at social criticism as "Main Street"', Sinclair Lewis's dark portrayal of small-town life in the American Midwest.[4] But many readers were less interested in social critique than in sexual escapades. Margueritte's middle-class heroine, Monique Lerbier, angered by her culture's hypocrisy, flagrantly and noisily rebels. Denied any choice about whom she will marry, she is betrothed by her parents to a dissolute man who, she discovers, is after her family's money. Her self-absorbed mother is no ally, focused as she is on a desperate effort to look twenty years younger. Monique refuses to be caught in a marriage to a man she detests; defying her parents, she runs away from her husband, determined to make a living on her own. Her rebellion entails a dramatic physical change: with a close-cropped haircut and tailored clothing, she deliberately takes on a mannish appearance, and she becomes as promiscuous as a man, too, treating lovers – men and women – as sex objects, to be toyed with and discarded when she wants someone new. But her sexual indulgences cause only isolation and despair, which she hopes to relieve by having a child. She is desolate when she finds that she is sterile – a punishment, the novel implies, for her transgressions. In the end, she is redeemed by a war veteran whom she nurses back to health, and with his love, she grows her hair long, embraces conventional femininity and marries him. Out of post-war disillusion, Margueritte gave readers a familiar plot of redemption through love and marriage, 'a stabilizing universe', as the historian Mary Louise Roberts put it, that emerged 'from the ruins of a civilization' to underscore 'a central cultural myth of the era'.[5] The dissolute woman was doomed; the womanly woman, like her nineteenth-century predecessor, thrived.

Despite Monique's shocking behaviour throughout most of the novel, something about the way she looked insinuated itself into popular culture. The image of the *garçonne*, sanitized and commercialized, quickly appeared in advertisements for clothing, hats and hairstyles. She became younger and more adorable, impish rather than decadent. Outfits with long, tunic blouses worn over mid-calf-length slim skirts became the '*garçonne*' style, appropriate, one fashion commentator advised, 'for Sunday chapel for the college girl or tea hours for the flapper. Older women can wear this model only if they are decidedly girlish in face and figure.'[6] An advertisement for Emile-Oil Permanent Wave touted the product for *la garçonne*'s 'Boyish Bob': 'It is essentially juvenile and irresistibly smart; it lends ineffable charm and piquant youthfulness to every woman.'[7] Transformed into a fashion statement, the *garçonne* look conveyed the wearer's modernity, 'a language of movement and change', Roberts notes, 'even when it was not'. Such fashion choices 'created a visual fantasy of liberation' that did not reflect most girls' lives.[8] 'The garconne look', agree fashion historians Valerie Mendes and Amy de la Haye, 'was in fact aspirational rather than rooted in reality, since relatively few women actually experienced radical social, economic, or political freedom.'[9] Most girls and women negotiated a reality that was not strikingly different from pre-war life.

While Fitzgerald and Margueritte attracted a great deal of critical attention and sold vast numbers of books, so did mainstream novelists such as Kathleen Norris, Temple Bailey, Viña Delmar and Dorothy Speare, to name a few. These writers' fictions offer a picture of more widely shared experiences; their fast-talking, short-skirted flappers became sensible girls, and they did what sensible girls were supposed to do: fall in love with good men, and marry them.

A version of that plot appeared in one of the most talked-about novels of the 1920s, as controversial surely as *La Garçonne*: Edith M. Hull's *The Sheik*, published in 1919. Sales were so strong that the book went into nineteen printings in its first nine months and was quickly made into a movie, with the sultry Rudolph Valentino in the title role. The story centres on Diana Mayo, a wealthy young Englishwoman who was raised without the gentle hand of a mother or the doting interest of a father. When her mother died shortly after her birth, her father killed himself in grief, leaving the infant in the care of her nineteen-year-old brother. Completely uninterested in raising a girl, he treats her like a boy, and she grows up disparaging all things feminine. 'She looks like a boy in petticoats, a damned pretty boy,' one observer remarks.[10] And throughout the novel, other characters, as well as the narrator, make the same observation about her boyish appearance. She is also beautiful, which she finds annoying: men are attracted to her, but they bore her. 'She's the coldest little fish in the world, without an idea in her head beyond sport and travel,' one man says.[11] She admits that she has never loved anyone, and is convinced that marriage means subservience, even 'marriage with a man who is a man, in spite of all that the most modern woman may say'.[12] Diana has yet to meet 'a man who is a man', but Hull presents her with a towering example of just such a being.

As the novel opens, Diana is in Algeria, about to embark on a month's trip into the desert. Her brother and friends warn her against making the trip. She is young and beautiful, and therefore vulnerable in ways that she cannot imagine, they tell her. But she has just reached the age of majority, and she insists on her freedom. 'I like wild places,' she proclaims.[13] Accompanied by an Arab guide, she has barely begun the adventure when her party is overtaken and Diana grabbed off her horse by a tall, broad-shouldered man with 'the handsomest and cruelest face that she had ever seen', marked by 'fierce burning eyes' and a 'passionate stare'.[14] This is Sheik Ahmed Ben Hassan, and he has claimed her for himself. That night, despite her tears and pleas, Diana, for the first time in her life, is dominated by a man: 'the touch of his scorching lips, the clasp of his arms, the close union with his warm, strong body robbed her of all strength, of all power of resistance.'[15] He rapes her, and for the next month, he continues to force himself upon her. 'What I want I take,' he tells her. 'I can tame you and I will.'[16]

Dark-skinned Ahmed, living beyond the borders of European civilization and its repressive social niceties, is as different as possible from Diana's adoring suitors. 'The men who had loved her', she reflects, 'had not had the power to touch her.'[17] They were pallid models of English manhood; some had been physically or mentally wounded by the war, others had yet to find a job, or career, or position of influence. Ahmed, though, striding as a giant in the vast, exotic desert, awakens her sexually and emotionally. She becomes not only tamed, but enslaved, willing to give up everything, willing to do anything he asks, passionately in love because of 'his very brutality and superb animal strength'.[18] And he, too, comes to realize – despite himself – that he loves her: 'The slim, boyish figure that rode beside him had a charm all its own, but it was the woman in her that sent the hot blood racing through his veins and made his heart beat as it was beating now.'[19] Hull's variation on Shakespeare's *The Taming of the Shrew* resonated with women readers. No matter how much a modern girl might protest for independence, what she really desired, the novel maintained, was to be swept off her feet by a ferociously sensual man.

According to the literary historian Patricia Raub, who investigated best-selling novels of the 1920s, the popularity of such plots reflected readers' ambivalent attitudes towards flappers. Most fictional flappers, Raub concludes, 'much like many of their real-life sisters, were more traditional at heart than their breezy demeanor – and F. Scott Fitzgerald's depictions of flappers – led observers to believe'.[20] Yet the idea of the transgressive flapper emerged as a cultural obsession.

Novissima

Just as the secret thoughts of adolescent girls posed a problem around the turn of the century, so, in the 1920s, the heart of the flapper seemed a dark mystery. Eighteen-year-old Ellen Welles Page, writing in the politically progressive *Outlook* magazine in 1922, tried to explain her contemporaries to mystified adults who dismissed or disparaged them. 'If one judges by appearances, I suppose I am a flapper,' she admitted. 'I am within the age limit. I wear bobbed hair, the badge of flapperhood. (And, oh, what a comfort it is!) I powder my nose. I wear fringed skirts and bright-colored sweaters, and scarfs,' and blouses with Peter Pan collars, which had not gone out of style since Maude Adams created her Peter Pan costume. 'I adore to dance,' Page wrote:

> I spend a large amount of time in automobiles. I attend hops, and proms, and ball-games, and crew races, and other affairs at men's colleges. But none the less some of the most thoroughbred superflappers might blush to claim sistership or even remote relationship with such as I. I don't use rouge, or lipstick, or pluck my eyebrows. I don't smoke (I've tried it, and don't like it), or drink, or tell 'peppy stories.' I don't pet. And, most unpardonable infringement

of all the rules and regulations of Flapperdom, I haven't
a line! But then – there are many degrees of flapper.
There is the semi-flapper; the flapper; the superflapper.
Each of these three main general divisions has its degrees
of variation. I might possibly be placed somewhere in the
middle of the first class.[21]

That is, Page was more or less a semi-flapper, and more or less like
any girl who had grown up in the 1910s.

Nevertheless, Page conceded that the end of war, while it
brought long-awaited relief, also generated disillusion, cynicism
and disorientation that came to be associated with the flapper. 'The
war tore away our spiritual foundations and challenged our faith,'
Page wrote, appealing to parents to help her, and others like her,
find their way. She pleaded with adults to stop criticizing flappers
and instead 'to appreciate our virtues' and offer advice, guidance
and understanding rather than the disdain that pervaded the media,
even directed towards a wholesome, thoughtful girl like herself.

Page's essay was published just months after G. Stanley Hall
rang in on the consternation over flappers, taking a new look at
the way girls had evolved since 1904, when *Adolescence* was published. Sadly for girls like Page, Hall reprised many views that
persisted among sceptical adults. The new young woman, whom
he designated with the mock-scientific term 'Flapper Americana
Novissima', shared many of the attributes he noted in his earlier
assessment: fickleness, flirtatiousness, susceptibility to peer pres-
sure. She was emotional, and not particularly interested in school,
unless she had an attractive male teacher. She knew all the popular dances, from the tango to the shimmy, and she gave up her
corsets – and with them her inhibitions – the better to move on

the dance floor. She loved jazz, 'with its shocks, discords, blariness, siren effects, animal and all other noises', which evidently offended Hall's sensibilities. She wore make-up and perfume, but she was not trying to attract boys her own age, who seemed to her callow, but instead hoped for attention from older men. Although accused of 'sublime selfishness', she was 'tinglingly sensitive' to other girls' opinions. The flapper novissima tended to rebel against her mother, assuming a sophistication that Hall found superficial. 'Her new consciousness is really naive,' he wrote, 'and in her affections she is simply trying out all the assortments of temperamental types, dispositions, and traits of character as she often tries out styles of handwriting before she settles upon one.' Hall lamented a flapper's 'mannish ways' in fashion and behaviour; he insisted, once again, that gender differences needed to be developed, 'pushed to the uttermost', if civilization was to progress. Women needed to become more feminine – gentle and submissive – and men more virile. Hall conceded that this new flapper was 'more or less a product of movies, the auto, woman suffrage, and, especially, of the war', but she was no less a puzzle to him than the adolescent girl of the turn of the century. Even a girl who seemed demure and obedient, he warned, 'is not the real girl and she knows it; for her true self is all the more securely masked by conformity to what we expect of her'. Just as in 1904, Hall felt both fearful of and attracted to this exuberant adolescent. But maybe, he cautiously suggested, she was 'the bud of a new and better womanhood'.[22]

Or maybe, as the British writer Arabella Kenealy wrote in her alarmist *Feminism and Sex-extinction*, flappers were a cultural blight. She condemned school sports for making girls weak and nervous, and cautioned against any 'strenuous' activities that sapped girls' energies: 'If young and fresh at 16, all at once we find them at 26

Fashions for very young flappers, 1920s.

in constitution and in temperament – a little lean, a little lined, a little wan, a little shrill, a little chill, and only too often more than a little disillusioned and cynical . . .'.[23] She noted increasing maleness in physique, skin and facial characteristics among girls and warned that with physical changes 'male mental proclivities develop; obsessions to wear trousers, to smoke, to stride, to kill, and otherwise to indulge the masculine bent'.[24] Girls were losing their 'youthful bloom', instead falling prey to 'the decadent and demoralizing vogue of the Flapper. Since, beyond all things, men seek vital youth and freshness in the other sex, to find it now-a-days, they must seek it in children.'[25] Kenealy's contemptuous views were no different from what girls heard in the 1890s, and they echoed throughout the 1920s.

Suspicion and attraction, fear and admiration: those were the feelings that poured out as the flapper image became increasingly popularized. 'Either she's the saving of this age or its ruination,' the novelist Edna Ferber told an interviewer in 1924. The brazen flapper, smoking, petting and drinking bootleg drinks from her boyfriend's hip flask, was, said 39-year-old Ferber, 'a passing craze'. But there was another kind of girl – Ellen Welles Page would fit her description – more serious and purposeful, who gave her hope. This girl, Ferber thought, represented a transition to a new 'real, vital interesting worthwhile, representative twentieth century woman'. Unlike Hall and Kenealy, Ferber felt celebratory: 'It's been glorious', she said, 'to actually see the changes come in women's dressing and thinking and living and planning. I can hardly wait to see what the next ten [years] will bring.' She added, however, with a note of wistfulness, that 'in waiting for my twentieth century woman to crystallize, I can only look at the more or less ephemeral girls of today, so vivid, so exquisite, so sure of themselves, and wish I were ten years younger.'[26]

Saplings

War did not unleash those vivid, exquisite, confident girls whom Ferber envied; war did not create flappers and Fitzgerald's baby vamps, but in the 1920s they became a marketed, and marketable, commodity. The rebellious daughters of the 1890s and the modern girls of the 1910s took on a new look. In the 1920s, a particular flapper image became a product, promoted through fashion magazines, advertisements, illustrations, cartoons and – as Hall rightly noted – movies; the flapper was a style that could be bought and behaviour that could be studied, practised and performed. In *This Side of Paradise*, one girl confesses that if she does not land a rich husband, she might go on the stage. 'Yes, you might as well get paid for the amount of acting you do,' her friend tells her.[27] 'This was the generation', F. Scott Fitzgerald noted in retrospect about the 1920s, 'whose girls dramatized themselves as flappers.'[28]

They dressed to fit their role: 'there was a first abortive shortening of the skirts,' Fitzgerald noticed, 'and girls all looked alike in sweater dresses.'[29] How short were flappers' skirts? The answer depends where, and when, one looks for evidence. Advertisements from the early 1920s show hems below the knee for day and evening, and even that modest length grew longer during the decade. Coco Chanel, heralded for liberating women from constricting clothing, never featured skirts anywhere near the knee, nor did any other French designer. In 1922 a news report on fashion in the *New York Times* decried short skirts as a fad that was quickly passing.[30] To be sure, skirts were shorter than before the war, when 15 centimetres (6 in.) from the ground was customary. By the end of the decade, knee-length skirts were common among girls in school and university who adopted a style that had long been associated with childhood: tomboys, let us remember, balked at having their skirts lengthened. However they dressed in real life, though, flappers are remembered today for a particular style: scanty dresses with skimpy skirts that revealed long legs and rolled stockings. For that indelible image, we can thank its inventor: the illustrator John Held Jr.

Held's drawings of saucy flappers appeared in *Vanity Fair* and *Puck*, and most notably on the covers of *Life*, a magazine with a readership of half a million. He illustrated the book jacket of F. Scott Fitzgerald's 1922 collection of stories *Tales of the Jazz Age*; and he created the widely read cartoon strip *Oh! Margy!* Held's flapper smoked, drank, danced with abandon, flirted with impunity, her skirts short, hair bobbed and stockings rolled. She was skinny, flat-chested, with spider-like, impossibly long legs. University men, in their own post-war style of raccoon coats and high-waisted, wide-legged trousers, flocked around her. Rotund, older men lusted after her, according to Held's illustrations, and he pictured her towering over them as they tried to keep up with her on the dance floor and, he implied, in bed.

Margy, whose comic strip adventures appeared from 1924 to 1927 in newspapers all over the u.s., was a girl whom Ellen Welles Page would have called a superflapper. Dressed in chic body-skimming outfits, she devoted herself to shopping, going to parties, shocking her elders and manipulating men. Looking up at them with adoring eyes, she assured them they were big and strong, and she was 'just little me'. With that strategy, she said, as her latest beau presented her with a huge bouquet of flowers, 'they always fall jibbering; it never fails.'[31] More than one episode ended with Margy kissing her boyfriend, a different one in each strip. Love, she reflected, is flavoured with lipstick, and kissing entailed no commitment – it was just fun. In one strip, she promises to wear fraternity pledge pins given to her by Spike, in one frame; Frank, in the next; and finally Spud, admitting that if she wore all the frat pins she accepted – signs that she was a boy's steady girlfriend – her outfit would be covered with them, neckline to hem.

Although she was content to be called a flapper, Margy suggested that girls like her more accurately should be called 'Saplings', because they were young, tall and willowy. The only drawback, she conceded, 'would be that her boy friend would be called a "sap"'. Margy, though, wants boyfriends who are 'sheiks'.[32] Just as 'flapper' became a term applied to all modern girls, 'sheik' entered the vocabulary to describe sexy, irresistible, indomitable men. Like the term 'flapper', 'sheik' was aspirational.

Along with Held in creating the flapper image was the graphic artist Ralph Barton, the magazine cartoonist and illustrator for

Anita Loos's *Gentlemen Prefer Blondes*. Barton's Lorelei Lee was slim and lithe; her blonde hair was close-cropped, the better to fit under her trendy cloche hats; and she gazed at men with girlish delight. She dressed in the latest slinky styles; her coats were collared deeply in fur, and her arms resplendent with expensive bangles. She coveted diamonds, she said, although she never turned down emeralds, a string of pearls or a large bottle of perfume. Adorable, manipulative, she was a girl, as she called herself, who knew how to get what she wanted.

Barton's depiction of Lorelei Lee was close to that of the 'butterfly woman', which historian Lucy Bland sees as a subspecies of the flapper. Frequenting nightclubs and parties, the butterfly woman was ephemeral, flighty and thrill-seeking; she was 'drawn to the bright lights of the night-time Metropolis, frequently singed her wings, and on occasion was fatally burnt. She was seen in effect as simultaneously butterfly and moth – fragile, short-lived insects of day and night.' But unlike Loos's shrewd heroine, the butterfly girl, Bland notes, 'was susceptible to bad influences and drawn to the consumption of bad substances (cigarettes, alcohol and drugs)'.[33] A butterfly girl illustration made it onto the cover of *Life* magazine in 1922, and her image decorated sets of cigarette cards, complete with a pseudo-scientific name and description of her habits and habitat. One flapper image even made its way into a classic children's book: in 1929 she found herself in a realm of magic and nonsense in Hungarian-born Willy Pogany's illustrations for *Alice's Adventures in Wonderland*.

In the 1920s a host of cartoons chronicled the misadventures of comely flappers. 'Who cartoons people who are of no importance?' suffragettes had remarked during their long campaign in Britain.[34] Flappers could well ask the same question, seeing themselves

The flapper as butterfly girl, illustration for *Life* magazine, 1922.

caricatured in syndicated strips such as 'Rosie of the Office'; 'Tillie the Toiler', featuring an attractive, independent girl who worked for a living and longed for a handsome boyfriend; and 'Winnie Winkle', a fashionable flapper who was her family's breadwinner. Among the most adorable was 'Flapper Fanny Says', a strip that began in 1924, imparting wisdom about life, looks and especially how to get a man. Flapper Fanny's maxims reveal the uneasiness and anxiety that many young women felt about independence, marriage and self-image – the same anxiety that had troubled them in decades past: 'the girl who acts out to be a "career woman" often altars her plans'; 'a girl uses clothes and a line to get a husband and then uses a clothes line to keep him'; 'many a girl would rather get a bachelor than a bachelor of arts'; 'girls who watch their figures are the ones who count – with men.'[35]

Flaming youth

Cartoons and caricatures portrayed girls as giddy flappers, and flappers as sexually liberated. But even Loos, who contributed to that portrayal, admitted that it was fanciful. Sex in the 1920s, she reported, 'took place against such naive backgrounds as *thés dansants*, where the most violent clutch was that of a tango, or in cozy corners where seldom did anything more sinful take place than the snapping of a garter.'[36] It was all 'pretty tame', she added. 'How could any epoch boast of passion with its hit love song bearing the title "When You Wore a Tulip, a Bright Yellow Tulip, and I Wore a Big Red Rose"?'[37] That song echoed in the minds of adolescents who had heard it in 1914, when it first became a hit, and they listened to it again when it was reprised in the 1920s. In 1922 *Billboard* magazine proclaimed that 'the jazz cycle appears to be on the wane', and saccharine ballads like 'When You Wore a Tulip', celebrating chaste lovers in a small town in Kentucky in bygone times, became popular with a public that was 'becoming sentimental again'.[38]

Sentimentality, though, had never gone out of fashion, not in music, not in novels and not in movies of the 1920s, in which adolescent flappers, glamorous and coy, were repeatedly reminded about morals; however gleefully they cavorted on screen, they ended up realizing that licentious behaviour led to disappointment.

Sexual freedom, in any case, hardly reflected most girls' experiences. According to the historian Paula Fass, sexuality among young people was marked not by promiscuity, but rather by 'two basic rituals of sexual interaction – dating and petting'.[39] Cars gave couples privacy, but what went on in those cars was mainly kissing and fondling, and petting often was carried out at petting parties, in the company of peers. Premarital sex was mostly limited to engaged couples, even though it incited much public hand-wringing. Nevertheless, as Smith College student Alice Parker said, it was fun to shock people, and girls learned how to do so from watching movies and by modelling themselves on stars like Olive Thomas, Clara Bow and Colleen Moore.

In 1920, at the age of 26, Thomas played a sixteen-year-old school-girl with a romantic imagination in *The Flapper*. Her escapades involved some older, predatory men, but no harm was done, and her innocence was preserved. Thomas herself served as a cautionary tale for her fans when she died mysteriously of poisoning a few months after the movie was released.

Bow and Moore were adolescents themselves when they rose to stardom in the 1920s, and both promoted themselves as tom-boys. In 1922 the feisty, Brooklyn-born Bow was sixteen when she appeared as Dot Morgan in *Down to the Sea in Ships*. 'Dot was a character Clara could relate to,' wrote Bow's biographer David Stenn, 'the spunky, chunky girl who beats up boys her age, then masquerades as one when stowing away on a whaler to escape her repressive Quaker family.'[40] In *Grit*, with a screenplay by Fitzgerald, she again admitted that her character was 'a little roughneck and a tomboy [like] I was'.[41] Bow became one of the most prominent examples of flapperdom, featured on the cover of *Motion Picture Classic* in 1925. 'There is something vital and compelling in her presence,' the magazine exulted. 'She is the spirit of youth. She is Young America rampant.'[42]

According to movies like *The Plastic Age*, based on a 1922 novel by Dartmouth College professor Percy Marks, young America consisted of 'sheiks and flappers who danced to the "jungle rhythm" of jazz, drank from silver flasks, and debated whether to "go the limit"'.[43] Like many other flapper movies, this one was set on a university campus, a hotbed of licentious behaviour in many people's minds, where, despite Prohibition, which had been enacted in the u.s. in 1919, alcohol lubricated social life.

The Volstead Act regulated the manufacture, sale and transport of alcohol – but not its consumption. Until it was repealed in 1933, not a day went by without Prohibition being debated in newspapers and magazines, and around dinner tables and on university campuses: 'It is perhaps the leading American problem,' announced the *New York Times* in 1927.[44] No one knew whether drunkenness had lessened because of Prohibition, or whether it had increased. One thing was certain: making the manufacture and distribution of alcoholic drinks illegal spurred crime. The law was unenforceable and flagrantly violated. Bootleggers proliferated, and it was easy to have bottles of whiskey, wine or gin – real or synthetic – delivered to one's home or party. Some university administrators attested that drinking had decreased on campuses, but others testified with just as much certainty that drinking was more prevalent, especially among girls who wanted to be popular.

The Plastic Age, with its depiction of drunken revelry, promoted Bow as 'the hottest jazz baby in films'.[45] According to Fitzgerald, Clara Bow was 'the quintessence of what the term "flapper" signifies as a definite description: pretty, impudent, superbly assured, as worldly-wise, briefly-clad and "hard-berled" as possible.' She was the model for many other actresses who took flapper roles, and for her many thousands of fans. 'It is rather futile to analyze flappers,' he added. 'They are just girls, all sorts of girls, their one common trait being that they are young things with a splendid talent for living.'[46] Even girls with a talent for living hoped to end up married, but, Bow insisted,

> Marriage ain't woman's only job no more . . . A girl who's worked hard and earned her place ain't gonna be satisfied as a wife . . . I wouldn't give up *my* work for marriage. I think a modern girl's capable of keepin' a job *and* a husband.[47]

In 1926 Bow starred in *Dancing Mothers*, playing Kitten, a young flapper with eyes for a man whom her mother knows is a philanderer. Trying to protect her daughter, the mother flirts with the man herself, but then falls for him. In an unexpected plot twist, the mother, disgusted with her husband's infidelity and her daughter's incorrigible selfishness, leaves them both and sets off for Europe, alone, to start a new, unencumbered life. Despite her unsavoury role, audiences flocked to see Bow. 'What a joy that little Clara Bow is!' exclaimed Grace Kingsley in the *Los Angeles Times*. 'What a wonder child!'[48]

By 1927 Bow, at 21, was not quite a wonder child, but she convincingly played adolescent flappers – brassy, irresistible and deceptively innocent. When Ben Schulberg read Elinor Glyn's novella *It*, he saw the potential for a huge career boost for the actress – not only by playing the lead in the movie he adapted from the novella, but by a new marketing strategy: Schulberg offered Glyn $50,000 to endorse Bow as the 'It' girl, embarking on a lecture tour advising girls on how to get the kind of animal magnetism

Clara Bow in *Dancing Mothers*, 1926.

that defined 'it'. The 63-year-old Glyn might have seemed an odd representative to promote youthful sex appeal. By all accounts, her appearance had become increasingly eccentric: she was heavily made up, with dyed red hair and bold red lips, and she habitually decked herself out with fake jewels. Nevertheless, Glyn drew audiences who desperately wanted to develop 'it'. By the time the movie opened, so much excitement fomented that ticket sales exceeded every other movie – doubling grosses in most cities. Bow 'just runs away with the film', *Variety* declared. 'Clara Bow really does it all, and how.'[49]

Competing with Bow in the early 1920s, Colleen Moore defined the popular boyish look: flat-chested, short hair and skirts, puckered lips and wide, wild eyes. 'Whenever a director has had a flapper picture to do,' noted one newspaper critic, 'he has turned to Miss Moore, as if F. Scott Fitzgerald himself wrote her!'[50] In fact, Fitzgerald praised Moore with as much enthusiasm as he praised Bow: 'I was the spark that lit up flaming youth,' he said, 'Colleen Moore the torch.'[51] Playing in movies that were often 'flashy Cinderella stories set to jazz', Moore understood her adolescent characters: 'Why, I'm a flapper myself,' she said: 'A flapper is just a girl trying to grow up. She wears flapper clothes out of a sense of mischief – because she thinks them rather smart and naughty.'[52]

Her movies, though, often condemned the behaviour that Moore presented as merely fun. In 1924 she starred in *Flaming Youth*, 'one of the strongest indictments of the jazz age', according to one critic from the *Washington Post*. The title 'is by no means too incendiary a description of the young generation – meaning youth from 14 to 40', whose behaviour stands as 'the latest plea for the good old traditions and the "safe and sane" life'. Moore's character serves as 'a veritable molecule of adolescence' around whom all the other characters revolve, like atoms around a nucleus.[53] And although she is an exuberantly energetic flapper, by the end of the movie she becomes a safe and sane girl.

That moralistic ending irritated the *New-York Tribune*'s reviewer, who panned the movie as 'one of those obvious, preachy, Hollywood-idea-of-New York-society pictures' that bore no relation to reality. Moore's character was 'the horrible example of what a flapper will flap into if her wings are not clipped or subdued by some good home influence'.[54] That same year, Moore acted against type in *The Perfect Flapper*, playing a girl so polite, obedient and

Colleen Moore, who played *The Perfect Flapper*.

Colleen Moore: 'just a girl trying to grow up', she said.

quiet that she is ignored by her peers and has no boyfriend. Seeing the kind of girl who attracts boys, she takes up drinking, smoking and partying, with great success. Yet this flapper, too, is reformed by the end of the movie, proving to her would-be suitor that she is a sensible girl at heart.

Surface freedom

With sex selling movies, and petting expected at the end of a date, it seems surprising that girls were as ignorant about the physiology of love-making as they had been decades earlier, which explains the success of British writer Marie Stopes's groundbreaking *Married Love*, published in 1918. According to her biographer June Rose, Stopes, like her readers,

> had been brought up to be romantically idealistic and abysmally ignorant about sex. Many girls feared that they would have a baby if they kissed a man; they knew little, if anything, of the female anatomy and nothing of the male.[55]

Stopes was an accomplished woman; she earned a doctorate in botany and pursued a career in science, but she felt that something was missing from her life. She yearned for romance with 'a knight who was exotic, as intellectually and aesthetically gifted as she was and, of course, abjectly in love'.[56] She fell in love with a married Japanese colleague whom she hoped would divorce his wife and marry her, but he did not, leaving her bereft. Not long after, she entered into an unfortunate marriage with a man who was probably impotent. 'In my own marriage,' she admitted in *Married Love*, 'I paid such a terrible price for sex-ignorance that I feel that knowledge gained at such a cost should be placed at the service of humanity.'[57] She believed that 'in spite of all our neurotic literature and plays', including Freud's theories – which she deemed filthy – and despite girls' 'surface freedom', most knew little about sex.[58]

In her own case, mutual frustration led to divorce, but Stopes mined that frustration to analyse her sexual needs; her conclusions made their way into a manual dedicated to young men, explaining women's physical and emotional needs and offering techniques in how to satisfy them. 'In *Married Love*', Rose says, Stokes 'managed to combine the idealistic, romantic and mystical approach to sex with a clinically detached description of how to enjoy it . . . Implicitly her book promised rapture ever after.'[59]

The book was published a month after women over thirty gained the vote in Britain, eight months before the war ended and in the midst of a well-publicized campaign against venereal disease. In the media and movies, horrifying statistics – more than 400,000 cases were discovered among British soldiers – struck fear in men and women.[60] Sex in marriage was touted as a social good and healthful choice, and Stopes promised sex that could be fulfilling for both partners. By 1927 *Married Love* had gone into its eighteenth edition, translated into twelve languages.[61]

Stopes's views on sexuality were complicated: she insisted that women desired and enjoyed sex, a shocking opinion, despite apparently burgeoning flapperdom. But she advised couples to keep separate bedrooms because she thought that too much familiarity would dampen romance. As a supporter of eugenics, a movement that was reinvigorated during the war, she pointedly addressed her manual to educated, middle- and upper-class readers. She believed that diseased, disabled and constitutionally weak people should be persuaded not to have children, so that humanity could progress to perfectibility.[62] She was a proponent of birth control – for all, not just those she considered unfit – and opened a clinic where she fitted women with a cervical cap that she had designed herself. Hailed by reformers such as H. G. Wells and George Bernard Shaw, she was derided, attacked and sued by conservative and religious groups. As strongly as she stood up to them, she took any criticism hard. Happily for her, in the U.S., where she lectured in 1921, an audience of more than a thousand acclaimed her warmly. Privately, she could be off-putting: on board ship returning to England, she met the young dramatist Noël Coward, who noted that Stopes 'had appropriately, the eyes of a fanatic'.[63]

Married Love transformed her life, turning her into an important, if controversial, public figure; and from the correspondence she received from readers, the book changed their lives, as well. Although it seemed, still, to be 'sex o'clock' in post-war movies and media, useful knowledge had not made its way into bedrooms, and Stopes's candid disclosures proved fascinating. She insisted that a woman needed foreplay before intercourse, every time, and suggested that a lover try kissing more than only a woman's lips. She recounted the frustration of a woman who wanted to be aroused by having her breasts fondled, only to have her husband plant a perfunctory kiss on one; she directed her readers' attention to the existence, and pleasurable potential, of the clitoris; she described the physiology of the erect penis; and she advised that couples try various positions for satisfying intercourse – all this intimate information, delivered in sometimes lyrical prose (Stopes considered herself a poet and novelist, as well as a science writer), was illuminating. Thanks, confessions and requests for advice poured in from men about to marry, from their fiancées, from newlyweds and from long-married couples hoping to reignite passion. Boys and girls read it, too, surreptitiously, hoping to sweep away 'the old evil conspiracy of secrecy', as one reader put it, which shrouded any mention of sex.[64]

Illusions

Girls in the 1920s, some of them enticed by a deluge of images of flappers, lived in a world of contradictions and decidedly mixed messages. The war had ended, and the media made it seem as if the single most dramatic result of those years of devastation was the flapper. 'Now with peace slinking through every loophole, we turn ourselves around to see just what has been happening,' one woman asserted.

> Peace . . . And the outcome of it all is the flapper. A very
> present evil according to some, a dire curse in the eyes
> of others, and to still others a transition from which will
> come something worth the heavy risk.[65]

Girls had been in transition for decades: towards more opportunities for education, more agency in making decisions about their own lives and more voice in civic life. After the war, girls on both sides of the Atlantic shared the bitterness of many returning soldiers. Daily reports of contentious peace talks underscored the fragility of peace itself; the world seemed ready to burst into another conflagration. Girls saw examples, every day, of prejudice, inequality and oppression; of the fear of anarchism and the threat of economic instability. The reform movements of the 1890s, in which women had taken leadership roles, continued to face endemic social problems, while the flapper, her fashions and her antics dominated the news.

In 1925 the Camp Fire Girls, an organization aimed at giving girls experiences in the outdoors, staged a protest: 'The young person of short skirts and bobbed hair, who looks the world in the face and tells it to go hang, objects to being called a "flapper",' the *New York Times* reported. That word, the girls said, implied that they were 'light, frivolous, vain and empty-headed characters'. Instead, they wanted to be seen as 'up-to-date', as girls of 'progress, ambition and common sense': they wanted to be known as 'modern', and they enlisted Colleen Moore to head their campaign.[66] Although Moore was the paragon of the frivolous flapper image, she consented with enthusiasm.

The Camp Fire Girls were responding rather militantly to what many girls perceived as blatant hypocrisy about their identity and their destiny. Looking towards their future, many girls dreamed of taking a job, finding a small apartment and steering themselves into the future. Wage earners were adventuresome women in charge of their own destiny, these girls wanted to believe. But they were barraged with another overwhelming message – from parents, movies and magazines – which told them that they needed to become wives and mothers. From those sources, girls learned that wage earners, as the historian Joanne Meyerowitz found, were women adrift.[67] Loose and carefree they might be, but working women risked falling into disrepute. In scores of movies, they were presented, just as in the 1910s, as gold diggers, preying on men's vulnerabilities.[68] Women adrift would not find their mooring until they married.

Girls intent on pursuing a career were faced with hostility by returning soldiers who wanted to regain the jobs that they had given up to women; and those girls competed, too, with other girls less interested in professional credibility, girls 'with hair as short as the brains it covered' and who used the workplace as a setting for flirtations. Those 'silly children', remarks an aspiring bookkeeper in a short story published in 1928, 'helped men to form their estimates of women [that] chained the ambitious ones to typewriters and adding machines'.[69] Girls with no interest in home-making were warned, as they had been before, of the folly of rejecting the lives their mothers led. 'How, in striving for emancipation, woman has reached such a dismal stage in her development is one of the saddest stories of our time,' lamented the poet and essayist Edwin Muir. Freedom to work outside of the home, he insisted, was 'a slave's idea of freedom. Instead of equal joys they have asked for equal obligations.'[70] The American writer and activist Victoria McAlmon caught the worried spirit of her contemporaries when she remarked,

> I feel no need for more freedom, but I want a world in
> which the freedom I now have can be used. We women
> are free, but free for what? I move from disillusionment to
> fresh illusions . . . Are we, while I live, going to get courage
> and wisdom to match our freedom? I am hopeful that we
> shall, but I suspect that I shall be disappointed as usual.[71]

And yet, throughout the 1920s, the media portrayed the flapper flapping with joy and abandon, and she continued to seduce girls with her image of sexual allure and youth everlasting. When *Black Oxen* opened as a movie in 1923, with Clara Bow as the irreverent flapper daughter, Gertrude Atherton's fantasy reached an even wider audience than her book had. Dieting, surgery, constricting undergarments and cigarettes continued their popularity among women longing for the boyish look of an adolescent.

Mothers, just as they had in the 1910s, tried to imitate their daughters, in spite of warnings by influential arbiters of fashion, such as Anne Rittenhouse, fashion editor of the *New York Times* and columnist for McClure's newspapers and *Vogue*. 'It is the girl, and not the woman,' she wrote regretfully, 'who is the purveyor of the dominant fashions of this generation.'[72] In her fashion guide *The Well-dressed Woman*, published in 1924, she cautioned her contemporaries against looking like adolescents. 'The mistake of mistakes, the way of error, the path of peril', she warned,

> is for the stout, middle-aged woman to ape youth. Slim, supple women of fifty may do it, in moderation, without endangering their appearance or their dignity, but the woman with flesh – even if it's admirably distributed – the woman with ugly bumps and curves in her figure must look upon youthful fashions with pleasant memories, not with eager desire. Regrets but not participation should be her mental attitude.[73]

But looking like a boyish adolescent persisted as an object of desire for women, and those women, in the 1920s and long after, evaluated themselves with regret.

The flapper was publicized, promoted and exuberantly celebrated throughout the 1920s, until, it seemed, styles began to change. In the summer of 1929, fashion observers remarked that the flapper's day had ended. Designers had created a new cultural icon: the sophisticated siren, seductive and cosmopolitan. Her skirts were longer, her dresses more sumptuous than diaphanous, but the styles still required youthful slenderness. And slenderness required repression by one means or another. By the autumn of that year, economic turmoil swept the U.S., Britain and Europe, and popular culture diverted its attention from the flapper's fabulous, voluptuous, seemingly endless party.

Hall was right about adolescent girls' secrets, desires, womanliness and sexuality. F. Scott Fitzgerald's jaded rich girls; Ellen Welles Page's semi-flapper; 'modern' Camp Fire Girls; Margy the comic-strip character; and all the girls that Colleen Moore played with such verve, harboured those secrets.

In 1922, 41-year-old writer Alma Whitaker reminisced about her youth. She was thirteen when 'The Revolt of the Daughters' shocked magazine readers; nineteen as the twentieth century began; and 23 when Stanley Hall published his groundbreaking *Adolescence*, investigating the stage of life from which she had so recently emerged. She saw the flapper look advertised in newspaper advertisements, touted in shop window displays and marketed vigorously in free fashion books distributed by department stores. She watched fast-talking, comical flappers in the movies. But Whitaker knew well that the modern flapper was no different from what she herself had been as a girl. 'Even we old-style flappers had our yearnings,' she wrote.

> We weren't allowed to express it in clothes – but we would have if we had dared. Consequently we were more hypo-critical, we mentally behaved a good deal like the flapper of today, felt peculiarly sophisticated, and if the thought is as culpable as the deed, the modern flapper has nothing on us . . . The only difference between us and the modern flapper is that our elders knew precious little about us and took our clothes as circumstantial evidence of our

superior virtue, whereas the modern chit has gained the right of 'self-expression'.

Women of her generation, Whitaker said, might pretend to scorn modern flappers, but their attitude was less 'an indictment of the modern girl as rankling jealousy. So, even while we frown, we look over the styles and do our best to make up for lost time.' After all, she said, the modern flapper has 'recaptured so much of a youth-time we were shamefully denied'. As a child, Whitaker looked forward to growing up and replacing her little-girl outfits with more sophisticated clothing; she imagined she would have some independence, but she discovered, instead, that 'the shackles of youth were replaced by the shackles of voluminous clothing and elder decorum.' The flapper, she realized, has 'dared to blaze the trail for mama and auntie'.[74]

That trail was elusive and mythical, blazed through a landscape that seemed, at times, as chimerical as Peter Pan's Neverland. Yet nearly a century after the flapper allegedly rose, shimmering, from the ashes of war, this girl – just a girl trying to grow up – still inspires envy. We imagine her in a smoky nightclub, beads, like lightning, flashing on her slip of a dress; we can hear a saxophone wail softly as she dances, and she dances with sinuous grace: as if she were moving – elegantly, fearlessly, inevitably – into a new world.

References

Introduction

1 Fanny Butcher, 'Tabloid Book Review', *Chicago Daily Tribune* (26 September 1920), p. 9.

2 Ruth Prigozy, 'Fitzgerald's Flappers and Flapper Films of the Jazz Age', in *A Historical Guide to F. Scott Fitzgerald*, ed. Kirk Curnutt (New York, 2004), p. 136.

3 Mildred R. Cram, 'The Extreme Adolescence of America', *Vogue* (1 February 1917), p. 66.

4 *The Times* (London) (20 February 1908), p. 15.

5 *New York Times* (31 March 1912), p. x10.

6 Quoted in Sally Mitchell, *The New Girl: Girls' Culture in England, 1880–1915* (New York, 1985), pp. 182–3.

7 Bonwit Teller display advertisement, *New York Times* (26 March 1916), p. ps8.

8 'Girls' Guides to Love', *Washington Post* (11 February 1906), p. sm5.

9 '"Flapper Girl" of Ten Years Ago Now Extinct, Say Educators', *Washington Post* (27 August 1913), p. 5.

10 *New York Times* (17 December 1911), p. c4.

11 '"Flapper" Takes London', *Detroit Free Press* (23 February 1913), p. 11.

12 Editor's Diary, *North American Review*, CLXXXIII/604 (7 December 1906), p. 1213.

13 Jane H. Hunter, *How Young Ladies Became Girls: The Victorian Origins of American Girlhood* (New Haven, CT, 2002), p. 394.

1 Angelfish

1 Quoted in John Cooley, ed., *Mark Twain's Aquarium: The Samuel Clemens Angelfish Correspondence, 1905–1910* (Athens, GA, 1991), p. xvii.

2 Ibid., p. 8. Gertrude Natkin to Mark Clemens, 27 December 1905.

3 Ibid., p. 9. Clemens to Natkin, 28 December 1905.

4 Ibid., pp. 14, 15. Clemens to Natkin, 20 February 1906; Natkin to Clemens, 22 February 1906.

5 Mark Twain, 'Marjorie Fleming, the Wonder Child', in *Mark Twain: The Complete Essays*, ed. Charles Neider (Garden City, NY, 1963), pp. 455–61.

6 Cooley, *Mark Twain's Aquarium*, p. 15. Clemens to Natkin, 14 February 1906; Natkin to Clemens, 17 February 1906.

7 Cooley, *Mark Twain's Aquarium*, p. 25. Clemens to Natkin, 8 April 1906.

8 Cooley, *Mark Twain's Aquarium*, p. 95.

9 'The Aquarium, Issued by The Admiral', in Cooley, *Mark Twain's Aquarium*, p. 191.

10 Cooley, *Mark Twain's Aquarium*, pp. 102–3.

11 Ibid., pp. 107, 137, 138.

12 'Mark Twain on the Secrets of Youth', *Leader* (London) (19 June 1907), p. 1. *Mark Twain: The Complete Interviews*, ed. Gary Scharnhorst (Tuscaloosa, AL, 2006), p. 614.

13 'Twain Home with English Jokes at 30 Cents a World', *New York American* (23 July 1907), p. 5. *Mark Twain: The Complete Interviews*, p. 638.

14 'Mark Twain Recalls Happy Days in Frisco', *New York Evening World* (23 July 1907). *Mark Twain: The Complete Interviews*, p. 645.

15 Cooley, *Mark Twain's Aquarium*, p. 154. Clemens to Dorothy Quick, 12 May 1908.

16 Ibid., p. 88. Clemens to Frances Nunnally, 29 December 1907.

17 Italics in original. Ibid., pp. 274–5.

18 Quotations from *New York Sun* and *New York Times* (23 July 1907), n.p. *Mark Twain: The Complete Interviews*, p. 644.

19 Ida Tarbell, *The Ways of Woman* (New York, 1915), pp. 122–3.

20 G. Stanley Hall, *Life and Confessions of a Psychologist* [1923] (New York, 1977), p. 7.

21 Ibid., p. 131.

22 Ibid., p. 132.

23 Ibid., pp. 42, 28.

24 Ibid., p. 135.

25 Ibid.

26 Ibid., pp. 220–22.

27 Ibid., pp. 199, 203.

28 Ibid., p. 199.

29 Ibid., p. 143.

30 G. Stanley Hall to William James, 26 October 1879, in *Correspondence of William James*, vol. v, ed. Ignas K. Skrupskelis and Elizabeth M. Berkeley (Charlottesville, VA, 1997), p. 66.

31 Hall to James, 15 February 1880, ibid., p. 87.

32 Hall, *Life and Confessions*, p. 261.

33 Ibid., p. 294.

34 Ibid., p. 576.

35 Ibid., p. 588.

36 H. Austin Akins, *Granville Stanley Hall*, ed. Louis N. Wilson (Worcester, MA, 1925), p. 57.

37 Hall, *Life and Confessions*, pp. 578–9.

38 William James to George Croom Robertson, 9 November 1887. *Correspondence of William James*, vol. vi, ed. Ignas K. Skrupskelis and Elizabeth M. Berkeley (Charlottesville, VA, 1998), p. 288.

39 James to Hugo Munsterberg, 11 August 1893. *Correspondence of William James*, vol. vii, ed. Ignas K. Skrupskelis and Elizabeth M. Berkeley (Charlottesville, VA, 1999), p. 451.

40 Théodore Flournoy to James, 13 July 1904, in *The Letters of William James and Théodore Flournoy*, ed. Robert Le Clair (Madison, WI, 1966), p. 159.

41 'What Have They Done?', *Washington Post* (27 May 1904), p. 6.

42 G. Stanley Hall, *Adolescence: Its Psychology and its Relation to Physiology, Anthropology, Sociology, Crime, Religion and Education* (New York, 1904), vol. II, p. 624.

43 Ibid., p. 566.

44 Ibid., pp. 644, 640.

45 Ibid., p. 645.

46 Hall, 'The Budding Girl', *Appleton's Magazine*, 13 (1909), p. 47.

47 Eliza Lynn Linton, *The Girl of the Period and Other Social Essays* (London, 1883), vol. I, p. 2.

48 Quoted in Jane H. Hunter, *How Young Ladies Became Girls: The Victorian Origins of American Girlhood* (New Haven, CT, 2002), p. 291.

49 Tarbell, *The Ways of Woman*, p. 122.

2 Daughters Revolt

1 Edward Alsworth Ross, 'Discerns Causes of Race Suicide', *Chicago Daily Tribune* (5 August 1905), p. 4.

2 Ibid.

3 Ibid.

4 Eliza Lynn Linton, 'Modern Mothers', in *The Girl of the Period and Other Social Essays* (London, 1883), vol. I, pp. 10–11.

5 G. Stanley Hall, 'Coeducation and Race Suicide', *Washington Post* (4 July 1904), p. 6.

6 G. Stanley Hall, 'Attack on Co-education', *New York Times* (11 July 1903), p. 6.

7 Edward H. Clarke, *Sex in Education; or, A Fair Chance for the Girls* (Boston, MA, 1873), available at www.gutenberg.org.

8 'Decay of Motherhood', *Chicago Daily Tribune* (20 August 1886), p. 9.

9 G. Stanley Hall, *Adolescence: Its Psychology and its Relation to Physiology, Anthropology, Sociology, Sex, Crime, Religion and Education* (New York, 1904), vol. II, p. 579.

10 Ibid., p. 626.

11 Ibid., p. 627.

12 Ibid., p. 579.

13 Mary Putnam Jacobi, 'The Education of Girls', *New York Times* (21 November 1897), p. 18.

14 G. Stanley Hall, 'The Kind of Women Colleges Produce', *Appleton's*, xii/3 (September 1908), p. 313.

15 LeBaron Russell Briggs, 'Co-eds and Race Suicide', *Washington Post* (19 July 1904), p. 6.

16 'Susan B. Anthony', *Atlanta Constitution* (26 August 1900), p. b4.

17 Arabella Kenealy, *Feminism and Sex-extinction* (London, 1920), pp. 123, 124.

18 Mary Lowe Dickinson, 'Girlhood to Motherhood', *Washington Post* (4 April 1897), p. 24.

19 Hall, *Adolescence*, vol. ii, pp. 628–9.

20 Quoted in Evelleen Richards, 'Darwin and the Descent of Woman', in *The Wider Domain of Evolutionary Thought*, ed. David Oldroyd and Ian Langham (Dordrecht, 1983), p. 92.

21 Ibid., p. 85.

22 Havelock Ellis, *Man and Woman* (London, 1894), p. 395.

23 Ibid., p. 179.

24 Ibid., p. 395.

25 Ross, 'Discerns Causes of Race Suicide', p. 4.

26 Theodore Roosevelt, 'Motherhood the Duty of Woman', *New York Times* (14 March 1905), p. 1.

27 Robert Baden-Powell, *Scouting for Boys*, ed. Elleke Boehmer (Oxford, 2004), pp. 184, xii.

28 Ibid., pp. 351–2.

29 George Robb, 'Race Motherhood: Moral Eugenics vs Progressive Eugenics, 1880–1920', in *Maternal Instincts: Visions of Motherhood and Sexuality in Britain, 1875–1925*, ed. Claudia Nelson (Basingtoke, 1997), p. 58.

30 Francis Galton, 'Parents May Improve the Race', *Chicago Daily Tribune* (5 July 1908), p. g5.

31 Leonard Darwin, 'Eugenics and National Economy: An Appeal' (12 June 1913), p. 13.

32 *The Observer* (London) (16 May 1909), p. 5.

33 Quoted in Michael Rosenthal, *The Character Factory: Baden-Powell and the Origins of the Boy Scout Movement* (New York, 1986), p. 151.

34 'Lovemaking', *Boston Daily Globe* (2 September 1906), p. SM7.

35 Quoted in Richards, 'Darwin and the Descent of Woman', p. 91.

36 Kathleen Cuffe, 'A Reply from the Daughters', in *Nineteenth Century Opinion*, ed. Michael Goodwin (Harmondsworth, 1951), pp. 85–8.

37 Alys Pearsall-Smith, 'A Reply from the Daughters', in *Nineteenth Century Opinion*, ed. Goodwin, pp. 89–91.

38 *The Speaker*, vol. IX (3 March 1894), p. 244.

39 Ibid., p. 245.

40 'Editor's Diary', *North American Review*, CLXXXIII/604 (7 December 1906), p. 1213.

41 Briggs, 'Co-eds and Race Suicide', p. 6.

42 William James, 'The Moral Equivalent of War', in *The Writings of William James*, ed. John J. McDermott (Chicago, IL, 1977), p. 664.

43 Quoted in Jeffrey Hantover, 'The Boy Scouts and the Validation of Masculinity', in *The American Man*, ed. Elizabeth H. Pleck and Joseph H. Pleck (Englewood Cliffs, NJ, 1980), p. 293.

44 Baden-Powell, *Scouting for Boys*, p. 44.

45 Ibid., p. 312.

46 Ibid., p. 14.

47 Juliette Gordon Low, *How Girls Can Help their Country, Adapted from Agnes Baden-Powell and Sir Robert Baden Powell's Handbook* (Savannah, GA, 1916), p. 9.

48 Ibid., pp. 15–16.

49 Ibid., p. 16.

3 The Happy Boy

1 Lancelyn Green, *Fifty Years of Peter Pan* (London, 1954), p. 126.

2 Bruce K. Hanson, *The Peter Pan Chronicles* (New York, 1993), pp. 55–6.

3 J. M. Barrie to Maude Adams, 18 April 1904. Quoted in Hanson, *Peter Pan Chronicles*, p. 53.

4 Ibid., p. 159.

5 *New York Times* (7 November 1905), p. 9.

6 *New York Daily Tribune* (18 January 1908), quoted in Armond Fields, *Maude Adams: Idol of American Theater, 1872–1953* (Jefferson, NC, 2004), p. 208.

7 Ibid., p. 209.

8 Ibid., p. 273.

9 Ibid., p. 214.

10 Elleke Boehmer, Introduction to Robert Baden-Powell, *Scouting for Boys* (Oxford, 2004), p. xxxii.

11 Quoted in Michael Rosenthal, *The Character Factory: Baden-Powell and the Origins of the Boy Scout Movement* (New York, 1986), pp. 16–17.

12 Mark Twain, *Mark Twain: The Complete Interviews,* ed. Gary Scharnhorst (Tuscaloosa, AL, 2006), p. 528.

13 J. M. Barrie, *Peter Pan and Other Plays*, ed. Peter Hollindale (Oxford, 1995), pp. 87–8.

14 Claudia Nelson, *Invisible Men: Fatherhood in Victorian Periodicals, 1850–1910* (Athens, GA, 1995), p. 205.

15 Ibid., p. 90.

16 Ibid., p. 89.

17 Ibid., p. 107.

18 Ibid., p. 116.

19 Ibid., p. 130.

20 R.D.S. Jack, 'The Manuscript of Peter Pan', *Children's Literature*, XVIII (1990), p. 107.

21 Barrie, *Peter Pan and Other Plays*, p. 132.

22 Ibid., p. 145.

23 Jack, 'The Manuscript of Peter Pan', p. 103.

24 Barrie, *Peter Pan and Other Plays*, p. 151.

25 'Woman's View of "Peter Pan"', *Washington Post* (23 October 1905), p. 9.

26 Andrew Birkin, *J. M. Barrie and the Lost Boys* (London, 1979), p. 95.

27 J. M. Barrie to Arthur Quiller-Couch, 25 July 1909, in Viola Meynell, ed., *Letters of J. M. Barrie* (New York, 1947), p. 21.

28 Birkin, *J. M. Barrie and the Lost Boys*, p. 43.

29 Ibid., p. 10.

30 Piers Dudgeon, *Captivated: J. M. Barrie, the du Mauriers and the Dark Side of Neverland* (London, 2008), p. 63.

31 Birkin, *J. M. Barrie and the Lost Boys*, p. 22.

32 Ibid., pp. 28, 29.

33 Dudgeon, *Captivated*, p. 167.

34 Ibid., p. 161.

35 Ibid.

36 Birkin, *J. M. Barrie and the Lost Boys*, p. 122.

37 Ibid., p. 95.

38 Dudgeon, *Captivated*, p. 18.

39 Birkin, *J. M. Barrie and the Lost Boys*, p. 130.

40 Ibid., p. 195.

41 Peter Davies, quoted ibid., p. 235.

42 Yvonne Blue, quoted in Joan Jacobs Brumberg, *The Body Project: An Intimate History of American Girls* (New York, 1997), pp. 100–101.

43 Daphne du Maurier to Ellen Doubleday, 10 December 1947. Quoted in Margaret Foster, *Daphne du Maurier* (London, 1993), p. 221.

44 Ibid., p. 13.

45 Daphne du Maurier, *Myself When Young* (Garden City, NY, 1977), pp. 55–7.

46 Angela Brazil, *The Terrible Tomboy* (1905, Gutenberg ebook), p. 10.

47 Ibid.

48 Ibid., p. 11.

49 Ibid., p. 284.

50 Lucy Rollin, *Twentieth Century Teen Culture by the Decades* (Westport, CT, 1999), p. 27.

51 Susan Coolidge, *What Katy Did* [1872] (London, 1918), p. 17.

52 Laura Lee Hope, *The Outdoor Girls of Deepdale* (New York, 1913), p. 21.

53 Ibid., p. 156.

54 Ibid., p. 160.

55 Frances Willard quoted in Sarah Wintle, 'Horses, Bikes and Automobiles: New Woman on the Move', in *The New Woman in Fiction and in Fact: Fin de siècle Feminisms*, ed. Angelique Richardson (New York, 2001), pp. 71–2.

56 Sally Mitchell, *The New Girl: Girls' Culture in England, 1880–1915* (New York, 1985), p. 131.

4 Private Lives

1 Sarah Grand, 'The Modern Girl' [1894], in *Sex, Social Purity, and Sarah Grand*, ed. Ann Heilman and Stephanie Forward, vol. 1: *Journalistic Writings and Contemporary Reception* (London, 2000), p. 37.

2 Ibid., p. 43.

3 William Arch McKeever, *Training the Girl* (New York, 1913), p. 160.

4 Ida Tarbell, *The Ways of Woman* (New York, 1915), pp. 12–13.

5 Clelia Duel Mosher, *The Mosher Survey: Sexual Attitudes of 45 Victorian Women*, ed. James MaHood and Kristine Wenburg (New York, 1980), p. 123.

6 Ibid., p. 426.

7 Ibid., pp. 225–6.

8 Alice B. Stockham, *Tokology: A Book for Every Woman* (Boston, MA, 1886), p. 162.

9 Ibid., p. 161.

10 Ibid., p. 162.

11 Mosher, *The Mosher Survey*, p. 139.

12 Ibid., p. 340.

13 Alice B. Stockham, *Creative Life: A Special Letter to Young Girls* (Chicago, IL, 1904), p. 30.

14 Ibid., p. 27.

15 Isabelle Thompson Smart, *What a Mother Should Tell Her Daughter*, Book Two (New York, 1911), p. 17.

16 Ibid., p. 33.

17 Ibid., pp. 45, 48.

18 Ibid., pp. 77–8.

19 John Cowan, *The Science of a New Life* (New York, 1869), p. 354.

20 Ibid.

21 Ibid., p. 53.

22 Ibid., pp. 380–82.

23 McKeever, *Training the Girl*, pp. 165, 163.

24 Ibid., p. 105.

25 Beverley Ellison Warner, *The Young Woman in Modern Life* (New York, 1903), p. 6.

26 Ibid., p. 7.

27 Ibid.

28 Ibid., pp. 24–5.

29 Ibid., p. 89.

30 Gertrude Hemery, 'Revolt of the Daughters', *Westminster Review*, CLXI (June 1894), pp. 680–81.

31 Sarah Grand, 'On Clubs and the Question of Intelligence', *Women at Home* (September 1900); Heilman and Forward, eds, *Sex, Social Purity, and Sarah Grand*, p. 97.

32 *The Times* (London) (25 October 1894), p. 14.

33 Sidney Grundy, 'The New Woman', in *The New Woman and Other Emancipated Woman Plays*, ed. Jean Chothia (Oxford, 1998), p. 5.

34 Ibid.

35 Ibid., p. 7.

36 Ibid., p. 17.

37 'Public Opinion is a Thing Difficult to Gauge With', *The Times* (London) (12 December 1894), p. 9.

38 Grand, 'The Modern Girl', p. 46.

39 Sarah Grand, 'The Man of the Moment', *North American Review* [1894], in Heilman and Forward, eds, *Sex, Social Purity, and Sarah Grand*, pp. 55–6.

40 Sarah Grand, 'The New Aspect of the Woman Question', *North American Review* [1894], in Heilman and Forward, eds, *Sex, Social Purity, and Sarah Grand*, p. 29.

41 Grand, 'The Man of the Moment', p. 51.

42 George Egerton, *A Leaf from the Yellow Book: The Correspondence of George Egerton*, ed. Terence De Vere White (London, 1958), p. 19.

43 Thomas Gill to Egerton, *c.* 1893, ibid., p. 26.

44 George Egerton to John J. Dunne, 15 March 1891, ibid., p. 11.

45 'George Egerton's Identity', *San Francisco Chronicle* (17 June 1894), p. 9.

46 George Egerton, 'A Cross Line' [1893], in *Daughters of Decadence: Women Writers of the Fin-de-siècle*, ed. Elaine Showalter (New Brunswick, NJ, 1993), pp. 58, 59.

47 Ibid., p. 57.

48 Ibid., pp. 62, 63.

49 George Egerton, 'Virgin Soil' [1894], in *Women Who Did: Stories by Men and Women, 1890–1914*, ed. Angelique Richardson (London, 2002), pp. 109–11.

50 Peter Morton, 'Grant Allen: A Biographical Essay', in *Grant Allen: Literature and Cultural Politics at the Fin de Siècle*, ed. William Greenslade and Terence Rodgers (Burlington, VT, 2005), p. 38.

51 Jeanette Gilder, 'A Loathsome Story', *Chicago Daily Tribune* (17 February 1895), p. 34.

52 Grant Allen, *The Woman Who Did* [1895] (Oxford, 1995), p. 56.

53 Ibid.

54 Ibid., pp. 57–8.

55 Chris Willis, '"Heaven Defend Me from Political or Highly-educated Women!" Packaging the New Woman for Mass Consumption', in *The New Woman in Fiction and in Fact: Fin de Siècle Feminisms*, ed. Angelique Richardson (New York, 2001), p. 55.

56 Ibid., p. 124.

57 'Grant Allen's Plain Talks', *San Francisco Chronicle* (27 March 1895), p. 12.

58 Grant Allen, *Miss Cayley's Adventures* (London, 1899), p. 140.

59 Mona Caird, 'The Yellow Drawing Room' [1892], in *Women Who Did: Stories by Men and Women, 1890–1914*, ed. Angelique Richardson (London, 2002), p. 22.

60 Ibid., p. 23.

61 Ibid., p. 26.

62 Ibid., p. 27.

63 Ibid., pp. 28–9.

64 Elisabeth Marbury, *My Crystal Ball* (New York, 1924), p. 151.

65 Ibid., p. 153.

5 Bodies in Motion

1 'The Nation-wide Wave of Moving Pictures', *New York Times* (3 January 1909), p. SM10.

2 Shelley Stamp, *Movie-struck Girls: Women and Motion Picture Culture After the Nickelodeon* (Princeton, NJ, 2000), pp. 125–30.

3 *Billboard* (27 June 1914), p. 15.

4 'The Adventures of Mary Fuller', *The Picturegoer* (1 November 1913), p. 98.

5 Eileen Bowser, *The Transformation of Cinema, 1907–1915* (New York, 1990), p. 126.

6 Stamp, *Movie-struck Girls*, p. 30.

7 Audrey Field, *Picture Palace* (London, 1974), pp. 46–7.

8 William Inglis, 'Morals and Moving Pictures', *Harper's Weekly*, LIV (30 July 1910), p. 12.

9 'Two-sided Attack on Picture Shows', *Chicago Daily Tribune* (3 December 1911), p. 1.

10 'End of Mrs Pankhurst's American Tour', *The Times* (London) (27 November 1913), p. 7.

11 'Virtue Not Dependent on Pay of Girls', *Atlanta Constitution* (23 April 1913), p. 11.

12 Howard A. Kelly, 'Calls White Slavery Worst Social Evil', *New York Tribune* (28 September 1912), p. 9.

13 'Nothing New in White Slavery', *Detroit Free Press* (27 December 1909), p. 7.

14 Ibid., p. 13.

15 Field, *Picture Palace*, p. 83.

16 Ellis P. Oberholtzer, 'What are the "Movies" Making of Our Children?', *World's Work*, XLI (January 1921), p. 254.

17 'Film Stars Tango and Gossip with 10,000 Happy Fans', *Chicago Daily Tribune* (15 May 1914), p. 1.

18 'Picture Personalities', *Pictures and the Picturegoer* (8 August 1914), p. 549.

19 'Mary Pickford', *The Billboard* (24 December 1910), p. 11.

20 'The Adventures of Mary Fuller', p. 98.

21 Grace Kingsley, 'How Famous Film Stars Have Been Discovered', *Los Angeles Times* (18 October 1914), p. 112.

22 Gertrude Price, 'Sees the Movies as Great, New Field for Women Folk', *Toledo News-Bee* (30 March 1914), p. 14. Excerpted in Richard Abel, *Americanizing the Movies and 'Movie Mad' Audiences, 1910–1914* (Berkeley, CA, 2005), pp. 255–6.

23 'Women Oppose Film O.K. on "Twilight Sleep"', *Chicago Daily Tribune* (4 April 1915), p. 12.

24 Bowser, *The Transformation of Cinema, 1907–1915*, p. 51.

25 'Tango and Turkey Trot', *Detroit Free Press* (19 October 1913), p. B4.

26 'Paris Has a New Dance', *New York Times* (15 January 1911), p. C3.

27 'Run Dance Hall Under City Rule', *Chicago Daily Tribune* (3 December 1911), p. 1.

28 'Mayor Won't Bar Proper Tea Dances', *New York Times* (8 April 1913), p. 22.

29 'Great Tea Dancing Boom Stirs Mayor', *New-York Tribune* (4 April 1913), p. 1.

30 F. Scott Fitzgerald, Appendix I, *Flappers and Philosophers* [1920], ed. James L. W. West III (Cambridge, 2000), p. 389.

31 Garland Smith, 'The Unpardonable Sin', in *These Modern Women: Autobiographical Essays From the Twenties*, ed. Elaine Showalter (New York, 1989), p. 118.

32 Rheta Childe Dorr, *What Eight Million Women Want* (Boston, MA, 1910), pp. 209–10.

33 Mark Knowles, *The Wicked Waltz and Other Scandalous Dances* (Jefferson, NC, 2009), p. 128.

34 Mary Grace, 'Turkey Trot Our National Dance', *Detroit Free Press* (14 September 1913), p. G7.

35 'Her Diary – The Day-to-day Story of a Modern Girl. Number II: The Hour of Thrills', *Ladies Home Journal* (November 1915), p. 17.

36 'Her Diary – The Day-to-day Story of a Modern Girl, Number I: The Hour of Her Debut', *Ladies Home Journal* (October, 1915), p. 10.

37 'Turkey Trot a la Mode Shown at Delmonico's', *New-York Tribune* (27 January 1912), p. 14.

38 Knowles, *The Wicked Waltz and Other Scandalous Dances*, p. 80.

39 Vernon and Irene Castle, *Modern Dancing*, intro. Elisabeth Marbury (New York, 1914), pp. 25–6.

40 'Miss Morgan Defies Uplifters', *New-York Tribune* (29 May 1915), p. 16.

41 Gladys Crozier quoted in Jo Baim, *The Tango: Creation of a Cultural Icon* (Bloomington, IN, 2007), p. 67.

42 Ibid., p. 68.

43 Ibid., p. 69.

44 Elisabeth Marbury, *My Crystal Ball* (New York, 1924), p. 248.

45 Ibid., p. 242.

46 Eve Golden, *Vernon and Irene Castle's Ragtime Revolution* (Lexington, KY, 2007), p. 45.

47 Marbury, *My Crystal Ball*, p. 244.

48 Ibid.

49 Seldes quoted in Golden, *Vernon and Irene Castle's Ragtime Revolution*, p. 87.

50 Elsie Janis, *So Far, So Good* (New York, 1932), p. 109.

51 Marbury, *My Crystal Ball*, p. 245.

52 Hariette Underhill, 'The Fetching Mrs Castle', *New-York Tribune* (3 December 1916), p. C4.

53 Irene Castle, *Castles in the Air* (Garden City, NY, 1958), p. 27.

54 Ibid., p. 117.

55 Ibid., p. 115.

56 Cecil Beaton quoted from *The Book of Beauty*, ibid., p. 117.

57 'Wilson Banned Ball Fearing Turkey Trot', *New York Times* (21 January 1913), p. 3.

58 'Mrs Taft Dances Turkey Trot at Final Reception in White House', *Detroit Free Press* (5 February 1913), p. 1.

59 'Tango and Turkey Trot', *Detroit Free Press* (9 October 1913), p. 4.

60 Castle, *Castles in the Air*, p. 85.

61 Vernon and Irene Castle, *Modern Dancing* (New York, 1914), p. 17.

62 Knowles, *The Wicked Waltz and Other Scandalous Dances*, pp. 99–100, 129.

63 Elizabeth Marbury, Introduction to Castle and Castle, *Modern Dancing*, p. 20.

64 Castle, *Castles in the Air*, p. 87.

6 A Culture of Their Own

1 'The Modern Girl', *Washington Post* (26 May 1914), p. 6.

2 'A Modern Girl', *The Billboard* (29 November 1913), p. 36.

3 'Risk of Modern Girls', *Washington Post* (18 September 1914), p. 4.

4 'The Modern Girl – She is Athletic, Alert and Businesslike', *San Francisco Chronicle* (12 October 1913), p. 9.

5 'Risk of Modern Girls', p. 4.

6 Anita Loos, *A Girl Like I* (New York, 1966), p. 31.

7 Ned McIntosh, '"Blindness of Virtue": Prose Play of Absorbing Interest', *Atlanta Constitution* (10 January 1914), p. 2.

8 Waldemar Young, 'Sex Propaganda in Play at Cort', *San Francisco Chronicle* (16 December 1913), p. 20.

9 Agnes Repplier, 'The Repeal of Reticence', *Atlantic Monthly*, XIII (March 1914), p. 303.

10 Florence B. Low, 'The Reading of the Modern Girl', *The Nineteenth Century and After*, LIX (1906), pp. 278–87.

11 H. L. Mencken, 'The Flapper', in *The American New Woman Revisited: A Reader, 1894–1930*, ed. Martha H. Patterson (New Brunswick, NJ, 2008), pp. 85–6.

12 Letter from 'Tango', 'Introduction at Dances', *The Times* (London) (20 May 1914), p. 9.

13 An American Girl in Germany, 'Idol of Flappers is German Crown Prince', *Boston Daily Globe* (3 January 1915), p. 51.

14 'Sex O'Clock in America', *Current Opinion*, LV (August 1913), pp. 113–14.

15 'Writers Turn Out to Book Trial', *New York Times* (7 February 1914), p. 9.

16 Jeannette Gilder, 'Elinor Glyn Outdoes Herself in the Line of Audacious Fiction', *Chicago Daily Tribune* (14 September 1907), p. 9.

17 Elinor Glyn, *Romantic Adventure* (London, 1936), p. 146.

18 Ibid., pp. 68–9.

19 Juliet Wilbor Tompkins, 'Shelter', *Good Housekeeping*, LXII/6 (June 1916). Maureen Honey, ed., *Breaking the Ties that Bind: Popular Stories of the New Woman, 1915–1930* (Norman, OK, 1992), pp. 68, 61.

20 Ibid., p. 69.

21 Ibid., p. 68.

22 'Laura Jean Libbey Talks Heart Topics', *Los Angeles Times* (3 October 1914), section II, p. 6.

23 'Laura Jean Libbey's Daily Heart Talks', *Los Angeles Times* (17 November 1913), section II, p. 7.

24 'Laura Jean Libbey Talks Heart Topics', *Los Angeles Times* (11 January 1914), section III, p. 23.

25 'Laura Jean Libbey's Heart Topics Talk', *Los Angeles Times* (3 December 1913), section II, p. 3.

26 Ibid.

27 'The New Woman', *Good Housekeeping*, XL/6 (June 1905), p. 700.

28 'An Open Letter to the American Girl Who Was Born Between January 1, 1892 and January 1, 1899', *Ladies Home Journal*, XXVII/10 (1 September 1910), pp. 5–6.

29 Helen Dare, 'Well! What Do You Think of This?', *San Francisco Chronicle* (5 May 1915), p. 7.

30 'The Flapper's Side of It', *New York Times Book Review* (26 March 1922), p. 51.

31 'Wanted, 35,000 "Daddy-Long-Legs"', *New-York Tribune* (9 November 1914), p. 7.

32 Rheta Childe Dorr, *What Eight Million Women Want* (Boston, MA, 1910), pp. 4–5.

33 Ibid., p. 23.

7 Votes for Flappers

1 'The Solitary Flapper', *The Observer* (London) (14 November 1909), p. 10.

2 Emmeline Pankhurst, *Suffragette: My Own Story* [1914] (London, 2015), p. 27.

3 Emmeline Pankhurst, 'Why We Are Militant', in *Suffrage and the Pankhursts*, ed. Jane Marcus (London, 2001), p. 155.

4 Ibid., p. 109.

5 Pankhurst, *Suffragette*, p. 36.

6 Emmeline Pethick-Lawrence, 'My Part in a Changing World', in *Voices and Votes: A Literary Anthology of the Women's Suffrage Campaign,* ed. Glenda Norquay (Manchester, 1995), p. 63.

7 Ibid., p. 257.

8 Ibid., p. 51.

9 Gertude Colmore, *Suffragettes: A Story of Three Women* [*Suffragette Sally*, 1911] (London, 1984), p. 29.

10 'The Outragettes', WSPU Leaflet, 1913, in *Suffrage and the Pankhursts*, ed. Marcus, p. 185.

11 Elizabeth Robins, 'Votes for Women!' [1907], in *The New Woman and Other Emancipated Woman Plays*, ed. Jean Chothia (New York, 1998), p. 173.

12 Pankhurst, 'Why We Are Militant', p. 160.

13 Emmeline Pankhurst, 'Why We Oppose the Liberal Government' [1908–9], in *Suffrage and the Pankhursts*, ed. Jane Marcus (London, 2001), p. 169.

14 Pankhurst, 'Why We Are Militant', p. 160.

15 Rheta Childe Dorr, *What Eight Million Women Want* (Boston, MA, 1910), p. 307; also, Pankhurst, *Suffragette*, p. 191.

16 Christabel Pankhurst, 'The Commons Debate on Woman Suffrage' [1908], ibid., p. 22.

17 Dorr, *What Eight Million Women Want*, p. 306.

18 Colmore, *Suffragettes*, p. 142.

19 Ibid., p. 143.

20 Evelyn Sharp, *Unfinished Adventure* [1933] (London, 2009), p. 52.

21 Henry James, *The Portrait of a Lady* [1880, revised 1908] (New York, 1995), p. 64.

22 Sharp, *Unfinished Adventure*, pp. 53–4.

23 Ibid., p. 56.

24 Ibid., p. 129.

25 Ibid., p. 133.

26 Evelyn Sharp, 'Filling the War Chest', in *Rebel Women* (London, 1910), p. 44.

27 Katherine Roberts, *Pages from the Diary of a Militant Suffragette* (Letchworth, 1910), p. 3.

28 Ibid., p. 41.

29 Ibid., p. 107.

30 Quoted in Lyndsey Jenkins, *Lady Constance Lytton* (London, 2015), p. 74.

31 Lady Constance Lytton, *Prisons and Prisoners* (London, 1914), pp. 13–14.

32 Quoted in Jenkins, *Lady Constance Lytton*, p. 104.

33 Lytton, *Prisons and Prisoners*, p. 238.

34 Margaret Haig, *This Was My World*, quoted in *Voices and Votes: A Literary Anthology of the Women's Suffrage Campaign*, ed. Glenda Norquay (Manchester, 1995), p. 257.

35 Pankhurst, *Suffragette*, p. 150.

36 'Tube Fed Girl Tells Woes', *Chicago Daily Tribune* (6 February 1910), p. 5.

37 Elinor Glyn, *Romantic Adventure* (London, 1936), p. 150.

38 Dorr, *What Eight Million Women Want*, p. 307.

39 Ibid., p. 302.

40 Ibid., p. 293.

41 Ibid., p. 297.

42 Pankhurst, 'Why We Are Militant', p. 162.

43 Rheta Childe Dorr, *A Woman of Fifty* (New York, 1924), p. 5.

44 Ibid., pp. 53, 55.

45 Ibid., p. 159.

46 'Votes for Husband', *Los Angeles Times* (14 March 1910), p. 11.

47 'No Vote, No Husband', *Atlanta Constitution* (2 August 1909), p. 9.

48 'Would Bribe with Kisses', *Los Angeles Times* (20 February 1910), p. 13.

49 'Won't Kiss to Get Votes', *New York Times* (21 February 1910), p. 2.

50 'Insulted at Albany, Girl Delegate Says', *New York Times* (10 March 1910), p. 1.

51 Florence Flynn, '"Attract and Allure", Cries the Suffragette', *New-York Tribune* (30 April 1911), p. C7.

52 Dorr, *Woman of Fifty*, p. 446.

53 Margaret Deland, 'The New Woman Who Would Do Things', *Ladies Home Journal*, XXIV/10 (September 1907), p. 17.

54 Margaret Deland, *The Rising Tide* (New York, 1916), p. 66.

55 Ibid., pp. 28, 64.

56 Ibid., p. 50.

57 Ibid., p. 31.

58 Deland, 'The New Woman', p. 17.

59 Deland, *The Rising Tide*, p. 203.

60 Ibid., pp. 238–9.

61 Ibid., pp. 14, 130.

62 Annie Nathan Meyer, Letter to the Editor, *New Republic* (1 December 1917), pp. 124–5.

63 Margaret Deland, 'The Change in the Feminine Ideal', *Atlantic Monthly*, CV/3 (March 1910), p. 290.

64 Ibid., p. 293.

65 Ibid., pp. 293–4.

66 Ibid., p. 296.

67 Shelley Stamp, *Movie-struck Girls: Women and Motion Picture Culture After the Nickelodeon* (Princeton, NJ, 2000), p. 157.

68 Elizabeth Robins, 'Votes for Women!' [1907], in *The New Woman and Other Emancipated Woman Plays*, ed. Jean Clothia (New York, 1988), pp. 164–5.

69 Ibid., p. 185.

8 The Age of the Girl

1 Henry Handel Richardson, *The Getting of Wisdom* [1910] (London, 1981), pp. 111–12.

2 Ibid., p. 130.

3 Ibid., pp. 75–6.

4 *Appleton's Magazine*, XII/3 (September 1908), pp. 258–9.

5 George Egerton, 'Nocturne', in *Women Who Did: Stories by Men and Women, 1890–1914*, ed. Angelique Richardson (London, 2002), p. 190.

6 J.O.B. Bland, 'The Youthfulness of Middle Age', *Chicago Daily Tribune* (21 June 1914), p. A3.

7 Nell Brinkley cited in James McGovern, 'The American Woman's Pre-world War I Freedom in Manners and Morals', *Journal of American History*, LV/2 (September 1968), p. 323.

8 Elisabeth Marbury, *My Crystal Ball* (New York, 1924), p. 177.

9 Kathy Lee Peiss, *Hope in a Jar* (New York, 1998), p. 97.

10 'Maison de Beauté Valaze', *The Times* (London) (6 July 1909), p. 12.

11 'Discover That Girls Paint', *New York Times* (22 May 1912), p. 21.

12 Nixola Greeley-Smith, 'Grandma and Flapper Dress Alike', *Washington Post* (19 November 1916), p. ES16.

13 'Cosmetics Triumphant in Debate on Beauty', *New-York Tribune* (11 December 1913), p. 6.

14 'Man's Refusal to Marry?', *New York Times* (5 August 1912), p. 8.

15 F. Scott Fitzgerald, 'Bernice Bobs Her Hair', in *Flappers and Philosophers* (New York, 1921), p. 163.

16 Ibid., p. 173.

17 Ibid., p. 156.

18 Warren Susman, '"Personality" and the Making of Twentieth Century Culture', in *Culture as History: The Transformation of American Society in the Twentieth Century* (New York, 1973), pp. 278–9.

19 Ibid., p. 280.

20 'Women to Slouch Around', *New-York Tribune* (12 July 1913), p. 8.

21 'The Failure of Fashion', *The Times* (London) (29 March 1913), p. 9.

22 Alma Whitaker, 'Slit Skirts and Legs', *Los Angeles Times* (1 August 1913), p. 116.

23 'Defense of Women's Dress', *Detroit Free Press* (17 August 1913), p. B3.

24 Georges Doeuillet, 'When All the World Looks Young', *Delineator* (August 1913), p. 20.

25 'Mental Aid for the Stout Supplants Tedious Dieting', *Washington Post* (18 June 1911), p. D8.

26 'Dieting, Swaying, Hopping to Make Over the Hip Line', *Washington Post* (4 December 1910), p. MS8.

27 'Looks Spoiled by Dieting', *Washington Post* (20 February 1910), p. MT4.

28 Hillel Schwartz, *Never Satisfied: A Cultural History of Fantasy and Fat* (New York, 1985), p. 181.

29 'Corsets are Longer', *Chicago Daily Tribune* (10 March 1909), p. 5.

30 *Vogue* (15 May 1923), p. 120.

31 Annette Donnelly, 'The Corseted Figure Back', *Chicago Daily Tribune* (15 October 1922), p. C6.

32 Paul Poiret cited in Genevieve Forbes, 'Are Women Slaves to Corsets?', *Chicago Daily Tribune* (8 June 1921), p. 21.

33 Jules-Bois quoted in Greeley-Smith, 'Grandma and Flapper Dress Alike', p. ES16.

34 Quoted in Rae Beth Gordon, *Dances with Darwin, 1875–1910: Vernacular Modernity in France* (Aldershot, 2009), p. 56.

35 Barbara Craydon, 'Who Wants to be Beautiful?', *San Francisco Chronicle* (8 August 1920), p. SM3.

36 Charles Willi and Charles Conrad Miller quoted in 'Cosmetic Surgery', *New York Times* (12 December 1920), p. x6.

37 Sander L. Gilman, *Making the Body Beautiful: A Cultural History of Aesthetic Surgery* (Princeton, NJ, 1999), p. 313.

38 Gertrude Atherton, *Adventures of a Novelist* (New York, 1932), p. 34.

39 Ibid., pp. 558–9.

40 Gertrude Atherton, *Black Oxen* [1923] (Buffalo, NY, 2012), p. 42.

41 Ibid., p. 73.

42 Ibid., p. 76.

43 Ibid., p. 221.

44 Ibid., p. 122.

45 Ibid., p. 124.

46 Ibid., p. 99.

47 Ibid., p. 252.

48 Ibid., pp. 315, 317.

49 Ibid., p. 305.

50 Atherton, *Adventures*, p. 560.

51 Ibid., p. 562.

52 Elsie Janis, *So Far, So Good* (New York, 1932), pp. 116, 128–9.

53 Matthew J. Bruccoli and Jackson R. Bryer, eds, *F. Scott Fitzgerald in His Own Time: A Miscellany* (Kent, OH, 1971), pp. 210, 208.

54 Ibid., p. 278.

55 A recording of Elsie Janis performing this song is available at www.youtube.com, accessed 25 September 2016.

9 The Flapper Paramount

1 F. Scott Fitzgerald, *This Side of Paradise* [1920] (New York, 2006), pp. 61–2.

2 Ibid., p. 171.

3 F. Scott Fitzgerald, 'Echoes of the Jazz Age', *Scribner's* (November 1931), p. 460.

4 William A. Drake, 'Books Abroad', *New York Herald* (16 November 1924), p. G7.

5 Mary Louise Roberts, *Civilization Without Sexes* (Chicago, IL, 1994), p. 62.

6 Corinne Lowe, 'We Never Cry "Peace" to the Two Piece Costume', *Chicago Daily Tribune* (29 October 1924), p. 23.

7 Advertisement, *Washington Post* (24 August 1924), p. PS4.

8 Roberts, *Civilization Without Sexes*, p. 84.

9 Valerie Mendes and Amy de la Haye, *Fashion Since 1900*, 2nd edn (London, 2010), p. 58.

10 E. M. Hull, *The Sheik* (Boston, MA, 1921), p. 2.

11 Ibid., p. 3.

12 Ibid., p. 11.

13 Ibid., p. 15.

14 Ibid., pp. 56–7.

15 Ibid., p. 58.

16 Ibid., pp. 78, 113.

17 Ibid., p. 133.

18 Ibid.

19 Ibid., p. 166.

20 Patricia Raub, 'A New Woman or An Old-fashioned Girl? The Portrayal of the Heroine in Popular Women's Novels of the Twenties', *American Studies*, XXXV/1 (Spring 1994), p. 112.

21 Ellen Welles Page, 'A Flapper's Appeal to Parents', *Outlook*, 132 (6 December 1922), p. 607.

22 G. Stanley Hall, 'Flapper Americana Novissima', *Atlantic Monthly*, 129 (June 1922), pp. 771–80.

23 Arabella Kenealy, *Feminism and Sex-extinction* (London, 1920), p. 84.

24 Ibid., p. 86.

25 Ibid., p. 85.

26 R. Heylbut Wollstein, 'Girls – As Seen By Edna Ferber', *New York Times* (11 May 1924), p. SM12.

27 Fitzgerald, *This Side of Paradise*, p. 168.

28 Fitzgerald, 'Echoes of the Jazz Age', p. 460.

29 Ibid., p. 465.

30 'Exit the Flapper Via Longer Skirts', *New York Times* (25 June 1922), p. E2.

31 'Oh, Margy', www.barnaclepress.com, accessed 6 April 2017.

32 Ibid.

33 Lucy Bland, *Modern Women on Trial: Sexual Transgression in the Age of the Flapper* (Oxford, 2013), p. 56.

34 Elizabeth Robins, 'Votes for Women!' [1907], in *The New Woman and Other Emancipated Woman Plays*, ed. Jean Chothia (New York, 1998), p. 173.

35 'Flapper Fanny Says', BANC PIC 2007.005-fALB, Bancroft Library, University of California, Berkeley.

36 Anita Loos, *A Girl Like I* (New York, 1966), p. 203.

37 Ibid., p. 118.

38 'Melody Mart', *The Billboard* (11 March 1922), p. 36.

39 Paula Fass, *The Damned and the Beautiful: American Youth in the 1920s* (New York, 1977), p. 262.

40 David Stenn, *Clara Bow: Runnin' Wild* (New York, 2000), p. 24.

41 Ibid., p. 29.

42 Ibid., p. 48.

43 Ibid., p. 52.

44 'Wet and Dry Talk Heard in 1791', *New York Times* (13 February 1927), p. XX5.

45 Stenn, *Clara Bow*, p. 55.

46 Fitzgerald quoted in Margaret Reid, 'Has the Flapper Changed?', *Motion Picture Magazine* (July 1927), www.21centuryflapper.com.

47 Stenn, *Clara Bow*, p. 105.

48 Grace Kingsley, 'New Jazz Picture', *Los Angeles Times* (6 March 1926), p. A7.

49 Stenn, *Clara Bow*, pp. 86–7.

50 Frank Vreeland, 'On the Screen', *New York Herald* (23 June 1924), p. 10.

51 Quoted in Kristine Somerville, 'Enemy of Men: The Vamps, Ice Princesses and Flappers of the Silent Screen', *Missouri Review*, XXXVII/2 (2014), p. 93.

52 Ibid., pp. 93, 91.

53 'Colleen Moore Hit in Flaming Youth', *Washington Post* (7 January 1924), p. 6.

54 Harriette Underhill, 'On the Screen', *New-York Tribune* (26 November 1923), p. 10.

55 June Rose, *Marie Stopes and the Sexual Revolution* (London, 1992), p. 112.

56 Ibid., p. 63.

57 Marie Stopes, *Married Love* (London, 1918), p. xiii.

58 Ibid., pp. xii, 9.

59 Rose, *Marie Stopes and the Sexual Revolution*, p. 113.

60 Ibid., pp. 111–12.

61 Ibid., p. 186.

62 Ibid., p. 134.

63 Ibid., p. 155.

64 Ibid., p. 115.

65 Ruth Hooper, 'Flapping Not Repented Of', *New York Times* (16 July 1922), p. BRM7.

66 'Want Flapper Called "Modern"', *New York Times* (6 October 1925), p. 29.

67 Joanne Meyerowitz, *Women Adrift: Independent Wage Earners in Chicago, 1880–1930* (Chicago, IL, 1988), p. 118.

68 Ibid., p. 128.

69 Emma Ramsay Richardson, 'Men Are Like That', *Ladies Home Journal*, XLV/5 (May 1928), p. 261.

70 Edwin Muir, 'Women – Free for What?', in *Our Changing Morality*, ed. Freda Kirchwey (New York, 1924), pp. 73, 82.

71 Victoria McAlmon, 'Free – for What?', in *These Modern Women: Autobiographical Essays from the Twenties*, ed. Elaine Showalter (New York, 1989), p. 115.

72 Anne Rittenhouse, *The Well-dressed Woman* (New York, 1924), p. 155.

73 Ibid., p. 150.

74 Alma Whitaker, 'The Flapper Paramount', *Los Angeles Times* (29 March 1922), p. 114.

Bibliography

Citations of essays, short stories and articles appear in the References.

Abate, Michelle A., *Tomboys: A Literary and Cultural History* (Philadelphia, PA, 2008)

Allen, Grant, *The Typewriter Girl* (Peterborough, Ontario, 2004)

—, *The Woman Who Did* [1895] (Oxford, 1995)

Armitage, Shelley, *John Held, Jr.: Illustrator of the Jazz Age* (Syracuse, NY, 1987)

Atherton, Gertrude, *Adventures of a Novelist* (New York, 1932)

—, *Black Oxen* [1923] (Buffalo, NY, 2012)

Auerbach, Nina, *Daphne du Maurier, Haunted Heiress* (Philadelphia, PA, 2000)

Baden-Powell, Sir Robert, *Scouting for Boys*, ed. Elleke Boehmer (Oxford, 2004)

Baim, Jo, *Tango: Creation of a Cultural Icon* (Bloomington, IN, 2007)

Barrie, James M., *Peter Pan and Other Plays*, ed. Peter Hollindale (Oxford, 1995)

Baxter, Kent, *The Modern Age: Turn-of-the-century American Culture and the Invention of Adolescence* (Tuscaloosa, AL, 2008)

Beaton, Cecil, *The Glass of Fashion* (Garden City, NY, 1954)

Bilston, Sarah, *The Awkward Age in Women's Popular Fiction, 1958–1900: Girls and the Transition to Womanhood* (Oxford, 2004)

Birkin, Andrew, *J. M. Barrie and the Lost Boys* (London, 1979)

Bowser, Eileen, *The Transformation of Cinema, 1907–15* (New York, 1990)

Bruccoli, Matthew, and Jackson Bryer, eds, *F. Scott Fitzgerald in His Own Time: A Miscellany* (Kent, OH, 1971)

Brumberg, Joan Jacobs, *The Body Project: An Intimate History of American Girls* (New York, 1997)

Castle, Irene, *Castles in the Air* (Garden City, NY, 1958)

Castle, Vernon and Irene, *Modern Dancing* (New York, 1914)

Chothia, Jean, ed., *The New Woman and Other Emancipated Woman Plays* (New York, 1998)

Colmore, Gertrude, *Suffragettes: A Story of Three Women* [1911] (London, 1984)

Connor, Holly Pyne, *Angels and Tomboys: Girlhood in 19th Century American Art* (Newark, NJ, 2012)

—, ed., *Off the Pedestal: New Women in the Art of Homer, Chase, and Sargent* (Newark, NJ, 2006)

Conor, Liz, *Spectacular Modern Women: Feminine Visibility in the 1920s* (Bloomington, IN, 2004)

Cooley, John, ed., *Mark Twain's Aquarium: The Samuel Clemens Angelfish Correspondence, 1905–1910* (Athens, GA, 1991)

Coolidge, Susan, *What Katy Did* [1872] (London, 1918)

Courtney, Florence, *Physical Beauty: How to Develop and Preserve It* (New York, 1922)

Cowan, John, *The Science of a New Life* (New York, 1869)

Cunningham, Patricia A., *Reforming Women's Fashion, 1850–1920: Politics, Health, and Art* (Kent, OH, 2013)

Curnutt, Kirk, ed., *A Historical Guide to F. Scott Fitzgerald* (Oxford, 2004)

Delamont, Sara, and Lorna Duffin, eds, *The Nineteenth Century Woman: Her Cultural and Physical World* (New York, 1978)

Deland, Margaret, *The Rising Tide* (New York, 1916)

Dellamora, Richard, ed., *Victorian Sexual Dissidence* (Chicago, IL, 1999)

Deluzio, Crista, *Female Adolescence in American Scientific Thought, 1830–1930* (Baltimore, MD, 2007)

Dorr, Rheta Childe, *What Eight Million Women Want* (Boston, MA, 1910)

—, *A Woman of Fifty* (New York, 1924)

Driscoll, Catherine, *Girls: Feminine Adolescence in Popular Culture and Cultural Theory* (New York, 2002)

Du Maurier, Daphne, *Myself When Young* (Garden City, NY, 1977)

Dudgeon, Piers, *Captivated: J. M. Barrie, the du Mauriers, and the Dark Side of Neverland* (London, 2008)

Dyhouse, Carol, *Girl Trouble: Panic and Progress in the History of Young Women* (London, 2013)

—, *Girls Growing Up in Late Victorian and Edwardian England* (London, 1981)

Egerton, George, *Keynotes and Discords* [1983] (London, 1995)

—, *A Leaf from the Yellow Book: The Correspondence of George Egerton*, ed. Terence De Vere White (London, 1958)

Etherington-Smith, Meredith, *The 'It' Girls* (London, 1986)

Fass, Paula S., *The Damned and the Beautiful: American Youth in the 1920s* (Oxford, 1977)

Ferrall, Charles, and Anna Jackson, *Juvenile Literature and British Society, 1850–1950: The Age of Adolescence* (London, 2010)

Field, Audrey, *Picture Palace* (London, 1974)

Fields, Armond, *Maude Adams: Idol of American Theater, 1872–1953* (Jefferson, NC, 2004)

Fischer, Lucy, ed., *American Cinema of the 1920s* (New Brunswick, NJ, 2009)

Fitzgerald, F. Scott, *Flappers and Philosophers* [1920], ed. James L.W. West III (Cambridge, 2000)

—, *Six Tales of the Jazz Age and Other Stories* (New York, 1960)

—, *This Side of Paradise* (New York, 1920)

Fitzgerald, Zelda, *Collected Writings*, ed. Matthew Bruccoli (Tuscaloosa, AL, 1997)

Foster, Margaret, *Daphne du Maurier* (London, 1993)

Friedman, Jean E., et al., eds, *Our American Sisters*, 4th edn (Lexington, MA, 1987)

Fryer, Sarah Beebe, *Fitzgerald's New Women* (Ann Arbor, MI, 1988)

Garber, Marjorie, *Vested Interests: Cross-dressing and Cultural Anxiety* (New York, 1992)

Gardiner, Juliet, *The New Woman* (London, 1993)

Gaudreault, André, *American Cinema, 1890–1905* (New Brunswick, NJ, 2009)

Gavin, Adrienne E., and Carolyn W. de la L. Oulton, eds, *Writing Women of the Fin de Siècle* (New York, 2012)

Gilman, Sander L., *Making the Body Beautiful: A Cultural History of Aesthetic Surgery* (Princeton, NJ, 1999)

Glyn, Elinor, *Romantic Adventure* (London, 1936)

Golden, Eve, *Golden Images: 41 Essays on Silent Film Stars* (Jefferson, NC, 2001)

—, *Vernon and Irene Castle's Ragtime Revolution* (Lexington, KY, 2007)

Green, Lancelyn, *Fifty Years of Peter Pan* (London, 1954)

Greenslade, William, and Terence Rodgers, eds, *Grant Allen: Literature and Cultural Politics at the Fin de Siècle* (Burlington, VT, 2005)

Grover, Kathryn, ed., *Fitness of America* (Amherst, MA, 1989)

Hale, Beatrice, *What's Wrong with Our Girls?* (New York, 1923)

Hall, G. Stanley, *Adolescence: Its Psychology and its Relation to Physiology, Anthropology, Sociology, Sex, Crime, Religion, and Education* [1904] (New York, 1914)

—, *Aspects of German Culture* (Boston, MA, 1881)

—, *Life and Confessions of a Psychologist* [1923] (New York, 1977)

—, *Recreations of a Psychologist* (New York, 1920)

—, *Youth: Its Regimen and Hygiene* (New York, 1906)

Hamilton-Honey, Emily, *Turning the Pages of American Girlhood: The Evolution of Girls' Series Fiction, 1865–1930* (Jefferson, NC, 2013)

Hanson, Bruce K., *The Peter Pan Chronicles* (New York, 1993)

Harrison, Patricia Greenwood, *Connecting Links: The British and American Woman Suffrage Movements, 1900–1914* (Westport, CT, 2000)

Hasian, Marouf A., Jr, *The Rhetoric of Eugenics in Anglo-American Thought* (Athens, GA, 1996)

Heilman, Ann, and Stephanie Forward, eds, *Sex, Social Purity, and Sarah Grand*, vol. I: *Journalistic Writings and Contemporary Reception* (London, 2000)

Higashi, Sukimo, *Virgins, Vamps and Flappers: The American Silent Movie Heroine* (St Albans, VT, 1978)

Honey, Maureen, ed., *Breaking the Ties that Bind: Popular Stories of the New Woman, 1915–1930* (Norman, OK, 1992)

Hope, Laura Lee, *The Outdoor Girls of Deepdale* (New York, 1913)

Hull, Edith M., *The Sheik* (Boston, MA, 1921)

Hunt, Felicity, ed., *Lessons for Life: The Schooling of Girls and Women, 1850–1950* (Oxford, 1987)

Hunter, Jane H., *How Young Ladies Became Girls: The Victorian Origins of American Girlhood* (New Haven, CT, 2002)

Jenkins, Lyndsey, *Lady Constance Lytton* (London, 2015)

Keil, Charles, and Ben Singer, eds, *American Cinema of the 1910s* (New Brunswick, NJ, 2009)

Kellerman, Annette, *Physical Beauty and How to Keep It* (New York, 1918)

Kelley, Mary, ed., *Woman's Being, Woman's Place: Female Identity and Vocation in American History* (Boston, MA, 1979)

Kenealy, Arabella, *Feminism and Sex-extinction* (London, 1920)

Kett, Joseph F., *Rites of Passage: Adolescence in America, 1790 to the Present* (New York, 1977)

Kimmel, Michael S., *The History of Men: Essays in the History of American and British Masculinities* (Albany, NY, 2005)

Kincaid, James, *Child-loving: The Erotic Child in Victorian Culture* (New York, 1992)

Kinney, Troy, and Margaret West, *Social Dancing of To-day* (New York, 1914)

Kirchwey, Freda, ed., *Our Changing Morality* (New York, 1924)

Knowles, Mark, *The Wicked Waltz and Other Scandalous Dances* (Jefferson, NC, 2009)

Ledger, Sally, *The New Woman: Fiction and Feminism at the Fin de Siècle* (Manchester, 1997)

Leider, Emily Wortis, *California's Daughter: Gertrude Atherton and Her Times* (Stanford, CA, 1991)

Leverenz, David, *Paternalism, Incorporated: Fables of American Fatherhood, 1865–1940* (Ithaca, NY, 2003)

Linton, Eliza Lynn, *The Girl of the Period and Other Social Essays*, vols I and II (London, 1883)

Loos, Anita, *A Girl Like I* (New York, 1966)

—, *Gentlemen Prefer Blondes* (New York, 1925)

Low, Juliette Gordon, *How Girls Can Help their Country, Adapted from Agnes Baden-Powell and Sir Robert Baden Powell's Handbook* (Savannah, GA, 1916)

Lowe, Margaret A., *Looking Good: College Women and Body Image, 1875–1930* (Baltimore, MD, 2003)

Lystra, Karen, *Dangerous Intimacy: The Untold Story of Mark Twain's Final Years* (Berkeley, CA, 2004)

Lytton, Lady Constance, *Prisons and Prisoners* (London, 1914)

McKeever, William Arch, *Training the Girl* (New York, 1913)

Mackrell, Judith, *Flappers: Six Women of a Dangerous Generation* (New York, 2013)

McVickar, Harry Whitney, *The Evolution of Woman* (New York, 1896)

Malnig, Julie, ed., *Ballroom, Boogie, Shimmy Sham Shake: A Social and Popular Dance Reader* (Urbana, IL, 2009)

Mangan, J. A., and James Walvin, eds, *Manliness and Morality: Middle-class Masculinity in Britain and America, 1800–1940* (New York, 1987)

Mangum, Teresa, *Married, Middlebrow, and Militant: Sarah Grand and the New Woman Novel* (Ann Arbor, MI, 1998)

Marbury, Elisabeth, *My Crystal Ball* (New York, 1924)

Marcus, Jane, ed., *Suffrage and the Pankhursts* (London, 2001)

Marks, Patricia, *Bicycles, Bangs, and Bloomers: The New Woman in the Popular Press* (Lexington, KY, 1990)

Marshall, Susan E., *Splintered Sisterhood: Gender and Class in the Campaign Against Woman Suffrage* (Madison, WI, 1997)

Melman, Billie, *Women and the Popular Imagination in the Twenties: Flappers and Nymphs* (New York, 1998)

Mencken, H. L., *In Defense of Woman* (New York, 1918)

Mendes, Valerie, and Amy de la Haye, *Fashion Since 1900*, 2nd edn (London, 2010)

Meyerowitz, Joanne, *Women Adrift: Independent Wage Earners in Chicago,
    1880–1930* (Chicago, IL, 1988)

Meynell, Viola, ed., *Letters of J. M. Barrie* (New York, 1947)

Mitchell, Sally, *The New Girl: Girls' Culture in England, 1880–1915*
    (New York, 1985)

Morgan, Anne Tracy, *The American Girl, Her Education, Her Responsibility,
    Her Recreation, Her Future* (New York, 1915)

Moruzi, Kristine, *Constructing Girlhood through the Periodical Press, 1850–1915*
    (Burlington, VT, 2012)

Mosher, Clelia Duel, *The Mosher Survey: Sexual Attitudes of 45
    Victorian Women,* ed. James MaHood and Kristine Wenberg
    (New York, 1980)

Mosher, Eliza M., *Health and Happiness: A Message to Girls About their
    Physical Life* (New York, 1912)

Mowry, George E., *The Twenties: Fords, Flappers and Fanatics* (Englewood
    Cliffs, NJ, 1963)

Nelson, Claudia, *Boys will be Girls: The Feminine Ethic and British Children's
    Fiction, 1857–1917* (New Brunswick, NJ, 1991)

—, *Invisible Men: Fatherhood in Victorian Periodicals, 1850–1910* (Athens,
    GA, 1995)

—, and Lynne Vallone, eds, *The Girl's Own: Cultural Histories of the
    Anglo-American Girl, 1830–1915* (Athens, GA, 1994)

Nicholson, Virginia, *Singled Out: How Two Million Women Survived
    Without Men After the First World War* (New York, 2007)

Norquay, Glenda, ed., *Voices and Votes: A Literary Anthology of the Women's
    Suffrage Campaign* (Manchester, 1995)

Pankhurst, Emmeline, *Suffragette: My Own Story* [1914] (London, 2015)

Petro, Patrice, ed., *Idols of Modernity: Movie Stars of the 1920s* (New
    Brunswick, NJ, 2010)

Pleck, Elizabeth H., and Joseph H. Pleck, eds, *The American Man*
    (Engelwood Cliffs, NJ, 1980)

Prigozy, Ruth, ed., *The Cambridge Companion to F. Scott Fitzgerald*
    (Cambridge, 2002)

Reep, Diana, *The Rescue and Romance: Popular Novels before World War i* (Bowling Green, OH, 1982)

Richards, Eveleen, David Oldroyd and Ian Langham, eds, *The Wider Domain of Evolutionary Thought* (Boston, MA, 1983)

Richardson, Angelique, *Love and Eugenics in the Late Nineteenth Century: Rational Reproduction and the New Woman* (Oxford, 2003)

—, ed., *The New Woman in Fiction and in Fact: Fin de Siècle Feminisms* (New York, 2001)

—, ed., *Women Who Did: Stories by Men and Women, 1890–1914* (London, 2002)

Rittenhouse, Anne, *The Well-dressed Woman* (New York, 1924)

Roberts, Katherine, *Pages from the Diary of a Militant Suffragette* (Letchworth, 1910)

Robson, Catherine, *Men in Wonderland: The Lost Girlhood of the Victorian Gentleman* (Princeton, NJ, 2001)

Rose, Jacqueline, *The Case of Peter Pan, or the Impossibility of Children's Fiction* (London, 1984)

Rosenthal, Michael, *The Character Factory: Baden-Powell and the Origins of the Boy Scout Movement* (New York, 1986)

Ross, Dorothy, *G. Stanley Hall: The Psychologist as Prophet* (Chicago, IL, 1992)

Rowbotham, Judith, *Good Girls Make Good Wives: Guidance for Girls in Victorian Fiction* (New York, 1989)

Russett, Cynthia Eagle, *Sexual Science: The Victorian Construction of Womanhood* (Cambridge, MA, 1989)

Scanlon, Jennifer, *Inarticulate Longings: The Ladies Home Journal, Gender, and the Promise of Consumer Culture* (New York, 1995)

Sharp, Evelyn, *Rebel Women* (London, 1910)

—, *Unfinished Adventure* [1933] (London, 2009)

Showalter, Elaine, ed., *Daughters of Decadence: Women Writers of the Fin-de-siècle* (New Brunswick, NJ, 1993)

—, ed., *These Modern Women: Autobiographical Essays from the Twenties* (New York, 1989)

Spacks, Patricia Meyer, *The Adolescent Idea: Myths of Youth and Adult Imagination* (New York, 1981)

Stamp, Shelley, *Movie-struck Girls: Women and Motion Picture Culture After the Nickelodeon* (Princeton, NJ, 2000)

Stanger, Janet, *Bad Women: Regulating Sexuality in Early American Cinema* (Minneapolis, MN, 1995)

Stirling, Kirsten, *Peter Pan's Shadows in the Literary Imagination* (New York, 2012)

Stockham, Alice B., *Tokology: A Book for Every Woman* (Boston, MA, 1886)

Stoneley, Peter, *Consumerism and American Girls' Literature, 1860–1940* (Cambridge, 2003)

Stopes, Marie, *Married Love* (London, 1918)

Tarbell, Ida, *The Ways of Woman* (New York, 1915)

Tickner, Lisa, *The Spectacle of Women: Imagery of the Suffrage Campaign, 1907–14* (Chicago, IL, 1988)

Tosh, John, *Manliness and Masculinities in Nineteenth-century Britain* (New York, 2005)

Tuitte, Patrick B., Allison B. Kavey and Lester D. Friedman, eds, *Second Star to the Right: Peter Pan in the Popular Imagination* (New Brunswick, NJ, 2009)

Twain, Mark, *The Complete Essays*, ed. Charles Neider (Garden City, NY, 1963)

—, *The Complete Interviews*, ed. Gary Scharnhorst (Tuscaloosa, AL, 2006)

Warner, Beverley Ellison, *The Young Woman in Modern Life* (New York, 1903)

Whitaker, Alma, *Trousers and Skirts* (Los Angeles, CA, 1923)

Wilson, Louis N., ed., *Granville Stanley Hall* (Worcester, MA, 1925)

Zeitz, Joshua, *Flapper: A Madcap Story of Sex, Style, Celebrity, and the Women Who Made America Modern* (New York, 2006)

Acknowledgements

My thanks to Skidmore College for Faculty Development Grants that support-ed my research, continued access to the Scribner Library and nimble responses from the Interlibrary Loan staff. Access to the libraries at the University of California, Berkeley, including the Bancroft, has been a great privilege.

For generously reading portions of this book and stimulating my thinking during long walks and fruitful conversations, I am grateful to my treasured friends and family: Alison Alkon, Ruth Copans, Catherine Golden, Sarah Goodwin, Sue Lonoff, Michele McGrady, Susannah Mintz, Samuel Perlin, Aaron Simon, Lanier Smythe, Mason Stokes and Thilo Ullmann.

Thank you to Nancy Von Rosk, for including my essay 'Flappers Before Fitzgerald' in her edited volume *Looking Back at the Jazz Age: New Essays on the Literature and Legacy of an Iconic Decade* (Cambridge Scholars Publishing, 2016). Portions of this book appear in different form in that essay, and I acknowledge permission to use this material.

The support and professionalism of the staff at Reaktion Books has been exemplary. Thanks to my editor Vivian Constantinopoulos for enthusiasm that truly buoyed me; to Maria Kilcoyne and Martha Jay, with whom it has been a pleasure to work; and to Amy Salter, for thoughtful and attentive copy-editing.

Photo Acknowledgements

ᘒ

The author and publishers wish to express their thanks to the below sources of illustrative material and/or permission to reproduce it.

Alamy/Chronicle: p. 215; published in *The Booklovers Magazine*, July–December 1904: p. 66; published in *Costumes Parisiens, Journal des Dames et des Modes*, 1913: p. 198; published in *Fancy Dresses Described or What to Wear at Fancy Balls*, 5th edition (p. 180): p. 36; Glasshouse Images/REX/Shutterstock: p. 62; Library Company of Philadelphia: p. 47; Library of Congress (Prints and Photographs division): pp. 6, 17, 31, 33, 40 (from *Puck* magazine, vol. LIV, no. 1401, 6 January 1904), 41, 46, 57, 110, 121, 125, 131, 134, 146, 148, 150, 161, 162, 163, 168, 179, 181, 182, 192, 208, 227; published in *Life* magazine, 1913: p. 197; from *Life* magazine, February 1922, by F. A. Levendecker: p. 232; LSE Library: p. 64; Margaret Herrick Library, Academy of Motion Picture Arts and Sciences: p. 113; National Institutes of Health, USA: p. 21; published in 'Notables of Britain: An Album of Portraits and Autographs of the Most Eminent Subjects of Her Majesty in the 60th Year of Her Reign', 1897: p. 101; U.S. National Archives and Records Administration: p. 18.

Index